DARK
TO LIGHT

To My favorite
foot doctor. I hope you
enjoy the read while you're
recouping. Thanks for all
you've done for me.

Arleta Carter

Dark to Light

Living Life after Death

Arlita Carter

MOUNTAIN ARBOR PRESS

MOUNTAIN ARBOR
PRESS

Alpharetta, GA

The author has tried to recreate events, locations, and conversations from his/her memories of them. In some instances, in order to maintain their anonymity, the author has changed the names of individuals and places. She may also have changed some identifying characteristics and details such as physical attributes, occupations, and places of residence.

ISBN: 978-1-63183-280-2

Library of Congress Control Number: 2018943943

10 9 8 7 6 5 4 3 2   0 5 1 4 1 8

Printed in the United States of America

⊗This paper meets the requirements of ANSI/NISO Z39.48-1992 (Permanence of Paper)

Scripture quotations are taken from the New King James Version ®. Copyright © 1982 by Thomas Nelson. Used by permission. All rights reserved.

Book cover design by Nnamdi Irving (NATIV Design Group)
Back cover photo courtesy of Neko Sheriff

For my late husband, Garry Carter (1949–2013):

*You were my biggest fan, my biggest cheerleader. Every time
I wanted to give up, I could hear your voice in my ear, saying,
"Come on, Kitten, you can do this!"
Because of your constant encouragement, and your unwavering faith
in me . . .
I did!*

Acknowledgments

First and foremost, I give my most sincere thanks to God for keeping, comforting, and protecting me always, but especially for these last five years. I thank him for giving me the courage to share my testimony, to lay bare my soul on the pages of this book. He spoke to my heart in the midst of my darkest hour and gave me an assignment. He then gave me the ability and provided the tools to complete it. I will be forever grateful for his guidance and unmerited favor.

To my family and my friends old and new, I thank you for your unwavering love and support. I thank you for keeping me lifted in prayer, for holding my hand, drying my tears, making me laugh, and for being my GPS back to the light. I hope as you read this book you will take pride and comfort in knowing you each in your own way were instrumental in helping me achieve this accomplishment.

To Shawn Hutchinson, my friend and mentor, thank you for believing in me. Thank you for encouraging me, and thank you for selflessly sharing your experience and your contacts. Your willingness to reach back and pull another forward helped to transition this book from a dream to a reality.

To my publisher Mountain Arbor Press, thank you for treating my manuscript with dignity and compassion. Your professionalism, attention to detail, and passion for my story produced a finished product I am, and you should be, extremely proud of.

To Nnamdi Irving, thank you for seeing and sharing my vision. Thank you for combining it with your own to create a book cover design that far exceeded my expectations. With your unique understanding of my journey along with your talent and expertise, you designed an outside that tells a story in and of itself and perfectly complements the words on the inside.

To Neko Sheriff, I am truly blessed by your constant encouragement, love, and unfailing support. Thank you for using your gift to make me look good.

To my mother, Evelyn Walker (RIH), my biggest regret is that you are not here with me to see this assignment completed. I hope you are looking down from heaven smiling with pride.

Last but certainly not least, to my sons Kevin and Kenneth Carter, your father told me before he died if anything ever happened to him, I could count on the two of you to take care of me. That's exactly what you did. I know he's smiling down from heaven, proud of the excellent job you have done. You held my hand, dried my tears, comforted and counseled me. Every step of the way, you were right there when I needed you. You believed in me when I didn't believe in myself, and your love and support gave me the courage to keep getting up and putting one foot in front of the other. I hope you are proud of the woman I have become and what I've accomplished, because you never gave up on me or allowed me to give up on myself. If for no one else, this book is a legacy of love for your father, my grandchildren, and especially for both of you.

INTRODUCTION

WHEN I FOUND OUT I had breast cancer, I thought it was the worst thing that could ever happen to me. When I survived, I felt like I had truly been through the fire. Sixteen years later when I lost my husband, I realized compared to losing him, breast cancer was a piece of cake!

My name is Arlita Carter, and this is my story. This is a story about recovery, not from an illness or an addiction, but a painful, life-shattering loss. Four months after my sixtieth birthday, my husband died suddenly, ten days after undergoing knee-replacement surgery. When Garry died, a part of me died too. I was no longer Mrs. Carter, no longer married, no longer the other half of a couple. I was lost and afraid, half the woman I had been.

I didn't think I'd ever get over the pain or survive the heartbreak. I didn't think I'd ever love or be loved again. I didn't believe I'd ever feel whole or safe again. I was absolutely certain that I'd never recover from such a devastating loss. But by the grace of God and the love and support of family and friends, I did. I have. This book is the sharing of my journey—a journey back to wholeness, a journey that revealed to me the woman I was and the woman I could be . . . the woman I am today. I'm sharing my story because I want you to know there is life after death, and *you* can recover too.

Chapter One

Friday, February 22, 2013

E ARLY ON THE MORNING of Friday, February 22, 2013, I begged
my husband for what seemed like the hundredth time to let me
take him back to the hospital. It was ten days after his surgery, and
instead of getting better, he was getting worse. My head, my heart,
and my gut kept screaming that there was something terribly
wrong, and I was desperately afraid that my absolute worst
nightmare was about to come to pass. He kept telling me he was
going to be okay and just needed to rest, so I decided to stop
nagging him for a while in the hopes that he would change his mind.

I tried to distract myself from the gnawing in my gut by doing
some housework, all the while praying that he'd give in and agree to
go back and get checked out. When I received his text at 3:15 that
afternoon, I felt a tiny sliver of hope that my gut was wrong and
everything was going to be all right. Less than an hour later, I
realized that the unease in my gut was not just a feeling—it was a
premonition.

He asked me to come upstairs because he had, in fact, decided to
go back to the hospital. When I walked into our bedroom, I could

see how bad he looked and could only imagine how bad he felt. I managed to get him dressed and was doing my best to get him downstairs. My heart was pounding so hard and so loud in my chest I could barely hear over the noise. Silently I kept praying, *Lord, please help me. Just let me get him to the hospital.*

I began to pray, *Please God, no, don't take him from me.* Halfway down the stairs he said, "I need to sit for a minute. I don't think I'm going to be able to walk."

"Just let me get you into the car," I pleaded. "I'll get someone to bring you a wheelchair."

After a few minutes he stood and made it down two more steps, but then he collapsed. His head fell forward and he began to heave. I watched in horror as he began to vomit blood. I remember screaming, "Garry! Garry! Are you okay?" But he didn't answer me. His eyes were closed, and he seemed to be gasping for air. I kept calling him: "Answer me, Garry. Please, baby, can you hear me? Please don't leave me!"

Everything was a blur after that. I vaguely remember calling 911 and somehow managed to give them my address. Between pacing and praying while the paramedics worked on him, I called my son Kevin, who thankfully was already on his way out to the house. After several minutes they took him out to the ambulance and transported him to the hospital. An officer waited with me till Kevin arrived. I tried not to look at all the blood on my kitchen floor, but that image will be forever etched into my brain for the rest of my life. We lived less than ten minutes from the nearest hospital, but when Kevin finally arrived, it seemed to take an eternity to get to the emergency room. All the way there I kept chanting, "Please God, let him be okay, please don't take him from me . . . not now . . . not yet!"

When we arrived at the hospital, I clung to the last vestiges of hope that I would wake up from this nightmare and everything would be all right. After a few minutes a doctor appeared, and I saw the truth on her face: nothing would ever be right again. I asked to see my husband, and as we started down the hall, she started giving us "the speech." I could see her lips moving, but the lights seemed to get dimmer the farther down the hall we went, and I could no longer hear what she was saying. Somewhere in the corner of my mind I wondered why I was staring up at her and Kevin was on his knees holding me. Then I realized I was on the floor and I couldn't hear her over my own screams. "No, no, no. Please God, no!" I screamed over and over again. It wasn't a dream. I was painfully awake, and this horrible thing was happening for real. The reality of it all hit me in the face like a ton of bricks, and suddenly my whole world went black.

♦

THE SCENE THAT UNFOLDED was surreal. My body was there, but my mind was observing the whole scenario play out in the life of someone else, because my heart was screaming, Surely this could not be happening to me—to us. They took me into this room and I remember calling my sisters Juanda, Donna, and my best friend, Joyce. I know that I talked to Kenny, my youngest son, but I can't remember if I called him or Kevin called him. It was not the kind of thing I wanted to tell him over the phone. I couldn't stop crying and telling him how sorry I was. I failed them, my sons, my grandchildren, our whole family . . . I let them all down.

It was my job to take care of him, my responsibility, and I failed. If I'd just gotten him here sooner, they could have fixed it. Whatever was wrong, they could have fixed it, and he'd be here now . . . he'd be alive, complaining that he wanted to go home. I should have fought him harder. I'd give anything to turn back the clock. I needed a do-over. I let my family down. How would I ever be able to make it up to them?

Our doctor arrived at the hospital shortly after we did. Garry really liked Tonja. Despite the fact that she was so young, he had complete confidence in her. It was obvious by the look on her face that she had a special fondness for him too. The look in her eyes said she was just as shocked and devastated by his death as we were. She held me in her arms as a continuous stream of tears cascaded down my face. Tonja wasn't just our doctor, she was a confidant, someone I trusted with my hopes, dreams, and plans for the future. She knew all about my concerns for Garry's health and his emotional well-being. She knew firsthand my desire for him to get better physically, to get some much-needed rest and some peace in his life. She held my hand and she listened as I recounted the events of the last few hours. She tried to get me to eat, but I had no appetite.

"I want you to know that I'm here for you, all of you," she said. "Whatever you need, just ask."

I knew she had put in a full day at her office; I knew she had a family that she should get home to. She didn't have to be there with us, but she was, and I was so grateful for her presence.

◆

AS I SAT BY Garry's side holding his hand, I looked around the room at my family. Donna and her family were there. They were all taking it pretty hard, especially my niece Staci. Garry's brother Ralph and my niece Raven had arrived too. I felt their pain, but the one whose pain I felt the sharpest was my son's. Kevin is so much like his father; he keeps his feelings all bottled up inside. He was the only one in the room who wasn't openly crying. I knew that was due in part to his attempt at being strong for me, but most of all I think he was just in shock. He'd been on his way out to the house to see his dad and lend his support to my campaign to get him to go back to the hospital. He'd only seen him once since the surgery and talked to him briefly on the phone. Now he stood looking down at his father's lifeless body, and I imagined he was thinking about all the things he didn't get to say to him, all the things he would never have the chance to say.

I felt so bad for him, and especially for Kenny trying to deal with this heartbreaking news all alone in Atlanta. My heart ached for them. I remembered how devastated Garry was when he lost his dad. I had always hoped and prayed my sons would be spared that kind of pain so young. I thought they had more time. I thought we all had so much more time.

Some of the members of our marriage ministry came to the hospital to express their condolences. I was really touched by their support and surprised that the word had spread so fast. By the time they all left, I was literally running on fumes. Tonja recognized that I was running out of gas.

"Kevin, I think you should take her home," she said. "She looks tired, and I think she needs to rest."

I hadn't slept much in the last few days, but at that moment sleep was the furthest thing from my mind. I didn't want to leave Garry there alone, and I really didn't want to go home without him.

"Doctor Austin, can you prescribe a sedative for Arlita?" my sister asked.

"Of course," she said. "I'll call it in now. I won't give her anything too strong, just something to help her relax so she can sleep."

Sensing my reluctance to go back to the house, Donna suggested I come home with her, at least for a little while. I didn't realize till later that Kevin had asked her to do so. He wanted to go to the house and clean up all the blood and any evidence of what had happened there earlier. He knew coming home without Garry would be hard enough; walking in and seeing all that blood would only make it worse.

I sat there for a few more minutes looking at my husband—this man I'd loved for over half my life—vacillating between heartache and anger. My heart ached for the love we shared, the love I'd lost.

I was angry at him for being so damn stubborn. *If you had just let me bring you back sooner,* I thought. I knew I had to go, but I didn't have the energy to move or the desire to leave.

"Mom, Mom, come on," Kevin said. "Dr. Austin said you need to go home and lie down."

I didn't want to go, but unable to stand the silence any longer, I allowed him to lead me from the room and out to the car. As we walked through the doors and out to the parking lot, I remember thinking how just a few hours ago I couldn't wait to get Garry here. Now I didn't want to ever see this place again.

By the time we arrived at Donna's, she had already picked up the sedative Dr. Austin prescribed and made a pot of tea. I wasn't ready for the sedative, but I drank the tea in the hopes that it would warm the chill that consumed my entire body. I tried to lie down, but my brain refused to settle down. My thoughts were scattered all over the place. There was so much I needed to do: people to call, arrangements to make, and I didn't have a clue where to start. I had so many questions and no answers. I wanted to know what happened. Why had Garry collapsed? Could he hear me calling out to him, begging him not to leave me? Did he know what was happening to him? Was there something he wanted to say to me? I would give anything to hear his voice again, to hear him say, "It's okay, Kitten, I got you." I was sitting in a room full of people, but I felt so alone.

I was still sitting on the couch staring into space when Kevin came back to take me home. I was trying really hard to focus my thoughts, trying to figure out what I was going to do with the rest of my life. All my hopes, dreams, and plans for the future died tonight with my husband. *Who are you kidding, Arlita,* I thought. *The future is the least of your worries. You don't even know what you're going to do tomorrow!*

"Mom, are you ready to go?" Kevin asked. "You need to try and get some sleep."

I knew I couldn't put it off any longer, so I agreed to go home, but going to sleep was another story altogether.

♦

WHEN WE ARRIVED AT the house, a coworker and friend of Kevin's was there along with three of my godsons—part of Kenny's crew from the neighborhood. They had come to help Kevin clean up the kitchen before I came home. As tired as I was, I still couldn't face going up to my bedroom, so I curled up on the couch in the family room. I lay there for a while listening to the guys reminisce about "Pops," the father and mentor they had known and loved since they were little boys.

"Ma . . . Ma, go to bed."

I must have zoned out for a minute. Kevin's voice sounded like it came from far away, so I was startled to look up and see him standing over me with his hand stretched toward me.

"Come on," he said. "Take your medicine and try and get some sleep."

I went up to my room and washed my face, changed into a gown, and took the pill. I got into bed, but I couldn't bring myself to turn off the light. I closed my eyes, and as soon as I did, I could feel the tears welling up behind my lids. Crying silently, I lay there waiting for the little pill to work its magic and put me out of my misery. Kevin walked in and sat on the side of the bed. He looked tired too, and I knew he had not yet begun to deal with his own feelings.

"You okay?" he asked.

I didn't want to be selfish. I knew he needed some time alone to grieve, to come to terms with all he had lost, but I couldn't lie.

"No," I said, shaking my head, and I thought to myself, *I don't think I'll ever be okay again.*

He lay down beside me, opened up his arms, and patted his chest, like his father had done a million times. I laid my head on his chest and let him hold me, and once again the floodgates opened up. He rubbed my back and held me tight.

"It's okay, Ma," he said. "You sleep now . . . It's going to be okay . . . We'll get through this."

Finally I could feel my body relax. My eyes were so heavy I couldn't keep them open any longer. As I succumbed to the medication, I thought to myself, *Kenny and Juanda will be here soon . . . They will know what to do. They'll help me.*

CHAPTER TWO

Saturday, February 23, 2013

WHEN I OPENED MY eyes, I could tell by the light coming through the blinds it was daylight. As I stretched and yawned, I could feel the cold creeping through my bones again, and I snuggled back into the covers. As I did so, I turned to my right and realized the bed was empty, and I thought Garry must be in the bathroom. I lay there for a few minutes straining to hear a noise, some sign that he was in there. There was nothing, no sound at all except the howl of the wind coming from outside. I sat up on the side of the bed, intending to get up, when suddenly—as if someone stabbed me with a knife—a sharp pain of clarity penetrated my heart. Memories from the night before flooded my brain with a force so painful it took my breath away.

I covered my mouth to stifle a sob and fell back on the bed. Curling up in a fetal position, I gave in to the pain and cried for what seemed like hours, but in fact was only a few minutes. *He's gone,* I thought, *and he's never coming back.* I wanted to put the covers over my head and stay there all day, perhaps for the rest of my life, but I knew that wasn't possible. I had things to do, people to call, and arrangements to make. *You're not the only one who lost him*, I told myself. *You're not the only one grieving. Your children need you, and you need them. Suck it up, Arlita!* No matter how much it hurt, I had to get up and face the day—the rest of my life without my Pooh.

When Kenny and Juanda arrived, I was overjoyed and relieved to see them, but I wished with all my heart they had come for any other reason. After everyone got settled, we sat around in the family room, and once again I recounted the events of the past week leading up to last night. We cried and we laughed as we shared memories of Garry, and then we cried again as we each dealt with our own individual grief. Finally, Juanda, who is the epitome of organization, broached the subject that nobody wanted to talk about.

"Sis," she said, taking my hand in hers. "We need to make arrangements to say goodbye. Are you ready?"

No, I'm not ready, I thought to myself. *It's too soon! We're supposed to celebrate our fortieth wedding anniversary in four months. We're going to Mexico . . .* I didn't want to do this again; I didn't want to cry. But the realization that none of that was going to happen was too much.

My heart broke again into a million pieces, and I felt like I couldn't catch my breath. *This wasn't supposed to happen*, I screamed inside, *not for years and years!* I looked up with tear-stained eyes and realized everyone was waiting for me to answer.

"There's something else I want to do first," I said. "I want to go back to the hospital. I want some answers. I want to know what happened."

"We'll take care of that," Kenny said. "Kev and I will go up there and talk to them. I also think we should call Dad's job and notify them so they can begin processing the paperwork for his insurance."

I was beyond grateful because the truth was, I really didn't want to go back to that hospital again, so I agreed to let them handle it. In the midst of my pain and grief, I was so proud and grateful for the way my sons stepped up and took control. I have absolutely no doubt that I wouldn't have gotten through those next few days without them.

Kevin and Kenny returned from the hospital a couple of hours later. The report from the ER stated that Garry had died as a result of a blood clot in his lung, a common complication of knee-replacement surgery. I thought knowing the reason for his death would take some of the sting out of losing him, give me some measure of peace. I was wrong. It was just the opposite; knowing just made me even more certain had I gotten him to the hospital sooner, he might still be alive. It hurt even more knowing that I couldn't go back and change anything. I lost my husband and the father of my children, and there was nothing I could do to bring him back. That was a pain I'd have to live with for the rest of my life.

While we waited to hear back from Garry's employer about the insurance, the next step was choosing a funeral home.

"Sis, I know you probably want to have the service at New Faith," Juanda said. "Do you know what funeral home you want to use?"

I don't have any idea, I thought. Garry never wanted to talk about this kind of thing. He avoided the subject like the plague, so we hadn't made any plans. Just a short while ago, I'd tried to talk to him about it. It came up when we applied for our passports in preparation for our anniversary trip to Puerto Vallarta.

"You know, baby," I said. "When you retire next year, we're going to be doing a lot more traveling, so I really think we should make some time to have our wills drawn up."

"I know," he said. "We'll get it done, don't worry."

Why do we always think we have plenty of time? I thought. It's not like we haven't been warned; the Bible tells us, "We know not the hour or the day."

"I don't have any idea," I said, pulling myself back into the present. "Until we hear back about the insurance, I don't even know how much money I have to work with." *I have no idea how much funerals cost these days,* I thought. I didn't have any idea how to pick a funeral home, but as usual, God was one step ahead of me. Kevin's girlfriend, Jillian, had come out to the house to stay with us and help out.

"I can call my friend Tyrone," she said. "He is the funeral director for Jones Funeral Home in the city. We've used them for several of our family members. They'll take good care of Dad, Ma, and make things real easy for you. Ty will work with the insurance company and make things as painless as possible. Do you want me to call him?"

There isn't going to be anything painless about this process, I thought, but since I didn't have any other places in mind, I agreed. "Yes, please call him, and thank you. See what's the earliest we can come in to make the arrangements."

Less than an hour later, Jillian's friend returned her call. He said that Jones would be happy to handle Garry's funeral, and as a special favor to her, he would come out to the house to make the arrangements. I was extremely impressed with their level of customer service and grateful that he was willing to come out to the house.

Trying to wrap my head around the idea of planning a funeral was hard enough; I didn't think I could handle going to the funeral home. I hoped that being in my own home surrounded by my family would make the whole ordeal a little easier to bear. While we waited for Tyrone to arrive, Kevin went to pick up my mom and bring her to the house. She was taking his death pretty hard. She had always considered Garry her son and never referred to him as her son-in-law. She'd been friends with his mother since long before we became involved. After Garry's parents retired and moved back South, she filled a void for him. Even more so in the last few years since Garry's mother had been diagnosed with Alzheimer's.

We had driven down to Mississippi to see his mother three months before his surgery. Her condition was advanced, and it had become too difficult for his stepfather to take care of her on his own. She was in a nursing home, and as hard as it was to see her in her own home and not have her recognize him, it was even more devastating to see her in there. By that time, she was completely unresponsive. All we could do was sit by her bedside and talk to her, even though we knew she probably couldn't hear us, and no longer knew who we were even if she could. It had been so hard watching the pain on my husband's face as he prayed and asked God to deliver his mother from the prison this horrible disease had imposed upon her. He asked God to take her, to release her from this life—a life that, as far as he was concerned, was no life at all.

On the way back home, he confided in me his fear that the next time he saw his mother would probably be at her funeral. Just thinking about that now produced a fresh batch of tears. It broke my heart to realize that it was my husband's funeral we would be attending, that once again another of her children had preceded her to the grave. More heartbreaking than that was the knowledge that she didn't, wouldn't, even know. I pondered whether God had seen fit to penetrate whatever part of her brain that had not been ravaged by the Alzheimer's and let her know that her son had made his transition. If not, perhaps it was a blessing she was spared the pain the rest of us were left to deal with.

My thoughts bounced back and forth from the past to the present. One minute I was stressing about all the decisions I had to make later that afternoon, and praying God would give me the strength to get through the next few days. The next minute I was reliving the past five days, remembering bits and pieces of conversations we had, wondering if somehow Garry sensed what was coming, if he knew he was living his last days. I was remembering the way he looked at me . . .

the way he held me . . . the comments he made . . . and wondered if in his own way, he was trying to prepare me for what I was about to face.

"GARRY, PLEASE, BABY, LET me take you back to the hospital," I begged. "You should be getting better by now. I know you're tired of me bugging you, but I just want—no, I need you to get better. I'm scared, Garry, something is wrong. You weren't like this before. I hate nagging you all the time, but I don't want anything to happen to you.

"You can't leave me, Garry, I can't do this without you. We have too much left to do. Besides, there's so much we haven't discussed, so many things you haven't told me. You always change the subject when I try to talk to you about what to do if you go before me. I wouldn't begin to know what to do if something happened to you. I'm not ready! I love you, and I don't want to live without you."

He looked at me in that way he did that said he thought I was overreacting. "I'm going to be okay, Kitten, but even if I'm not . . . you'll be fine," he said. "You're a strong woman, an intelligent woman. And besides, your boys will take care of you, and you have Ralph. They'll know what to do." *I'm not that strong,* I thought.

I was frustrated and angry. I didn't think he was taking my concern seriously. I couldn't seem to make him understand how frightened I was. I just couldn't ignore that nagging in my stomach, that nervousness that always warned me something was terribly wrong, that awful feeling that a storm was brewing. When I was going through my cancer treatment, when I thought I might not beat it, I was more sad than scared about the possibility that I wouldn't be around to see my babies grow up. I was sick at the thought that I wouldn't get to grow old with my soul mate, to see all our dreams and plans fulfilled. I never worried about leaving Garry alone, because he was our rock. I knew he would be all right. I knew he would keep it together and take care of our children. I knew he could make it without me. I survived the cancer, but in a cruel twist of fate, God had flipped the script and I was the one left behind. I was scared as hell I couldn't make it without him.

I loved my husband more than I think he ever really knew. I had a crush on the boy when I was ten years old. I was crazy about the teenager, and I fell in love with the man he grew into. He'd been my hero for the last forty years. I unintentionally took for granted all the things he did for me—for us. It never occurred to me that he would ever not be there. Long after I survived the cancer, I continued to believe, because of my medical history, it was more than likely I would be the first to go. Now I felt like I was wandering around in a desert with no map, no GPS, no direction…and no water. Before today, when I thought of the future, I saw a kaleidoscope of images flash before my eyes, images of all the wonderful moments we would share with our children and grandchildren. It was like watching the previews of an upcoming movie: the story of our lives. Now when I tried to look into the future, the screen was dark and the images were gone.

STICKING TO THE CHECKLIST Juanda prepared for me, I called the church earlier that day. I left a message for Reverend Powell to express my desire to have Garry's homegoing service there. His return call interrupted my thoughts and transported me back to the present. He said as a member of the church, of course I could have the service there. There was no cost except a small love offering for the officiating minister, and the musicians if we needed them. I wanted to have the service on that coming Friday, but the church was closed on Fridays, so I had to have it on Saturday.

The more I thought about it, Saturday was actually better. It would give out-of-town family members more time to get there. Unfortunately, the banquet hall wouldn't be available for the repast because of another event already scheduled for that day. *We'll just have to have it at the house*, I thought. He expressed his deepest sympathy once again and made an appointment to come and see me in the next couple of days to discuss the eulogy.

"I want to talk to you about who Garry was to you," he said. "The husband, the father, whatever you want to share with me so I can make sure I do right by him."

"Thank you so much, Reverend Powell," I said. "I look forward to seeing you."

I breathed a sigh of relief after my conversation with Rev. Powell. I had some money in savings, and I hoped it was going to be enough to cover everything with a little left over just in case it took a while for the insurance claim to process. In May of 2010, the company I'd given twenty-one years of my life to was sold to another company based in Atlanta. We were planning to relocate to Houston when Garry retired in 2014, so I didn't accept a job with the new company. I was told if I stayed until they completed the transition, I would receive additional weeks of severance pay on top of what I was already entitled to, and I would also be able to collect unemployment. So six months ago in August of 2012, they completed the transition of our office operations to Atlanta and I was out of a job. It had been my plan to quit in 2014, which would have been my twenty-fifth year with the company. Losing my job two years earlier put a serious crimp in our plans, but Garry had assured me we'd be all right.

I was still receiving severance pay and unemployment, but I knew that wasn't going to be enough without Garry's salary. I had lost my job and my husband in the span of six months, and there was a very real possibility I might also lose my home. We had planned to move. We remodeled the kitchen and made a few other minor changes in preparation for putting the house up for sale next February. Now I didn't have any idea what I was going to do next week, let alone next year. It wasn't that I didn't want to leave the house; I didn't think I could stand to be there without Garry. I just wanted to be able to leave on my own terms.

The young man who walked though my door later that day took me completely by surprise. I expected Tyrone to be around my age or even older, but this young man looked like a teenager. He was a prime example of the saying "You can't judge a book by its cover." It only took a few minutes for me to realize he possessed an abundance of patience, compassion, and an extensive knowledge of his business. He put me at ease immediately.

"The first thing we need to do," he said to Kevin and Kenny, "is check with your father's HR department and confirm that the insurance company will agree to a second-party payout. We'll go ahead and make the arrangements today. If they agree, when they process the claim, they'll cut a check directly to us for our services."

"I don't know how long it will take," I said, wondering what would happen if they didn't agree. "Will you be able to wait for your payment?" I asked.

"Yes ma'am," he said. "We do this kind of thing all the time. They will send you a form to sign authorizing the payment to us, and then you will send me a copy of that form. They will cut a separate check to you for the remainder of the claim. Everything will be okay," he said reassuringly.

He went on to say that he would contact the hospital about releasing my husband's body to them, and he would take care of obtaining all the death certificates we would need. We went on to talk about where the service was going to be, and what time; programs, flowers, and how many cars we would need. I was doing okay until Tyrone asked whether me and my husband had burial plots, and if so, at what cemetery? We hadn't had a chance to discuss this in advance, and I didn't know how my sons were going to respond to the one and only decision their father had made and actually discussed with me about his death.

IT CAME COMPLETELY OUT of the blue. One of Garry's coworkers had lost her mother. When she returned to work after the funeral, she told him all about how prepared her mother had been, all the arrangements she had made in advance. She showed him a brochure from the company that handled all the arrangements, and he brought it home to show to me. I remember the front of the brochure said, "Take the burden off your loved ones, plan in advance." As I read further, I realized it was all about cremation, and I was totally shocked.

"You want to be cremated?" I asked, dumbfounded. "I thought you would want to be buried with your brother and your grandfather." His dad was buried in Mississippi, and I was sure when the time came, his mother would be buried beside him, even though she had remarried.

"That might have been true if we were planning to stay here," he said. "But we're not, and just suppose I die before we get a chance to get out of here, or you die. I wouldn't want to leave you here, and I know you won't want to leave me here. More importantly, funerals are getting more and more expensive every year.

"Hopefully, I'll still be working if I kick the bucket anytime soon, because I don't have any insurance other than what I have through my job. I've worked too long and too hard for that money for you to spend a ton of it putting me in the ground. I don't know what kind of financial position you'll be in when I die, and I want you to have as much money as you can. So I want you to promise me you won't let some sleazy funeral director guilt you into spending a penny more than you absolutely have to."

I had always envisioned us buried side by side, with our tombstones reading "Beloved Husband" and "Beloved Wife." But everything he said made sense. Still, it was hard for me to accept at first. I knew other people who had loved ones cremated, but it just never occurred to me that either of us would do it. Over time, I made peace with his decision and even decided that I wanted to do the same in the event I died before him. I wished he had written his wishes down somewhere so I could show them to my sons now. I hoped they believed me when I told them it had been his choice. I didn't want them to think that I was just being cheap and wanted to keep all the money for myself.

"I KNOW THIS MAY be hard to hear and even harder to accept," I said, looking at my boys, "but your father told me he wanted to be cremated." I waited for a few minutes to let that sink in, and then went on to explain his reasons. As I expected, they were shocked at first, but they believed that he had told me what he wanted, and they both agreed that I should honor his wishes. It was my mother who was completely unsettled by my announcement. Her disapproval was written all over her face. My mother was very old school, and she did not believe in cremation.

I silently prayed she wouldn't make a big fuss and make things more difficult than they already were. With as much respect as I could muster, I told her that I understood how she felt, and when the time came, I would definitely honor her wishes. What I didn't say, but she must have picked up on from my tone, was that this was not about her and what she did or did not want. Gratefully, she let it drop, and we continued on finalizing the arrangements. Everybody helped out with the remaining arrangements. We all sifted through my many photo albums selecting pictures to go in the program.

Ralph made phone calls to family members and friends and helped to write the obituary. Donna took care of coordinating food for the repast. People were already calling for information about the service and wanting to know what they could do to help, and she told me to direct those calls to her.

Garry had a thing about flowers—he hated them. He couldn't stand the smell of them and said they reminded him of funerals. When we were dating and throughout our marriage, he never gave me flowers; he would give me plants instead. At first it bothered me that he never gave me flowers, but after attending so many funerals of family members and friends, I began to see his point of view.

"Sis, would you do me a favor?" I asked. "Would you send out an email and ask people not to send flowers? I don't mind plants—I would prefer plants—but no flowers!"

"I'll do you one better," she said. "I was going to talk to you and the boys about this later, but since you brought it up . . . I've been thinking, since you're not working and you don't know how long it will be before you get the insurance check, I want to request in lieu of flowers they send a financial donation in Garry's honor. You should go to the bank and open an account to receive the funds. Every little bit helps, and it will hold you until the dust settles and you know where you are financially."

"I hate to sound like I'm begging for money," I said.

"You're not begging, sweetie, you're just being practical. They'll spend all that money on flowers and they're going to die in a few days. You can't eat those flowers. Anybody who really cares about you, and cared about Garry, won't see it as begging."

Kevin and Kenny agreed, and we made plans to go to the bank the following Monday.

While we were there, I wanted to find out how much we owed on the house. I hoped that with the insurance money, maybe I'd have enough to either pay it off or at least lower the monthly payment. I still didn't know what I was going to do, or where I was going to go from here, but I hoped I could manage to keep a roof over my head until I made that decision.

CHAPTER THREE

Friday, March 1, 2013

I HAD SPENT MOST of the last forty years learning how to sleep through Garry's snoring. It was one of the most difficult adjustments I had to make when we got married. Every night it sounded like a freight train was running right through the middle of our bedroom. We tried changing positions, extra pillows, nasal strips; nothing worked. Even nasal surgery failed to rid him of the problem. Things did improve, though; his roar became a gentle purr, and only when he was extremely tired did it once again rise to a level that made me wish for noise-cancelling headphones.

I eventually got used to his snoring, which evolved from a nuisance to a strange comforting sound that provided a sense of peace and security. It reminded me that I wasn't alone, that he was there, and as long as he was, I was safe. It cancelled out all those bumps in the night and other strange sounds that kept me up, depriving me of sleep whenever he wasn't home. I had almost forgotten that my sister snored too. I thought it very amusing the first time I heard it while visiting her in Houston. I'd never heard a woman snore before. It didn't seem possible that so much noise could come from such a little body.

I hadn't noticed it those first few nights after she arrived because I was taking the sedatives to help me sleep. For the first time since Garry died, I decided to try and sleep without it. I was desperately afraid of becoming addicted to prescription drugs, and decided to try and wean myself off of them before my body got used to them.

When she first started shortly after we went to bed, I smiled and thought to myself, *Maybe I should have taken the pill.* After a few minutes, though, I found the noise comforting. It reminded me of Garry, of the peace and security I'd been missing. It wasn't long after that I drifted off to sleep. I opened my eyes and looked at the clock. It was four o'clock, and I lay there wondering what woke me. Then it hit me—it was too quiet. I looked to my right and saw that the bed was empty. Juanda was gone. There was no light coming from beneath the bathroom door, and no sounds to indicate she was in there. I got out of bed and headed downstairs. When I got to the bottom step, I could just barely hear her muffled sobs, and following the noise, I found her sitting on the couch in the family room.

"I'm sorry, sis," she said when I sat down beside her. "I came down here because I didn't want to wake you. I tried, I really tried, but I couldn't hold it in any longer. I know what I'm feeling is nothing compared to what you're going through . . . but I miss him so much, I miss my big brother. I miss his smile, his laugh . . . I keep waiting for him to walk through the door. I miss his hugs. I miss seeing him love up on you. You guys had something really special, the kinda love I wish I had."

"I know you loved him," I said. "And I know how much he loved you and your boys. Everybody is walking around on eggshells trying to be strong for me, and as much as I appreciate it, I don't want you to hide your feelings or your grief from me, okay? It's comforting to me to know I'm not alone in my grief, that I'm not the only one who loved him and misses him. I realize I'm not the only one who lost him—we're a family, and we're all in this together. If we cry, we cry together," I said, hugging her.

We talked, cried, laughed, and reminisced a little while longer. "Sis, it's six o'clock. You need to try and lie back down for a while. You've got a long day ahead."

Yes, I thought, although I doubted I'd be able to sleep. In a couple of hours it would be time to get ready to go and say goodbye. In just a little while, I would see my husband again for the first time since he died, and I'd have to face the fact that after today, I would never see him again.

Saturday, March 2, 2013

FOR SOME REASON MY husband, bless his heart, had no idea the impact he had on others. Outside of his family, his wife, children, grandchildren, and siblings, he had no clue how many people he had inspired, encouraged, enlightened, and empowered. He never realized through his mentoring, coaching, and befriending how many lives he touched—how many lives he blessed. That's why I know without a shadow of doubt, he would have been amazed to see how many people attended his homegoing.

The church had not been able to accommodate us for the repast because of a prior commitment in the banquet hall. They did, however, provide us with a pre-past. They set aside a smaller room for us before the service so that we might fellowship with family and friends who came to pay their respects. They served coffee and juice, fruit and pastries, and the grief ministry was on hand to lend support if we needed it.

When we arrived at the church that morning, we were directed to that room. I walked through the door and was immediately overwhelmed and deeply moved by the number of people there waiting for us. There were family members, friends, coworkers—his and mine—neighbors, and members of our congregation. I looked around the room through eyes that were quickly filling with tears and thought to myself, *I wish you could be here, baby... to see how much you were loved.*

Eight days after his death, I stood over my husband's casket to say my goodbyes. It took everything in me not to climb in with him. For more than forty years, he'd been the center of my world. The thought of going on, of living without him, was inconceivable. The brave words I spoke at the service were a sham to disguise my real pain. I was not only numb with grief, but I was all but paralyzed by fear.

Proverbs 18:22 says, "He who finds a wife finds a good thing, and obtains favor from the Lord." I don't know if my Pooh was looking for me when we met, but I have no doubt he was heaven sent. I don't recall consciously giving God a wish list for the man of my dreams, but Garry was everything I ever wanted and so much more.

As a woman of faith, I knew we weren't supposed to question God. I knew we were supposed to accept his wisdom and will for our lives, but underneath the pain, the sorrow, and the utter disbelief was a whole lot of anger, and more than a few questions. Like, why had God sent this wonderful man into my life so many years ago, only to take him away just when we were about to realize all our dreams... just when we were about to reap the rewards of our joint labor? We were so close to living our dream! Long before he became my husband, Garry was my big brother, my protector, my confidant—and my best friend. When we were wed, he became my lover, my provider, and more importantly, my partner. He was my biggest fan, my own personal cheerleader, and my constant encourager. Everything I ever did, every accomplishment, was made possible because of the secure knowledge that, success or failure, he always had my back.

As I sat and listened to my sons speak about the father they idolized, my heart bled for them. I wondered if they were thinking the same thing I was thinking: how in the world were we going to make it without him? I looked around at all the people who had come to pay their respects and show their support.

I saw the pain on their faces, and my heart went out to them. I knew many of them loved him and would miss him as much as we would. There was a special sharp pain in my heart for my grandchildren. I thought about all the vacations we planned to take them on, all the places we wanted to show them together, all the special times we would never have. They'd been robbed, cheated out of a relationship with a grandfather who worshipped them.

I was trying to hold it together, but when I looked at my youngest grandson, Mason, the tears I could no longer hold back threatened to drown me. Mason only met his Papa one time, and he was so young I feared he wouldn't remember. I could only hope and pray that in that moment when Garry held him for the first and last time, he could feel the love and pride his grandfather felt. I prayed that somewhere in the recesses of his tiny little heart, a memory was stored.

Sitting there in the front of the church staring at the closed casket, I had to resist the urge to scream at them to open it up again. The more I heard about the good man my husband was, the more I listened to the recollections of what a great brother and outstanding husband and father he was . . . the more I wanted to climb in there with him. I closed my eyes and thought about the future, the days, weeks, and months and years ahead. I couldn't envision a life without him. *There is nothing left for me here*, I thought. The love of my life was gone; all the light in my world had been extinguished. No one would ever love me or want me the way he had. I would never find another love like my Pooh.

CHAPTER FOUR

IN THE DAYS IMMEDIATELY following Garry's service, I was overwhelmed by intense grief and mind-numbing fear. Every day there were new details to address, decisions to make, and questions I had no answers to. There was no Garry to encourage and reassure me, and I began to second-guess every thought that entered my head. I was desperately afraid that I would make some irreversible decision that would negatively impact my life, and my family's as well. It wasn't just about me; every decision I made would affect my children, grandchildren, and my mother. I was stressed out, and at times very angry.

I walked around my house through every empty room talking to Garry. "Why did you leave me?" I cried. "You promised me. You said you'd be okay, but you weren't okay! You said I'd be okay, but I'm not! I don't know what I'm doing, I can't do this by myself, I don't want to do this by myself. You're supposed to be here, we're supposed to be together!" These tirades usually ended with me collapsing on my bed too exhausted to cry or even speak anymore, thinking if anyone had walked in and caught me screaming at my dead husband, they'd lock me up.

I could really appreciate the saying "You never miss your water until the well runs dry." I missed him so much. I missed having him to confide in, to bounce ideas off of. I missed knowing that if I messed up, he was there to help me straighten things out. There were so many things he took care of in the day-to-day running of our household, things that I didn't even know about. Just thinking about all the things I didn't know gave me a headache. *You should be here*, I thought again as the tears flowed.

My appetite was practically nonexistent, and despite the fact that I felt exhausted all the time, sleep eluded me. Every time I thought I had no tears left, something as simple as a TV commercial would produce another flood of fresh tears. In the past, when the pressures of life wore me down, I found solace and comfort in my church. The soulful gospel songs that seemed to be written just for me, and the comforting words of wisdom from my pastor, who seemed to know just what I needed to hear. Now instead of looking forward to the comforting warmth of my congregation, I felt only dread. The first time I attended church after Garry's death, I saw couples worshipping together, and they were a painful reminder that I was alone.

They were the same couples who had been there all the time, but now seeing them, I felt disconnected and displaced. I felt like I no longer belonged.

Friends and family went out of their way to include me in their lives, but the more they did, the more alone I felt. I knew it was irrational for me to be jealous of their closeness, their happiness, and yet I couldn't help but resent it because it was a constant reminder of what I'd lost, what I felt I'd never have again.

Everyone kept telling me that things would get better with time. I had even spoken those very same words to others in the past, and now they tasted bitter in my throat. I felt like time had stopped the night the ER doctor told me Garry was gone, but in truth, time kept moving, and the pain and deep sense of loss I felt had not diminished one bit. It was as sharp and searing now as it was the night I sat staring in utter disbelief at my husband's still body. The touch I could no longer feel, the voice I could no longer hear haunted me day and night. The more I tried to get past it, the harder I tried to adjust to my new reality, the more I craved the past. I desperately wanted to believe that one day I would wake up to a world without pain, a world absent of the emptiness that now defined my every waking hour, but my heart simply refused to accept that the passing of any amount of time would ever make that happen.

◆

IT HAPPENED AGAIN. I passed out from sheer exhaustion three hours ago, but once again I was denied the merciful escape of sleep. As soon as I closed my eyes, the dreams began again. Bittersweet panoramic scenes flickered through my brain, representing the most memorable moments of our forty years together. They were all there, all the memories: the night Garry proposed, our first wedding, our first apartment. The birth of our first child, a boy we named Kevin. As if someone else were operating the remote, my brain fast-forwarded through the years to our first house, our starter home, and the birth of our second child, another boy we named Kenneth. Next came the move to our second home, our dream house.

No life is without adversity, a fact reflected in my dreams. Some of the memories were reminders of the storms we weathered together. My trip down memory lane took me back sixteen years to when my doctor spoke what at the time I believed were the four most devastating words I'd ever hear in my life: "You have breast cancer."

Like a fly on the wall, I saw and heard once again Garry's reaction to those words. I saw him holding my head and massaging my back as I puked my guts up after chemo, and I saw him changing my bandages after my radiation treatments. I saw him tenderly holding me and reassuring me that we'd get through it and I'd be all right.

That was the first of many storms that would test our faith and our marriage. Just when I thought the worst was over, it was my turn to hold him and reassure him that God was able. A company physical revealed that he had kidney cancer. I prayed to the same God who had delivered me, and hoped he would do the same for him—and he did. We survived that storm and went on a few months later to renew our wedding vows on our thirtieth anniversary.

They say love is better the second time around, and I can truly say our second wedding was definitely better. Not because it was everything our first wedding wasn't, but because our love had been tested, strained, and strengthened. When we married the first time, we were just two kids in love with the idea of love. Thirty years later when we stood before God, our family, and friends and recited our vows for the second time, we were two mature adults who really understood the words we spoke. We'd been through hell and back, and we were truly grateful that we never gave up on our love, or each other.

We thought we'd been through the worst; we thought we were finally back on track. Just a few short months ago, we were sitting in the swing on our patio talking about our future. Making plans for our retirement, we discussed our move to Houston far away from the cold of the windy city. We daydreamed about our plans to travel, all the places we wanted to go, the things we wanted to do and share with our grandbabies. We imagined out loud the joy we would experience being free to spend more time with them, watching them grow.

Suddenly without warning, my journey into my past was abruptly halted and I was unceremoniously catapulted back to the present. Standing in my kitchen, in a scene straight out of *Grey's*

Anatomy, I stared in horror as the paramedics shocked Garry over and over again with the defibrillator. The police officer tried to turn me away, but I was glued to the spot praying for some reaction, for any sign that he was still alive.

Standing on my front porch, I shivered with dread as much as from the cold as they transported him to the ambulance and drove away. I tried to hold on to a tiny shred of hope, all the while wondering why there were no lights and no siren.

The tape in my head sped up again, and I was walking down the hall in the hospital listening to the doctor tell me they did everything they could, but . . .

I was sitting next to his body holding his still-warm hand, willing him to open his eyes and tell me everything was going to be all right. I was not alone; there were others in the room. Everybody was crying. My face felt wet, and I opened my eyes to the reality of my dark bedroom and realized I was crying too. Once again I shivered in my cold and lonely bed, missing the warmth of his body . . . the comforting purr of his snoring, the safety of his loving arms. The tears continued to stream down my face while I stared up at the ceiling, wishing I could close my eyes and . . . just sleep.

Asleep he could still hold me, kiss me, and make love to me. Asleep we could still talk and laugh and plan. But when I was awake, I had to face the silence, the loneliness, the emptiness. Awake I had to face every inch of my house that was filled with reminders of him—his pictures, his clothes, his scent . . . the ghost of his laughter. Everywhere I turned he was there, and yet he wasn't. Some days I felt like I was losing my mind!

♦

MY MIND HAD BEEN turned upside down. I still had no clue what I was going to do with the rest of my life, but what I did know was that I needed a change of scenery, even if it was only temporary. Juanda had suggested before she left that I come to Houston for a visit: "Come spend a few days with me," she said, "just to clear your head." Deciding to take her up on her offer, I picked up the calendar and chose the days I wanted to go. Afterward, I called her to see if those days were okay with her.

"When I said you needed to get a way, sis, I meant for more than four days," she said. "I was hoping you would stay for at least ten days, and don't tell me you can't. You aren't doing anything else but sitting in that house going crazy. I want to spend some real time with you, and besides, you can help me find a new place."

As much as I hated to admit it, she had a point. I wasn't doing anything but feeling sorry for myself. Maybe getting away would give me some new perspective. Besides, I really needed to talk to someone about everything I was feeling, about everything that was keeping me up at night. Someone, that is, who could talk back.

After discussing my plans with Kevin, I sat down to make my reservations. It was just another thing in a long list of things that I would have to get used to doing for myself. Garry always made our travel arrangements. I had flown alone plenty of times for business and pleasure, but I never actually made the reservations myself. I was nervous and afraid I was going to make a mistake, but I took my time, and it wasn't as hard as I thought it would be. When I finished, I was really proud of myself, and with a tinge of sadness I wondered if Garry was proud of me too.

In the days leading up to the funeral, Kevin and Kenny had talked to me a lot about my plans for the future, or lack thereof. They wanted to know what I was going to do, but I couldn't make any definite plans until I received the insurance money. I didn't have a job, I didn't have a husband, and I didn't have a snowball's chance in hell of holding on to my house without one or the other. If there wasn't enough money left over after the funeral expenses to pay off the mortgage, I definitely couldn't afford to stay.

I wanted to follow through with our plans. I wanted to go ahead and relocate to Houston. It would be just me and Mom. All her relatives had either died or relocated to another state, and I couldn't leave her alone. We had always planned to sell the house, but another idea had started to form in my brain. If I could get the mortgage payment reduced to an amount Kevin could afford, I could rent the house to him and keep it in the family. I found out I was eligible to begin receiving Garry's social security benefit, and the rent from the house would provide another source of income. I was counting on my trip to Houston to give me a chance to think, and while there I could check out housing for me and Mom. It would give me a chance to see what was available and what we could possibly afford with our combined income. Hopefully by the time I returned home, I'd have a more definitive plan of action.

March 2013

WHEN IT WAS TIME for my trip, Kevin dropped me off at the airport. I hadn't traveled alone in a very long time. Walking through the airport, I missed my travel buddy. He always joked that I only brought him along to carry my bags. "Marry me," he said the night he proposed, "and I'll show you the world." He'd kept his promise and taken me to several of the places that I'd only dreamed of, read about in books, or seen on TV. I still had a long list of places I wanted to see, and I wondered if I'd ever get to see the rest of the world he promised.

Juanda was there to meet me when I arrived in Houston, and on the drive from the airport to her apartment, I saw so many landmarks that reminded me of all our previous visits there. On our last visit we'd spent a couple of days looking at houses in anticipation of our move there. Originally we had planned to buy a little ranch big enough for the three of us, but while we were there, he changed his mind and decided he didn't want to buy another house.

"When I retire, I don't want to take on that kind of debt again," he said. "Besides, if something happens to me, I don't want you to get stuck trying to sell another house. If, God forbid, something happens to both of us, I don't want to leave that burden on the kids."

Like so many other Americans, our house was seriously underwater due to the crash of the housing market. We hoped we'd be able to find a buyer and at least break even and not owe any money to the bank. Taking that into consideration, his decision to rent instead of trying to buy made sense. I didn't care one way or the other, as long as we were together.

"Sis . . . hello . . . earth to sis, where are you?"

"What?" I asked.

"I asked, where were you?" she answered. "I've been talking to you for the past five minutes. Did you even hear a word I said?"

"No," I admitted. "I'm sorry, I was thinking about the last time we were here. What did you say?"

"I asked if you wanted to stop at the store for anything before we go home."

"I could use a glass of wine," I answered, smiling.

"Just one?" she asked, grinning at me.

"Well . . . let's start with one," I replied, laughing.

CHAPTER FIVE

August 2012

MY LAST DAY AT work was August 30, 2012. In the weeks leading up to that day, I asked Garry repeatedly if he was absolutely certain he didn't want me to try and find another job.

"It's probably going to be at least two years before we're ready to move," I said. "How are we going to save up money to make the move if I'm not bringing in a paycheck?"

"I wish you would stop worrying, Kitten," he answered. "You know we've been through this before, more than once. God brought us through before, and like you keep telling me: if he did it once, he can and will do it again."

It wasn't that I doubted God's power, but this move was something I had been dreaming about and praying for the last ten years. I lived each day with great anticipation for the day we could finally escape the Midwest and move to a warmer climate. We weren't getting any younger, and the extreme cold was really taking a toll on our bodies. I looked forward to the day Garry could retire and enjoy the much-needed rest he had earned and so richly deserved. We could see the finish line off in the distance, but I just couldn't shake this awful feeling that we wouldn't get there.

"I've been thinking," he said. "This is the perfect time for us to go ahead and remodel the kitchen. Since you won't be working, you can take your time looking for a contractor, buying all the materials we'll need, and supervising the work. Besides, I want you home after I have this other knee replaced, so you can help me with my rehab. As far as I'm concerned, baby, as far as work goes . . . you're done. You've put in twenty-three years with Smurfit-Stone, and that doesn't count all the years you worked before that. It's totally up to you if you just want to get another job when we get to Houston. What I'd really like to see you do is start working on your catering business. You'll have a new dream kitchen to work in, for at least a year. So, I think you should use that time to test the waters. Start building up a clientele here, and you can get the business started in Houston once we get settled."

I am tired of working my behind off making somebody else rich, I thought. It would be nice to do something that really made me happy instead of doing something I hated just to get a paycheck. Getting started here would give me a chance to see if I really had the skills to build a business.

"I know exactly what you're thinking, Kitten," he said. "Trust me, I have no doubt you can do it. You've been baking your goodies and giving them away free for years. Don't you think it's time you got paid?"

From your lips to God's ear, I thought. "Okay, all right," I said. "I'll give it a try when the kitchen is finished, but if things get too tight, you just say the word and I'll start pounding the pavement."

By the end of October, I was able to locate and hire a contractor. At the end of November, we'd purchased all the materials, and the contractor and his crew began working the first week in December. They finished the remodel three days before Christmas.

January 2013

I WAS IN LOVE with my new kitchen. The remodel turned out even better than I imagined, and I knew it was going to be hard giving it up when we were ready to move. Everybody who saw it liked it too and thought it would be a great selling point for the house. After the holidays, I started working on recipes and making samples for family and friends. Garry appointed himself my chief taster and quality-control manager, a job he thoroughly enjoyed.

Donna was responsible for my first paid order. The general consensus throughout my family and circle of friends was that my peach cobbler and red-velvet cake should be my two signature desserts. Donna secured an order for red-velvet cupcakes from her job. Little by little, through word of mouth I began to build a small clientele. Things were just starting to take off and I was beginning to feel very optimistic about my chances for success, when everything I feared came to pass. Garry underwent his second knee-replacement surgery on February 12, and ten days later, he was gone.

After the funeral, after I had time to review my finances, I realized it was more important than ever that I find a way to supplement my very limited income. I knew I had to get serious if I wanted to make any real money. I knew I would have to take and pass a food-service class in order to apply for a license. I found a course I could take online and signed up. I was about two weeks into the course when I flew to Houston.

March 2013

I HADN'T HAD ANY hard liquor in years. After my bout with breast cancer, I only drank wine every once in a while, and even then I rarely drank more than one or two glasses. We stopped at the store on the way from the airport and picked up something to eat and a few bottles of wine. After we ate, we sat down to talk and sip on the wine. We'd already killed one bottle and started on the second when Juanda told me her schedule for the week.

"I've made some appointments in the evening after work to go and look at some houses," she said. "I'm off on Friday, so we can do some shopping, get some lunch, and check out some houses for you and Mom. You'll have the whole place to yourself during the day until then. What are you going to do?"

I told her about the class I had started before I left. "I brought my laptop," I said. "I'm going to try and finish this class, or at least do as much as I can while I'm here. That should keep my mind occupied while you're at work. I guess I'll have plenty of time to think about my future, and try and figure out what I'm going to do with the rest of my life."

"One day at a time, sis. One day and one step at a time," she said, hugging me.

Later that night I lay in the bed in her guest room trying to fall asleep. Every time I tried to close my eyes and envision what life would be like in Houston for me and Mom, nothing surfaced. All I could see were the dreams I had of the life Garry and I had planned to share there, a life that was no longer a part of the equation. I didn't want to wake Juanda since she had to go to work the next day, so I got up as quietly as I could and poured myself another glass of wine. Taking it back to the bedroom, I turned on the TV and drank the wine. Sometime later, a combination of the wine and the sound of the TV I wasn't really watching enabled me to drift off.

◆

I SHOULD HAVE BEEN excited about looking for a home for me and Mom. But as we drove from one subdivision to another and looked at one house after another, all I kept thinking was, *You ought to be here, Garry. We should be doing this together.* The housing market was slowly starting to recover. It was rebounding a little faster in Houston versus Chicago. Interest rates were low, and Juanda was convinced I could buy a house for less than what it would cost me to rent one. I still had my doubts as to whether I could afford to buy a house, or even if I wanted to.

It didn't really matter what I wanted at that point. Everything was contingent upon what I would be able to do with the house I was currently living in.

We visited a couple of new subdivisions and looked at some new construction. I took brochures of the houses that I liked, to take home and show to Mom. If it turned out we wanted to buy, or even if we decided to rent, it would take both our incomes to pull it off. She said she trusted my judgment, but if she was going to be paying her share of the mortgage or the rent, she was entitled to a say in what the place looked like.

◆

WHEN I RETURNED HOME, the insurance check had finally arrived in the mail. Much to my disappointment, it was not, as I had hoped, enough to pay off the mortgage. That had been my plan A. Now I would have to come up with a plan B, and I hadn't quite figured out what that was going to be. Fortunately, the state of Illinois allowed people like me the ability to collect unemployment while still receiving severance pay from a former employer. When I started receiving my unemployment, I put all my severance pay in savings, with the intention of only using it after my unemployment ran out. Garry had already paid the mortgage for March, and I received two more paychecks still owed to him, a couple of weeks after his death. That took care of April and May, but I knew I would have to come up with something else before the end of May. I thought the day

Garry died was the worst day of my life, but I had no idea how much worse it would get until I went to the bank.

As painful as it was to stay alone in the house I had shared with Garry for the last thirty years, the reality was, it wasn't just our house. My children had grown up in the house. They made lifelong friends in the community, and those friends considered it their home as well. My boys had accumulated just as many memories in the house as we had. I felt like I owed it to them to pursue every option available to me in an effort to keep it.

Kevin wasn't in any position to buy the house outright, but if I could get the mortgage payment reduced to a reasonable amount, he could rent it. Going that route would keep the house in the family and possibly provide me with an additional source of income. If I couldn't get any help from the bank and I had to dip into the insurance money, it might last me about three years—with an emphasis on "might." I really wanted to move, though, to relocate to Houston like we planned, and I would need that money to make a new start.

I thought I had it all worked out, and I was very optimistic about my plan B when I marched into the bank. It took less than twenty minutes for them to burst my bubble. I explained to the bank officer that my husband had recently passed, and I was currently unemployed. The last time we refinanced the loan, we had failed to purchase the insurance that would pay off the mortgage in the event of either of our deaths. I went on to say that I had recently received my husband's life insurance, but after paying off all the expenses, I still didn't have enough to completely pay off the mortgage.

"So," I said, "I'd like to make a lump-sum payment toward the principal in the amount of fifty thousand dollars to lower the monthly payment."

"Well, Mrs. Carter," he said with a look of sympathy, "first of all, let me say how sorry I am for your loss. We would be more than happy to accept your lump-sum payment, but unfortunately, I'm afraid that wouldn't accomplish what you want." He paused for a minute to allow me time to digest what he said, and I saw my plan B circling the drain. "Making a lump-sum payment," he began again, "would only result in reducing the length of your mortgage, but it wouldn't lower the monthly payment."

That made absolutely no sense to me, a fact that must have been written all over my face. "I'm afraid," he continued, "the only way to reduce the monthly payment is to lower the interest rate. In order to do that, you'd have to refinance the loan. I know you said you were unemployed. What exactly is your current monthly income, if you don't mind my asking?"

"I'm collecting unemployment and severance pay from my former employer," I said, "and I've also started receiving my husband's social security."

He gave me that sympathetic look again, and with his next words proceeded to throw dirt on my hopes and dreams. "Well, you could apply for a refi," he said, "but I'm afraid without a more stable income it's highly unlikely you would get approved."

What he really meant was no job, no loan!

How can this be? I thought, sitting there totally dumbfounded. I could feel my eyes begin to sting, but I was determined not to cry. What I really wanted to do was scream at the top of my lungs, "WHAT'S THE MATTER WITH YOU PEOPLE!" What happened to all those government programs I kept hearing about? They were supposed to help people like me who had suffered a financial hardship, so they could keep their homes. In the space of six months, I'd lost my job and then my husband. In effect I'd lost not one, but two incomes. If that didn't qualify as a hardship, what the hell did?

"What about a loan modification?" I asked. "I thought there were programs in place to help people in my situation."

"There are," he said, as he began typing on his keyboard and looking at his computer screen. "There are certain criteria that must be met in order to qualify for a modification."

"Which are?" I asked.

"Well, you have to have purchased or refinanced your home before June 2009, for one," he said. "You also have to be at least three or more months behind in your mortgage payments."

My emotions ranged from severe frustration to boiling anger, and I could feel my blood pressure starting to rise. Garry and I had always worked very hard to maintain a good credit rating. We took pride in the fact that we always managed to pay our bills on time, even in the worst of times.

"So what you're telling me is, if I purchased my home or refinanced it after June 2009, I'm screwed. No help for me." He started to speak and I held my hand up. "Let me finish," I said. "Even if I was within the time frame, I would have to jeopardize the good credit rating my husband and I worked so hard to achieve by allowing my mortgage payment to get three months or more in the rear. Does that about cover it?" I asked.

The fact that my voice had raised a couple of octaves, and I looked like I was ready to kill somebody, was not lost on him.

"I'm sorry, Mrs. Carter," he said. "I know it seems unfair, but these are the guidelines we have to follow."

Seems unfair? I thought. *Are you kidding me?* I had to get out of there! I was starting to have difficulty breathing. I started gathering up my things and rose to my feet, preparing to leave.

"We have a program," he said, rushing ahead. "It's designed to provide temporary help for people who are unemployed." He paused for a second to see if I would sit back down. When I did, he continued. "It's called unemployment forbearance. Based on your mortgage payment, plus all your other household expenses and your current income, whatever that may be, they will adjust your mortgage payment to an amount you can afford to pay for a period of anywhere from three months to nine months. If you still haven't found employment after that period is up, you can reapply for additional assistance. If you can wait a few more minutes, I can make a call and have the application forms sent to you."

I wasn't looking for a temporary fix. What I needed was a permanent solution, but the end of May was looming. *Maybe this program will buy me some time,* I thought. *At least until I can figure out something else.* I agreed to try it, and he made the call.

CHAPTER SIX

April 2013

A FTER MY VISIT TO the bank, I was more depressed than ever. The finish line I had once seen clearly was now just a blur, and it was moving farther and farther away. I remembered telling my boys a long time ago that money wouldn't buy them happiness. I could tell by the look in their tiny little eyes they didn't believe me. Truth be told, I didn't really believe it myself. Secretly I believed if I had money—real money—I could buy whatever I needed to make me happy. Now I realized how foolish I had been. I was as naive as my children. I was by no means rich, but because of the insurance money, I had more money than I would have made in a year had I still been working. And yet, I might as well have been penniless. In a battle against the bureaucracy of the federal banking system, my money was worthless. It wasn't enough to buy the freedom I desired, and I was afraid it wouldn't get me to the finish line. I was disappointed and disillusioned, but I wasn't ready to give up.

Once I'd had time to regroup and think, I realized the bank that held my mortgage wasn't the only game in town. Just as I had done when I received my breast-cancer diagnosis, I would seek a second opinion. There were too many people in the world like me, people going through the same thing. I had to believe there was another way. *This is just a temporary setback,* I told myself. It had only been a couple of months since Garry died. I needed to take time to think things through. I needed to calm down and exercise some patience. I knew from past experience, I wasn't going anywhere until God decided I was ready to go.

I could just barely tolerate the days, but it was the nights I had a real problem with. It was hard enough sleeping alone, but being in the house all alone at night was really working my nerves. If it wasn't my dreams keeping me awake, it was all the strange night noises that kept me on edge. Even though we had an alarm, I slept with a knife under my pillow. The only time I got even a little bit of sleep was the nights Kevin and Jillian stayed over.

They had started coming out two to three nights a week to check on me. I knew it was taking a toll on them, both physically and financially. They both worked on the far north side of Chicago past the loop. It made for a really long drive to and from my house, and gas was at an all-time high. Part of me wanted to tell them it wasn't necessary, that I was okay; but to tell the truth, I was really grateful for their presence. It gave me something to look forward to, and it was the only time I got any real rest.

Garry and I spent the better part of our youth in the suburbs. It's where we met, became friends, fell in love, and got married. After the wedding, we moved to the city. We lived there until Kevin was a little over a year old. We decided we wanted to raise our children in the suburbs and give them the same opportunities our parents had given us. At that time it was much safer, and the schools were better. We wanted our children to have fresh air and a backyard to play in. We wanted to shelter them from drugs and gangs, and give them the best possible chance to grow up and become young men we could be proud of.

It wasn't until after his marriage and subsequent divorce that Kevin returned to the city. He'd become quite accustomed to and comfortable with urban life. He lived on the north side and walked, biked, or took public transit to and from work. The only reason he even owned a car was so he could pick up his son on his weekend visitations. He usually spent those weekends at the house with us, so we could spend time with our grandson, Noah.

I hadn't given up on the hope of keeping the house, but I wasn't sure Kevin really wanted to return to the suburbs. I wasn't sure he wanted the responsibility of owning a home. It was that uncertainty that prompted me to make a suggestion. One evening after they returned from work, I presented them with my plan.

"The two of you have been spending more time out here than you have at your apartment," I said. "Have you considered moving out here with me, at least until I figure out what I'm going to do? You could give me half of what you're paying now for rent toward the mortgage, along with a little for groceries, and you can bank the rest. If things don't work out, at least you'll have a nice little nest egg to help you get relocated."

They looked at each other, and I could tell they were weighing the pros and cons.

"The time you spend out here would give you a chance to see if you'd really like living in the suburbs again," I said. "It would also give you the opportunity to see if you really want the responsibility of owning a home. You don't have to give me an answer right now, just think about it for a couple of days."

"Our lease is up in June," Kevin said. "We do want to move, so yeah, we'll think about it and let you know."

"What would we do with all our stuff?" Jillian asked.

"Well, I plan to leave this house one way or another," I said. "I'm going to have to start getting rid of anything I don't plan to take with me, so you can move as much as you can in here. You could put the rest in storage." I didn't want to push, but I could tell they were warming up to the idea. "Let's all think about it," I said. "You can let me know what you decide in a few days."

While I waited for the kids to make a decision, I scoured the internet for any and all information I could find about mortgage modification. I was overwhelmed by all the sites I found. I had to be careful. I'd heard horror stories about all the scammers who made false promises they couldn't deliver on. Some people ended up in worse shape than when they started out. People were losing all their savings and retirement money, and when they had exhausted all their assets, the banks foreclosed on them and they wound up on the street.

Every company I researched offered one piece of information in common. Before the banks or mortgage companies would even consider a modification, an individual had to be at least three months or more behind.

"As long as you keep paying the mortgage, Mrs. Carter," one representative told me, "you're demonstrating that you can pay. They don't care how you pay or what sacrifices you have to make to come up with the payment. You won't get their attention until you stop paying."

It went against everything I believed in . . . everything I'd been taught. I wasn't some deadbeat; I didn't have bill collectors calling my house all hours of the day and night. We always found a way to pay our bills, even if we had to rob Peter to pay Paul. I just couldn't wrap my head around the idea of intentionally not paying my mortgage. I had to face a harsh reality. The game had changed, my husband was gone; I didn't have a safety net anymore. I was on my own, and I'd have to do whatever it took to survive.

While I attempted to decipher all the information I found on the internet, the application for unemployment forbearance arrived via Fed-Ex. The inch-thick packet of forms I had to complete made me feel more like I was applying for a position with the secret service instead of a temporary mortgage reduction. In addition to filling out the application, I had to supply bank statements, tax returns, and proof of any and all income. They wanted to know exactly how much money I had and what I spent it on. About the only thing they didn't ask for was my DNA.

On top of everything else, there was a time limit on when I had to complete and return the application. Much later down the road, I would come to understand that time only mattered when they wanted my information. When it came to getting a response from them, suddenly time was no longer important. It took me a couple of days to compile all the information they asked for, but I managed to get it all done and returned before the deadline. While I waited for them to receive and process my application, I continued my quest to find a permanent solution to my problem.

I went back to the internet and completed one of those multilender applications requesting information about refinancing my loan at a lower interest rate. What a nightmare that turned into. Not five minutes after I hit the enter button on my keyboard, I was bombarded with calls from everybody and their mother. Some of the names of the lending institutions were familiar, but others I'd never heard of.

All the conversations started out the same. They were all very cordial in the beginning, and so sure they could help me out. I repeated my story over and over again, until at one point I considered making a recording and just hitting the play button at the appropriate time. The conversations all ended the same as well. Everyone agreed I had excellent credit, but as soon as I revealed that I wasn't working, all the doors closed with a loud bang. The overall consensus was they couldn't count my unemployment compensation when looking at my income, and without it, I simply didn't have enough income to qualify for a loan.

I just didn't get it! I didn't make enough money to pay the current mortgage, but I didn't make enough money to qualify for a loan to reduce the mortgage to an amount I could afford to pay. So, if I didn't make enough money to qualify for a loan to pay at a lower rate, how did they expect me to pay the higher rate with that same income? Everyone kept asking the same question: Was I planning to go back to work? HELLO? It didn't matter what *I* planned, jobs just weren't that easy to find, especially for someone my age. Besides, even if I had been working, I still couldn't afford my mortgage on my own. Why couldn't I get anybody to understand I hadn't lost just one income—I'd lost two! I was so frustrated, and the more I tried to see the light at the end of the tunnel, the dimmer it got.

I was so grateful I'd never been a heavy drinker. I'd seen too many people try and drown their sorrows at the bottom of a bottle. It never worked; if anything, it only made things worse. I just kept trying to remember what my pastor was always saying: when the fire's burning hot and you're afraid you'll be consumed, you gotta throw some word on it. I kept telling myself, *I'm battered and bruised, but I'm not broken. I'm down, but I'm not defeated. I can do all things through Christ who strengthens me.* I was in a battle for my life, and I wouldn't go down without a fight!

Days went by as I waited to hear back from the bank about my application. I was nervous, restless, cranky, and very lonely. What if they didn't approve my application? I really didn't want to have to start dipping into the insurance money. I wanted to move, to start over, and I knew I was going to need every penny of that money that I could hold onto. I missed having my best friend there to talk to. Whenever I was struggling with a problem, he would always let me vent. I would go on and on talking it out and he'd just listen. By the time I reached the end of my tirade, I usually knew what I needed to do. I'd thank him for his help and he'd laugh. Hours and sometimes days later I'd think back on the conversation, and I'd realize he hadn't said a word. Sadly I realized now more than ever, it was just his being there . . . that's how he helped.

Just because your mind knows something doesn't mean your heart will accept it. My mind knew that my husband was gone and he wasn't coming back, but my heart wasn't ready to accept it. I was there. I saw him lying in his casket. I had the death certificate. For the past three months, I'd been trying without much success to get used to the empty space beside me in bed. I'd tried to adjust to the constant silence, but a part of me kept waiting for him to walk through the door. A part of me kept waiting for him to come home and rescue me from this nightmare. Like he'd done so many times before, I was waiting for my partner to guide me through the murky waters and help me find my way. I would sit for hours trying to recall all our past conversations. I tried to remember all the rough patches we made it through together. I would think to myself over and over again, *What would Garry do?*

So many times I heard him say to our sons, "You have to have a plan. If you don't have a plan, then you plan to fail." *But I have a plan*, I said to myself. Why is it so hard to execute my plan? And there it was—the answer was right in front of my face. Proverbs 16:9 says, "A man's heart plans his way, but the Lord directs his steps." My pastor often says, "Man makes plans, and God laughs!" I was so focused on what *I* wanted, on "my plans," it never occurred to me that what I wanted wasn't what God wanted for me. Everything was so hard because my plans didn't line up with God's will for my life. Our timing is not God's timing, and his reasoning is beyond our comprehension. For whatever reason, God wasn't ready for me to move. Obviously there were some things that needed to be revealed to me, some lessons I had yet to learn. Important information I would need to prepare me for the rest of my life. My mind knew, and my heart would just have to get with the program. I needed to sit still and wait on the Lord. I had to believe that in due season, he would work all this out. He would clear a path to my future.

As hard as it was to accept, I had to come to terms with one essential reality: I couldn't move forward until I could let go of the past, and my heart wasn't ready to do that yet. I needed time to heal. God knows what we need better than we know ourselves. I needed time, and maybe, just maybe, that's exactly what he was trying to give me.

I wasn't giving up on my plan. I still believed that letting go of the past meant eventually getting out of this house, but I was finally accepting that getting to where I wanted—needed—to be wasn't going to happen overnight. When I thought about our relationship and where we were in our marriage, I realized the love and trust we shared, the happiness and peace we found in each other, had been cultivated over time. There was a lot I needed to learn and do before I was ready to close the door on this chapter of my life, and it would more than likely take several months—not days.

It was time for me to give myself a reprieve from my self-imposed exile. It hadn't been intentional, I hadn't deliberately cut myself off from my friends and family; it had just happened a little bit at a time. Prior to Garry's death, I had been active in my church, and even though I was no longer working, I still kept in touch with my former coworkers. We talked on the phone, emailed, texted, and met for lunch or dinner. Garry and I had long given up the club scene, but we loved going to the movies, we attended the occasional house party, and we liked to sneak off whenever we could for long weekends.

After Garry died . . . after the first couple of weeks, everyone returned to their normal routines—everyone except me. There was no normal for me anymore. I forced myself to go back to church even though it felt so uncomfortable being there alone, and it got harder and harder to go back every week. I knew they meant well and they were probably genuinely concerned, but I was tired of people asking me how I was doing. "How do you think I'm doing?" I wanted to ask.

On the outside, I knew they didn't mean any harm; they probably thought they were being supportive. But on the inside, I was hurt, and more than a little angry. They asked me how I was feeling, and then proceeded to tell me how I should be feeling.

"You should give thanks for all the years you had together," they said. "Think about how blessed you are to have experienced a love many live a whole lifetime and never know."

Duh, I thought. Did they really think I wasn't grateful for our life together? Yes, I knew how blessed I was to have had a love that most people only dreamed about; that's precisely why it hurt so badly. Was I wrong for wanting more of the life I had? Did that mean I didn't have the right to grieve? After a while I felt compelled to say what they wanted to hear. I felt like I had to lie about my true feelings to make them feel better, and slowly, little by little, I began to retreat. I couldn't take it anymore. I didn't want to be around people who even unintentionally made me feel guilty for mourning my husband.

Eventually loneliness outweighed my hypersensitivity and I realized I'd either have to grow a thicker skin or become a hermit. Standing in front of my fireplace staring at Garry's ashes, I got an eerie feeling that he was frowning at me, shaking his head with disapproval. He had always encouraged me to have a life apart from him.

"You need to get out and spend time with your friends," he'd say. "You can't appreciate me if you never give yourself a chance to miss me. You know what they say—absence makes the heart grow fonder!" I knew he wouldn't want me to cut myself off from the rest of the world.

"All right, all right," I said, remembering his smile . . . that crooked smile that stole my heart a lifetime ago. *I hear ya. I hear ya! You're right*, I thought. *It's time to come out of hiding.*

We all have a person or a group of people in our lives we consider friends. Special people we trust with our secrets, our hopes and dreams; a select few we trust to have our backs through thick and thin. I believe in times of great adversity God gives us wisdom and discernment. He opens our eyes and enables us to see those true friends in our circle. Joyce and I clicked from the very beginning. We met when we joined a marriage ministry at our church. We named the ministry "Foundations." Its sole purpose was to provide spiritual encouragement, enlightenment, and support to all the couples involved. We met once a month to fellowship, pray for one another, and discuss the challenges we faced every day in our relationships. Through our testimonies we learned that our problems were not unique, but often universal, and we helped each other work through them with prayer and counseling. It was evident after the first few meetings that Joyce and her husband, Reggie, had a lot in common with me and Garry. A short time later, Joyce encouraged me to join the women's choir at our church, which only strengthened our bond. It was for that reason Joyce was the first person I called outside of my immediate family the night Garry died.

She understood my incoherent babbling, assessed my need, and immediately called in the troops. She was at work when I called and was unable to come herself, but she assured me she would be there as soon as she could for whatever I needed. Less than an hour later, members of our marriage ministry arrived at the hospital to provide prayer and comfort to me and my family. Without being asked, she worked with Donna to secure food donations for the repast. She made sure the food arrived at my house as promised, and had it set up and ready for me and my family when we returned home from the service. Everyone was so impressed by how well organized everything was. I was impressed as well and grateful, but not surprised. Time and time again I had seen her minister to grieving families in our church community, and I didn't doubt for a minute she would do the same for me.

After the funeral, she called periodically to check on me and encourage me, but she didn't push. She gave me the space I needed, and when I reached out to her, she was right there to comfort me. Because of all the things we had in common, I knew Joyce was someone I could really talk to. I could let it all hang out, bare my soul without fear of recrimination or judgment. It was so comforting to know I didn't have to be some spiritual superwoman in her presence. I could be vulnerable and flawed, and she would understand.

Even before Garry died, Joyce and I shared our hopes and dreams for the future. We often discussed our mutual concerns and fears regarding the health challenges our husbands faced, and how they impacted our lives. We shared the same frustrations over their unwillingness to take our concerns seriously. I called her, and we made a date to go out to lunch. I hadn't been out of the house in a while to do anything other than go to church or to the grocery store, so I was really looking forward to our lunch date.

I didn't realize how badly I needed to get out—to talk to someone other than myself. I'd been keeping so much bottled up inside, so the minute we sat down, I started talking and couldn't stop. I told her everything I'd been going through and the reasons why I'd been keeping to myself.

"Girl, Garry was *your* husband, and nobody knows better than you how much you loved him and he loved you. You don't have to apologize to anyone for your grief. Nobody has the right to tell you how to grieve or how long it should take. Everybody grieves differently and at their own pace. You will never forget Garry, and I doubt you'll ever get over losing him. In time, God will ease your pain, but only you can determine when you're ready to move on."

"I'm so glad to hear you say that," I said, relieved. "Some days I really feel like I'm losing my mind! Every day is a roller-coaster ride. I'm so lonely, and one minute I'm sad, the next I'm angry, and then there's that nagging feeling of guilt."

"Wait, hold up. What are you feeling guilty about?" she asked.

"Joyce, I think about Garry every minute of every day. I relive that last day over and over again. I can't help feeling that if I had gotten him to the hospital sooner, he'd still be here. I'm angry with myself because I didn't push harder, and I'm angry with him because he didn't take my concern seriously until it was too late."

Saying all of that out loud brought all those feelings bubbling to the surface. I took a deep breath and tried my best to keep the tears pooling behind my eyes from spilling down my face.

Joyce gave me a minute to pull myself together, and then she said, "Listen, girlfriend, everything you're feeling is normal. After all, it's only been a few months. But you need to stop with the shoulda, woulda, couldas. It's not like you knew something was wrong and you deliberately didn't do anything about it. You weren't responsible for living Garry's life, and you certainly weren't responsible for saving his life. He had some responsibility in that. When it comes right down to it, though, none us have any real control over that. I believe ultimately it was God's choice, and his alone. I know you don't want to hear this, sis, but you need to try and accept that maybe it was just Garry's time."

She was right; I didn't want to hear that. I wasn't ready to accept it either. It would be so much easier if I could, but I just couldn't.

"I guess I'm not ready to accept that," I said. "I still can't wrap my head around the idea that I'm never going to see him or talk to him again. I find myself still waiting for him to come home. I have so many questions. I'm so afraid I'm gonna make a mistake or a bad decision about the house, or about relocating. I just wish I could talk to him . . . ask him what to do."

"I understand," she said. "Anybody who knew the two of you could see how much Garry loved you, and how well he took care of you. You say he spoiled you—well, he did, but you don't give yourself enough credit. You're smarter and stronger than you think, and more than capable of making decisions for you and your family. You just need to take your time, give yourself some time to grieve. With God's love and his guidance, everything will fall into place when it's supposed to."

I enjoyed the meal and the fellowship with Joyce, and when I went home that day, I felt better than I had in a long time. It felt good to talk about my feelings, to admit out loud my fears and concerns. When I was going through my cancer treatment, my oncologist encouraged me to join a support group, but I never did. I went to work every day and pasted a smile on my face. I held my head up, squared my shoulders, and never let on to anyone how terrified I was. Even though the doctors assured me they had gotten all the cancer, I spent the better part of five years after my treatment waiting for the cancer to come back. I was waiting to die. There were resources available to help me deal with my fear, to help me get past it so I could live the life God had spared. I didn't take advantage, and I wasted precious time.

Older and wiser now, I knew I didn't have time to waste. I needed to accept my new reality and take advantage of any help offered to get me to that place. My family was depending upon me, and I didn't have the luxury of wasting time wallowing in self-pity.

CHAPTER SEVEN

May 1973

"WHAT DO YOU MEAN, why did I do that?" I asked incredulously. "It's your birthday, silly, it was just cake and ice cream. If it wasn't so close to our wedding, I would have thrown you a real party. Next year," I said, smiling. "Next year. I promise."

He was looking at me like I'd suggested a trip to the moon.

"What's the matter?" I asked. "You act like you've never had a birthday party before."

A look of pain crossed his face briefly. He looked at me again and said stiffly, "Not really. I can't remember ever having a birthday party."

"Yeah right," I said, laughing. I thought he was joking until I saw the expression on his face.

I couldn't find the words to express the sincere pain I felt on his behalf. I couldn't begin to imagine a child growing up without ever having a birthday party. I wanted to put my arms around him. I wanted to hold him and never let go. The love I had for him intensified a hundredfold after that revelation. I made a vow that day to never let another birthday, or any other milestone in his life, go unrecognized or uncelebrated.

May 2012

OVER THE YEARS I kept my promise. I made it my mission to acknowledge his birthday and every other special day. I wanted to make sure he always felt loved and appreciated. After our boys were born and old enough to understand, I made sure they did too. It took a while for him to get used to me fussing over him and making such a big deal out of his birthday and other special days, but eventually my enthusiasm began to wear off on him and he began to reciprocate in kind.

I always strived to make the next year better than the year before, and I was really proud of myself in 2012. Garry was turning sixty-three, and I decided to take him away for a long weekend. I'd been saving my money and making plans for weeks, and I was so excited to finally tell him about them. I wanted to go somewhere fairly close so we could drive, so I decided on St. Louis. I found a hotel online and made reservations. Then I went to MapQuest and printed out the directions. I also checked out the restaurants in the area and decided to take him to Morton's for his birthday dinner. I could hardly wait for him to get home from work so I could tell him.

After we ate dinner, we went upstairs to watch TV. "So, Mr. Carter . . . you've got a birthday coming up next week," I said.

"Yeah," he replied, already glued to the TV screen.

"Well, I thought I'd whisk you away for the weekend. How does that sound?" I asked.

"Where are you planning to whisk me away to?" he asked, smiling.

"I thought we'd go someplace close enough to drive, so I picked St. Louis. We haven't been there in a while. We can go check out the Arch, and that restaurant featured on Oprah's network, Sweetie Pies. There's a mall across from the hotel with a movie theatre, and I plan to take you to Morton's steakhouse for your birthday dinner. Does that sound okay?"

"Wow," he said, smiling again. "You've really put a lot of thought into this."

"So . . . is that a yes?" I asked.

"Of course it is," he said, hugging me. "It sounds great. What's the name of the hotel? I'll go online and make the reservation."

"Not necessary," I said with pride. "I already made the reservation, and I printed out the directions to the hotel. I also printed out the directions from the hotel to Sweetie Pies, and to Morton's from the hotel."

"You didn't need my card?" he asked, looking surprised.

"No, baby, I said I was taking *you* away for *your* birthday, which means *I'm* paying for everything."

Looking thoroughly pleased, he smiled that smile that always melted my heart and kissed me on the forehead. "Well, look at you," he said. "My baby's all grown up, making her own reservations and stuff."

I knew he was teasing me, but I could tell by the look on his face he was proud of me. The weekend was wonderful. The weather was perfect. The ride was long enough to feel like we'd really gotten away, but not long enough to tire us out. I was relieved the hotel lived up to the pictures posted on the internet, and the staff was very nice.

When we checked into our room, Garry looked around, visibly impressed, and said, "You done good, babe."

After getting settled, we went to Sweetie Pies that evening for dinner. It wasn't bad, but as far as we were concerned, it didn't live up to the hype.

"I'm sorry," I said, disappointed.

"Why are you apologizing?" he asked. "It wasn't that bad, but your food is way better."

"I'm flattered," I said, smiling. "But you're not exactly unbiased."

"Hey, I'm just calling it like I taste it," he said, laughing. "After thirty-plus years of your cooking, I know what good food tastes like."

The next morning we enjoyed the free breakfast at the hotel and then went shopping at the mall. We went to a movie that afternoon and then picked up some ribs from a local rib joint we found by accident. While we ate, we watched Sunday-night football. Garry had been working so hard, it was really good to see him getting some much-deserved rest and relaxation. I know he really enjoyed his birthday weekend, but I'm absolutely certain the last day was hands down the highlight of the trip. It began with a huge breakfast in bed, followed by a lazy afternoon of cuddling and bingeing on HGTV and the Food Network. In anticipation of his birthday dinner, we decided to skip lunch and snacked on microwave popcorn instead.

Garry knew I had made reservations at Morton's, but he had no idea what was in store for him when we arrived. When I called and made the reservation, I told them it was a birthday celebration. They promised to make it a special celebration, and they far exceeded my expectations. I was expecting a slice of cake with a candle and maybe a song, but they went way beyond that.

We were greeted like royalty and then escorted to a special booth. They presented Garry with a personalized menu with his name and the date on it. They provided a complimentary bottle of wine and took a lovely picture of us to take home as a keepsake. The food was excellent and worth every penny, but the smile of satisfaction Garry gifted me with throughout the evening was priceless. When we returned to the hotel, he couldn't stop thanking me and telling me how much he enjoyed his weekend.

"You outdid yourself, Kitten," he said, beaming. "I don't know what you're going to do next year to top this!"

I kept looking at that photo they gave us and marveling at how relaxed and happy he looked. I had no idea at the time it would be the last photo we would ever take together . . . or the last birthday of his we would ever celebrate.

When I reflect back on that weekend with joy tinged with sadness, I'm truly grateful I made every effort to make it a birthday he would always remember—and as it turned out, one I will never, ever forget!

May 2013

MY FAMILY AND FRIENDS kept telling me time heals all. The problem with that was nobody could tell me how much time. Days, weeks, and months had passed, and I wasn't feeling any healing. They say, "Weeping endures for a night, but joy cometh in the morning" (Psalm 30:5). Well, I seemed to be having trouble distinguishing night from day, because my tears endured way past night and my mornings were devoid of any sustainable joy.

I wasn't hiding anymore, but when I was alone, I found it increasingly hard to concentrate. I was distracted, depressed, and stressed out about the status of the house and my future or possible lack thereof. My headaches were coming more frequently and lasting longer. I was afraid to go to the doctor because even though I was on medication, I was pretty sure my blood pressure was through the roof.

It was always there. It never went away; it was lying there just below the surface—the pain and the anger. I had been extremely moody and emotional the past several days, which more than anything had to do with the calendar, specifically the month and the date. It was May. The seventh of May. It was Garry's birthday. If I could turn back the clock, we'd be celebrating his sixty-fourth birthday. We'd be out to dinner or maybe off on another one of our little getaways. But I was forced to live in the present, and in the present, there was no celebration; there was no birthday. There wouldn't be any more birthdays . . . ever.

That painful reality consumed me with an emptiness I couldn't even begin to comprehend, let alone describe. I didn't want to bring anybody else down, so I kept my pain to myself. From the minute I woke up that morning and was forced to acknowledge the significance of the day, I just wanted it to be over. But, as if to spite me, it seemed to last forever.

June 2013

THE LAST TEN MONTHS of 2013 were without a doubt absolutely the worst of my life. Looking back at that period of my life reminded me of the time my old boss brought this punching bag to work. Actually, it was more like a large balloon made of heavy plastic, painted to look like a man with no legs. He put it in a storage room adjacent to our offices and brought us all in to see it.

"This is Ernie," he said. "I know you all get angry and frustrated with each other, our customers, and mostly me," he said, smiling and backing up a few steps. "It's not healthy for you to keep all that aggression all bottled up inside. So rather than having a stroke or a heart attack, the next time you feel like exploding, I want you to come in here and take it out on Ernie."

We all looked at each other and then at Ernie and laughed.

"Go ahead," he said. "Try it."

We hesitated for about a minute, and then one at a time we started punching Ernie. I remember feeling sorry for Ernie; every time he got punched, he would tilt to one side or the other, but he never fell down. I remember thinking, *Poor guy, he can't recover from one blow before he gets hit with another one.* That's how I felt about 2013.

I couldn't seem to catch my breath. When Garry died, I felt like someone had punched me in the gut, like I got knocked down, and every time I tried to get up . . . I got hit again. The fire was burning hot and I kept trying to pour word on it, but it was like pouring water on a grease fire. I tried to stay positive, I tried not to give up or give in, but it was like the enemy had detected a weakness and he was hell bent on exploiting it.

The calendar said June 7. I was supposed to be getting ready for my anniversary dinner tomorrow. The plan was to have a big dinner for family and friends to celebrate our fortieth wedding anniversary. Donna was going to organize the dinner, and to show our appreciation for all her hard work, we had invited her and Karl to join us on our trip to Puerto Vallarta. Ironically, the passports we applied for arrived a week after the funeral, painfully reminding me that I needed to call the resort and cancel the trip.

Now I had to face the fact that there wouldn't be a fortieth anniversary, or any other anniversaries for that matter. People kept telling me that I had to accept my loss and move on, but how could I do that when every time I turned around, something happened to remind me of that loss? How could I get up when life kept knocking me down?

I wanted more than anything for time to move at warp speed through the weekend and the week to follow. I didn't want to spend one more minute thinking about where I was supposed to be and who I was supposed to be with.

Time, however, was not on my side. As if to punish me, it moved at a snail's pace. It didn't help that I still hadn't heard from the bank about my application for temporary mortgage assistance. I didn't want to think about the anniversary dinner we weren't going to have and the trip we'd never take. I didn't want to think about what I was going to do if I couldn't get some kind of help paying my mortgage. I needed to do something, anything, to take my mind off everything. Sitting down at my vanity, I opened one of the drawers and started throwing out all my old makeup. As I picked up one half-used container of lipstick after another, I suddenly remembered some very expensive lipstick I purchased back in March and had never used. It's funny how the mind works. I don't know why that stupid lipstick suddenly became so important, but I was determined to find it. I was dumping everything out of one particular drawer when I came upon a small, black box pushed all the way to the back of the drawer. I pulled it out and stared at it for a long time.

When Garry proposed to me, he was still in the service. He bought my engagement ring in the commissary on base. I was so excited that he'd asked me to marry him, and thrilled with the ring, but he always felt bad that he hadn't been able to afford a larger diamond. He spent the next thirty-nine years trying to make it up to me, even though I did my best to convince him it wasn't necessary. On our tenth anniversary, he bought me a new ring, a larger diamond, and he gave me a new ring every major anniversary after that. So I received a new ring for our twenty-fifth and another one on our thirtieth when we renewed our vows.

Since we were planning to have a big dinner, followed by the trip, I wasn't expecting a new ring this year. Considering the fact that he died four months before our anniversary, a new ring was really the last thing on my mind. And yet there I was sitting on the floor in my bedroom, holding this box in my hand trying to summon the courage to open it. I knew I hadn't put it there, and there was only one other person who could have. I don't know how long I sat there staring at that innocent-looking box. I wasn't afraid to open it; I was pretty sure I already knew what was inside. I just didn't want to feel the pain I knew I would experience once its contents were revealed.

As I expected, when I finally opened it, the very sight of what it held inside evoked a strange mixture of joy and immense pain. At first there was joy, because my Pooh had completely outdone himself. The ring was unusual, and the most beautiful thing I'd ever seen. It was so unlike anything he'd ever given me before: a beautiful, diamond-encrusted ring shaped like a belt buckle. When had he bought it, I wondered, and when had he snuck it into my vanity? When and how had he planned to give it to me?

The answers to all those questions would forever go unanswered. The undeniable truth of it all produced an onslaught of pain and tears. I curled up on the floor and allowed them to flow unchecked. Hugging the ring close to my chest, I wished with all my heart he was there to place it on my finger.

When I finally pulled myself together, I returned the ring to the box, and put it back in the drawer. I couldn't bring myself to wear it . . . not yet. I looked at it every day, and I was torn between wanting to wear it and not wanting to be reminded that the man who loved me enough to purchase it would never have a chance to see how it looked on my finger.

Later that month, Donna called to say she was throwing an impromptu dinner party for her birthday. I tried to get out of going, but she wasn't having it.

"Look, sis," she said. "I know you're hurting, but staying cooped up in that house by yourself isn't helping. You need to get out and have some fun, be around your family, allow yourself to laugh a little. I know Garry would want that."

"Okay, okay," I said. "I know you're right. I'll come."

When I started getting dressed, I had to admit it did feel good to put on something other than leggings and a T-shirt, and put on some makeup. I realized I was actually looking forward to being around family and friends and having somebody to talk to other than myself. At the last minute before leaving the house, I decided to wear my ring. Part of me wanted to show it off the minute I walked through the door, but I was afraid if I started talking about it, I'd start bawling all over again. It was Donna's night, her birthday celebration, and I didn't want to bring everybody down with my sad story. I decided not to say anything, but I didn't have to. The ring was so spectacular it spoke for itself. I noticed everyone stealing looks at it throughout the night, and finally someone commented on how beautiful it was.

I was planning to just say thank you and leave it at that, but Donna commented that she'd never seen it before. "Is that a new ring, sis?" she asked.

"Yes," I answered, and then I proceeded to tell them the story of how and when I found it. When I finished, I wasn't the only one whose eyes were misting. Their verbal and emotional response to the story confirmed what I already knew. I was very blessed to have been loved by such an extraordinary man!

June 2012

WHEN KENNY BROUGHT APRIL and my grandbabies up from Atlanta for the funeral, I could hardly believe my eyes. I was amazed at how much they had grown in the last eight months. I hadn't seen them since our vacation in Atlanta last June. We booked a resort in Villa Rica, about an hour outside of Atlanta. It was the kind of vacation I'd always dreamed about—a real family vacation, me and Garry, our children and grandchildren.

It's a vacation I'll never forget because we had such a good time, but most of all because it was the one and only time Garry ever saw his grandson Mason. I flew to Atlanta the year before to help out after Mason was born, but Garry had to save his vacation days for his upcoming surgery, so he couldn't join me. He was scheduled to have his first knee-replacement surgery later that year. Because of his rehab, we weren't able to travel until the following year.

I took lots of pictures and told him all about his new grandson, but he couldn't wait to meet him in person. We decided to make it a real family vacation, and we even arranged to take Kevin's son Noah with us. On the flight to Atlanta, he seemed really nervous. I knew he wasn't nervous about flying, so I asked him what was wrong.

"What's up, Pooh?" I asked. "Why are you so antsy?"

He was looking out the window, and he took so long to answer me I thought maybe he hadn't heard me. Before I could ask again, he finally turned to me and said, "He's already a year old. I've never seen him, and he's never seen me . . . he won't know who I am. What if he doesn't like me?"

That's ridiculous, I thought to myself. I would have laughed if I hadn't seen the serious look on his face. "You're his grandfather, silly," I said. "Of course he's going to like you; he'll love you the minute he sees you, just like all your other grandchildren."

"I hope you're right," he said, looking doubtful.

Noah did his best to distract him during the flight, but once we landed, he seemed to get more and more agitated the closer we got to Kenny's house. Thinking about what he said on the plane, I knew he would be devastated if Mason didn't take to him, so I began to pray that their first meeting would go well. When we arrived at Kenny's house, he opened the door with Mason in his arms. Instantly, I watched as Garry's heart melted when he saw him producing a smile that lit up the room.

I didn't miss the look of pride on Kenny's face either. He finally had the son he'd always wanted, and I could tell how much it meant to him to present him to his father.

Kenny sat Mason on the floor at Garry's feet and said, "Mason, meet your grandpa."

For a few seconds we all nervously waited for Mason's reaction to this revelation. Silently I prayed, *Please God, Please God.* Mason looked back over his shoulder at his daddy, and then he looked up at Garry, who I'm sure to him must have seemed a million miles away from where he was sitting. Suddenly, as if on cue, his little face broke into a huge grin and he held his arms up toward Garry, indicating he wanted to be picked up. I let out a sigh of relief and said silently, *Thank you, God!*

Garry picked him up and held him close. I could tell he was having difficulty controlling his emotions. With tears forming in his eyes, he said a shaky, "Hello, little man. I'm your grandpa. You can call me Papa."

My instincts were right on target; as soon as Garry picked him up in his arms, he and Mason were inseparable. I, on the other hand, might as well have been invisible. Standing there watching them, it suddenly hit me: it had been a year since I last saw Mason.

I had held Mason, smothered him with kisses, changed his diapers, fed him, and rocked him to sleep over a period of one week. He was just an infant. I believed we had established a bond, but the truth was I didn't know before the minute Kenny opened the door if he would remember me. His smile indicated that maybe he had some idea of who I was—he did, after all, grant me a kiss on the cheek—but for the rest of the vacation, it was all about his Papa. Another grandma might have been a little jealous, but I was absolutely thrilled. I was also used to it; it had been the same with all of our grandchildren.

I had no doubt my grandchildren loved me, but I had long ago accepted that I took a back seat to Papa. There was something magical about the relationship between my husband and his grandchildren; they absolutely adored him. Papa was the man, and I was all right with that. It was one of the things I loved the most about him. After getting the introductions out of the way, we all went to lunch, and from there to get groceries for the resort. We took our granddaughters, McKenzie and Londyn, with us and headed for the resort. The plan was for Kenny, April, and Mason to meet us there later after April got home from work.

◆

WE ARRIVED AT THE resort a couple of hours before nightfall. It was a nice place, a two-bedroom unit with a large family room and a big enclosed porch that led out to a large backyard a few feet from the resort pool. It was an average place in comparison to other places we'd been to, but our grandbabies made us feel like we'd taken them to the Taj Mahal. They oohed and aahed over the inside and outside. We knew their reaction was a result of their lack of travel experience, but their excitement and enthusiasm made us feel good nonetheless.

While we waited for the rest of the family to arrive, we put away the groceries and took a quick tour around the grounds of our unit. The kid's excitement was contagious. So far everything was going even better than my dreams, and I couldn't wait to see what the rest of the week held. When Kenny and April arrived, the love fest between Garry and Mason resumed. Mason proceeded to make his Papa his own personal jungle gym. He climbed up into his lap, up onto his shoulders, and down the other side over and over again, all the while giggling with glee. He was having a ball, and Papa was eating it up.

I'll never forget the joy I felt inside watching them interact, because I knew how much it meant to him. They played and played until Mason wore himself out, and then like all the other grandbabies before him, he curled up on Papa's shoulder and fell fast asleep. I will always treasure the pictures I took of them laughing, kissing, hugging, and bonding. They are all the more special now, knowing it was all the time they had. I'm sure McKenzie and Londyn would have been a little jealous of all the attention Mason was getting from their Papa, had it not been for their cousin Noah.

He was like a big brother to them, and it was obvious to anyone how much they adored him. It really warmed my heart to watch them interacting. It was my greatest hope that they would bond and experience a loving, lasting relationship like the one I shared with my cousins when I was their age. Family was important. I knew if a solid foundation was developed in their early years and maintained as they grew, they would always be able to count on one another later in life.

After Mason went down for the count, Noah and the girls binged on the Disney Channel until they too succumbed to sleep. When we retired to our room, I couldn't help but notice how happy and relaxed Garry looked. I knew it had been a long day and he was physically exhausted, but considering the fact that he and Mason had gotten along so well, mentally he was on top of the world. He couldn't stop talking about him.

"He's such a handsome little boy. He's all boy too," he said, grinning. "Did you see the way he was climbing all over me? He's not afraid of anything."

"Of course he's handsome," I said, smiling. "He takes after his granddaddy. He's smart too, smart enough to have you wrapped around his little finger already!"

"Yeah, yeah, yeah," he said laughing.

He didn't bother to deny it, because he knew I spoke the truth. Before I fell asleep that night, I thanked God again for fulfilling my dream of a real family vacation. I thought about my children and grandchildren asleep on the other side of the condo, and I prayed it would be the first of many.

I woke up the next morning to the sound of my grandbabies trying to outtalk each other over the sound of their favorite Disney characters. I opened my eyes, and the first thing I saw was Garry's grinning face.

"How long have you been awake?" I asked, yawning and stretching.

"About thirty minutes or so, I guess," he replied.

I groaned and pulled the covers up over my head.

He playfully pulled them back down and said, "Be careful what you wish for!"

We lay there for a few more minutes talking quietly. When the noise outside our door continued to escalate, I turned to him and said, "The natives are getting restless. I think it's time to get up and feed them some breakfast."

The condo we reserved was a lot larger on the inside than it looked on the outside. On one side of the large family room was an equally large master bedroom and private bath, which Garry and I occupied. On the other side was another bedroom with two queen-size beds, which Kenny and April shared with Mason and the girls.

They had their own TV and their own private bath. The family room had a very nice queen-size sofa sleeper. The plan was for Noah to sleep out there, but when I emerged from our bedroom that morning, it was obvious my grandchildren had their own plans. The chaos in the family room indicated they'd had a major pajama party last night. As I headed toward the kitchen to a chorus of "Hey Grandma," I smiled to myself. My main objective for the vacation was for my grandchildren to bond; I couldn't help thinking, *Mission accomplished.*

"Where's Papa?" they asked as I started pulling food out of the fridge for breakfast.

"Taking a shower," I answered. "He'll be out in a minute. Are you all hungry?" I asked.

I received a resounding yes from all of them. By the time I got the bacon and sausage ready to go in the oven, Garry had joined me in the kitchen to help, and Kenny along with April and Mason emerged from their bedroom.

Breakfast preparations became a family affair. The kitchen was probably the smallest room in the condo, but we managed to function like a well-oiled machine. It had been a long time since we'd all been in the kitchen cooking together, and despite the close quarters, I was enjoying every minute of it.

All of my grandbabies shared their Papa's love of bacon, and they also liked the Mississippi sausage we introduced them to. So much so, I made a mental note during breakfast to pick up more while we were out later that day. Watching them put away all of that bacon, sausage, cheesy eggs, and toast that morning, I had to laugh. I was thinking about the future when I suggested to Garry later that day that one of us would probably have to get a part-time job when we retired.

"Why?" he asked, looking confused.

"Did you not see how much food your grandchildren put away this morning?" I asked, laughing. "That was just breakfast! If they eat like that three times a day, we're going to need the extra income to buy all those groceries."

"Yeah," he said, laughing. "They did put away a lot of food this morning. I think the girls were just trying to keep up with Noah."

"Maybe," I said, smiling. "We'll see over the next few days, but I think we better be prepared. The older they get, the more they're gonna eat. Mark my word, we're gonna need to keep the fridge fully stocked at all times."

After a quick kitchen cleanup, we decided to go to the mall to do some shopping and walk off our hearty breakfast. Noah had some spending money from his parents, and it was burning a hole in his pocket. We had to take two cars, and of course the girls wanted to ride with us so they could be with Noah.

The resort was nestled in the midst of a lovely community comprised of beautiful homes of various sizes populated with big, beautiful trees. There were lots of hilly, winding roads, and it got very dark after the sun set. The combination of hills, winding roads, and spooky darkness made for a fun and scary ride, much like a roller coaster. The children loved it! They laughed and squealed with delight as their Papa whipped up and down the hills and around the curves. Striving to be the adult in the car, I admonished Garry to be careful, but eventually that funny feeling in the pit of my stomach took over and the kid in me began laughing and giggling with the rest of them. It was hard to tell who was having more fun, the adults or the children.

When we arrived at the mall, the children were laughing and talking over each other trying to tell Kenny and April how much fun they had.

As they looked at Garry, all bright eyes and smiles of admiration, there was no doubt in my mind: as far as they were concerned, Garry was officially the coolest grandpa in the world. The look on Kenny's face as he watched his children and his father was confirmation that these encounters meant as much to him as they did to me.

For the next several hours, we walked and shopped and walked some more, until the breakfast we had that morning became a distant memory. We decided to stop for some lunch, at which time my grandchildren confirmed what I already knew: that morning had not been a fluke. As I watched them eat, I stole a glance at Garry and he started laughing, having read my mind.

After we finished lunch and looked in a few more stores, all the eating and walking had taken its toll. We were all ready to head back to the resort to chill out. Mason was past ready for a nap, and he wasn't the only one. I've always been grateful that Garry had an excellent sense of direction. He always teased me about being directionally challenged. Every time we went on vacation, I struggled to remember landmarks to and from our location. He, however, always had the route memorized after the first day. I was especially grateful for that gift on this vacation.

By the time we stopped at the grocery store to restock the fridge and headed back to the resort, it was already starting to get dark. Street signs were far and few between. That coupled with the descending sunlight meant you absolutely had to know where you were going. I could barely see anything, let alone landmarks. My directionally gifted husband, on the other hand, seemed to have some invisible map inside his head. He not only knew where he was going, but he had the nerve to have discovered a shortcut on the way back. Fortunately, his shortcut included enough hills and twists and turns to delight his grandchildren and preserve his Cool Grandpa status. They had been quiet and on the verge of falling asleep for most of the ride back, but once the roller-coaster ride began, they were awake and wound up again.

After a light dinner, the kids resumed their Disney marathon. It was just as well; *Jessie, iCarly,* and *Austin and Ally* seemed to be the only thing on TV, besides *Cold Case* and *Law and Order: Special Victims Unit.* While the older kids were caught up in their programs, we were content to be entertained by our one-year-old grandson, who impressed us with his amazing agility. He took a short nap when we returned from the mall and woke full of energy.

Technically he wasn't walking yet, but he managed to maneuver his way around the family room by pulling up on various pieces of furniture and sidestepping or crawling from one to the other. Mason was like a kid in a candy store. He had the undivided attention of his parents and grandparents; he knew it, and he made the most of it.

I watched April as she watched her son moving across the room barely missing the corner of the cocktail table. I saw her flinch and restrain herself when he tripped over his own little feet and fell face forward to the carpeted floor. I smiled to myself, identifying with her distress. I remembered all too well what it was like when Kevin and Kenny were that age. Wanting to protect them and at the same time not wanting to let my fear rub off on them. I remembered Garry telling me not to coddle them. "Give them a beat," he said. "They'll get up, dust themselves off, and keep moving. If you don't make a big deal out of it, they won't."

I wanted to know what made him think he knew so much about it; after all, he was a first-time parent too. Then I remembered he was the oldest of four boys, so he probably did know more about it than I did. As usual, he had been right. They fell and they got up; they knew I was always there if they needed me, but ninety percent of the time they didn't.

"I know it's hard to watch them fall," I said. "Your first instinct is to rush to them and comfort them and check for broken bones. Raising boys is a lot harder than girls, although if memory serves me, Mac and Londyn were just as rambunctious at his age. They tell us we have to teach them to be strong and independent, but what they don't tell you is how hard it is to stand by when they fall and let them get up on their own."

April looked at her son with a mixture of pride and awe. "I know," she said, shaking her head. "He has no fear! My heart is in my mouth all the time. Kenny keeps telling me if I don't make a big deal out of it when he falls, he won't."

I looked from my husband to my son and smiled. "Hmm," I said. "I wonder where he got that from."

While initially Mason's energy seemed endless, eventually he ran out of steam. Like the night before, Garry seized the opportunity to do what he did best. He gathered him up in his arms, and within minutes, he was sound asleep on his shoulder. I could tell he was reluctant to let him go when Kenny came to take him to bed. Kevin had a son, and now Kenny finally had one too. That meant the Carter name would live on through his two grandsons.

I knew he adored his granddaughters, but I had only to look at my husband's face to know how much it meant to him that the Carter name would carry on for generations.

Lying in bed later that night, he turned to me and said, "I love that little boy."

"Really," I said, trying to keep a straight face. "I never would have guessed."

He ignored my sarcasm and pulled me into his arms. Kissing my forehead as I lay my head on his shoulder, he said, "Seriously, I really love that little boy!"

"Seriously," I said, snuggling closer. "I'm a hundred percent sure the feeling is mutual."

I was so happy at that moment. I was so grateful we only had two more years before we could retire and be free to spend more time with our grandchildren. I dreamed that night like I had done so many nights before about all the fun vacations we wanted to take with them. I dreamed about all the places we wanted to show them and experience with them. Two years was only twenty-four months, and yet it seemed like an eternity. *Please, God,* I prayed. *Please let us get there.*

Sunday started off a lot like Saturday, only a little later. I don't know what time the kids went to bed Saturday night, but I was grateful they didn't get up at the crack of dawn on Sunday. Everyone was feeling a little lazy that morning and that was just fine; we were, after all, on vacation. When we finally started stirring, the first thing the kids wanted to know was when they could go to the pool.

"You need to eat some breakfast first," Kenny said.

That pacified them for a little while, but as soon as the last piece of bacon was consumed, they were ready to go.

By the time we finally allowed them to put on their swimsuits, and collected beach towels, pool toys, sunscreen, and goggles, they were like little convicts just released from prison. They couldn't get to the pool fast enough. Between Kenny and their Papa, they had a ball. I stayed on the patio to catch up on some reading, but I couldn't concentrate. There was so much squealing, laughing, and splashing coming from the pool, I finally put my book down and went to join in on the fun.

I watched them play in the pool, each one vying for their grandpa's attention. It was hard to tell who was having more fun, the kids or Garry. All I could do was smile and think to myself, *This is what it's gonna be like.* I didn't want this vacation to end, and I was already looking forward to the next one.

◆

WE SPENT THE REST of Sunday and all day Monday together, the whole family, but Monday evening Kenny and April had to head back home because they had to go back to work. They took Mason with them but left the girls so they could continue to bond with Noah. The plan was for us to spend the next couple of days with the kids, check out on Friday morning, and return to Kenny's house, where we would spend the night and fly back to Chicago on Saturday.

Garry had that one last evening with Mason on Friday, and he made the most of it. It was an emotional departure on Saturday when we left for the airport. We hugged and kissed the girls and told them how much we enjoyed them, and how much we were looking forward to our next vacation with them. Garry held Mason an extra-long time and seemed reluctant to let him go. He kissed and hugged him.

"I'm so glad I got to meet you, little man," he said. "I promise Papa's going to see you again soon."

It never occurred to any of us standing in the foyer of Kenny's house that day, it was a promise he would not be able to keep.

On the return flight, Noah said over and over again how much fun he'd had with us, but there was an underlying sadness in his voice. I knew that he really enjoyed spending time with his cousins and wished he was able to see them more often. It was the reason I was so looking forward to future vacations with all of them.

When we finally made it home, we were exhausted from traveling, but not too tired to replay every detail of our time with our grandbabies. We talked and laughed about every cute and outrageous thing they did or said as we looked through the pictures we took and relived every precious moment.

The joy of that vacation stayed with us and lifted our spirits for weeks. I will always be grateful for the time we had, however short, and I pray that as my grandchildren grow, the memories of that vacation and those last days with their beloved Papa will remain in their hearts and minds, as precious to them as they are to me.

When we returned to work following our trip, I found that I was no longer angry about my impending job loss and the resulting changes to our plans for the future. The family trip had somehow calmed me and given me hope. That peaceful and joyous time had enabled me to embrace my husband's prediction that God would see us through yet another transition in our lives and work it all out for our good.

As much as I would miss my fellow coworkers, the other family that I'd spent the last twenty-three years of my life with, I was no longer dreading or fearful about my last days on the job. Instead, I was looking forward to what I believed would mark the start of a new beginning for me and Garry. I'd finally have the time to tackle some long-neglected projects around the house, like purging some of the junk we'd accumulated over the last thirty years. It would also give us an opportunity to make some repairs around the house that hopefully would increase the value of our property and make it easier to sell in the current real-estate market.

At home I made countless to-do lists. My plan was to give myself a few days to enjoy not having to go to work, and once we returned from our trip to San Diego in early September, I'd get down to business. At work I immersed myself in the task of training my replacement and gradually turning over all my daily responsibilities to him. If everything went according to the new company's plans, by the time we reached my last week of employment, I would be functioning in a purely supervisory capacity.

Teaching someone else to do my job, a job that had become second nature to me, proved to be a lot harder than I anticipated. Over the last several years, the job had become extremely stressful, and constant changes in systems and management made it equally frustrating. I took pride in what I did and the way I did it, so in those final weeks, I struggled with mixed emotions. Part of me was grateful and looking forward to being relieved of the stress, yet another part of me was a little reluctant to let go. I found myself not wanting to share the knowledge I'd accumulated over the past twenty-three years, to pass the torch, so to speak.

In retrospect, I believe it had a lot to do with the fact that it had not been my choice to do so. Once again, the course of my life had been changed by the decisions of people who gave no thought to how their decisions impacted my life. They may have given me no choice with regard to my job, but I had to believe that God's plans for me were bigger and better. They may have forced me to change direction, but my destiny was ordained by God, and that was something they lacked the power to change.

CHAPTER EIGHT

August 2012

I T WAS THE TWENTY-NINTH of August. My last work day had finally arrived. I got up at 4:45 a.m. like I'd done every other work day. I drove to the train station and rode the train downtown for the last time, and then walked the six blocks to the office. If you'd asked me a month ago, I would have sworn that when this day arrived I would be skipping all the way to the office.

The closer I got to the office, though, I realized it was a bittersweet end to a long journey. As I thought about saying goodbye to my fellow coworkers, about the prospect of perhaps never seeing some of them ever again, I found it hard to summon the joy I had been so sure I would feel.

There was no work to do that day. My cubicle had been cleaned out, and all my work had been turned over to my replacement. The only thing left to do was my exit interview and turn in my employee ID. After that formality, my last hours were spent walking around the office saying my goodbyes. A lot of employees had been released earlier in the month, so there weren't many of us left on that day. Everywhere you looked, there were clusters of us standing around reminiscing about the many years we had spent together, and all the people we had watched come and go. We discussed our future plans, said our goodbyes, shared some hugs, and fought back tears.

On any other day we would be watching the clock, counting the seconds until we could escape. But on that last day, nobody seemed in any hurry to leave. It was if we all knew once we walked out those doors for the last time, the life we'd known up until then was finally over, and nothing would ever be the same.

The walk back to the train station was long and devoid of the excitement I had expected to feel. For years I had looked forward to no longer being a slave to the Metra trains, but as I boarded the train to return home for the last time, it was with a tinge of sadness. Just like I would miss my coworkers, so too would I miss my train buddies. We'd put in a lot of years together on those train rides to and from work, and I would truly miss our time together. My stop at the Flossmoor station was the last stop on the line. On August 29, 2012, it was the last stop for me in more ways than one.

The day after my last day, I fully intended to sleep late and languish in my bed until at least noon. I wanted to take full advantage of my new unemployed status. At least, that had been the plan when I turned off my alarm and went to bed the night before. On the morning of August 30, however, my body betrayed me and I woke at 4:45 a.m., just as I had done every work day. As soon as my eyes popped open, I knew it was way too early, so I closed my eyes tightly and took deep breaths hoping to fall back to sleep. After ten minutes of tossing and turning, I knew it was futile and got out of bed. I made my bed, took a shower, and dressed. Then I noticed for the first time how quiet the house was. Garry had left for work early. I sat on the bed for a while trying to figure out what I was going to do with myself. After taking my medication, I opened the refrigerator looking for something to cook for breakfast, but realized I wasn't hungry and decided to go for a walk.

It was a beautiful day outside, not too hot despite the brilliant sunshine. It was almost as quiet outside as it had been in the house. Except for a few birds chirping and an occasional car passing by, I seemed to be the only other living soul in my subdivision. I was used to the hustle and bustle of the streets of Chicago, and after thirty minutes of suburban solitude, I felt lonely and bored so I decided to go back home.

Just as I walked back into the house my phone rang, and I smiled when I saw it was my Pooh.

"Hey," I said.

"Hey girl," he said in that sultry voice. "You up?"

"Yeah," I groaned. "Unfortunately, I've been up. I just came in from taking a walk. It's only nine thirty, and I'm already bored to tears!"

"Poor baby," he said, laughing. "It's tough being retired, huh?"

"I can't believe I'm saying this, but I don't know what I'm going to do with myself," I said, ignoring his sarcasm. "I feel like I need to be doing something, but I don't know where to start."

"Babe, you've been doing something for the last twenty-three years," he said. "This is your time to relax and enjoy yourself. Read a book, write a book . . . better yet, I know what you can do."

"What?" I asked.

"Why don't you get the suitcases out and start packing for our trip? That should keep you busy for a while," he said, laughing. "When I get home, I'll think of something else you can do."

I could see him grinning through the phone. "Dirty old man," I said. "Any chance you can come home early?" I asked seductively.

"Don't tempt me, woman," he said, laughing again.

"You started it," I laughed. "Now get off this phone and get back to work!"

We joked back and forth for a few more minutes, and then we hung up so he really could get back to work.

My short walk around the subdivision may have been less than stimulating, but I did succeed in working up an appetite. I decided to fix myself a snack before retrieving our luggage as Garry had suggested. While I ate, I browsed through one of our photo albums. We'd traveled a lot in our thirty-nine years together. As I perused the pictures from some of our previous vacations, my trip into the past evoked fond memories of all the places we'd explored together. I started thinking about our upcoming trip to San Diego, and I could feel the excitement building up.

I was really looking forward to this trip because I'd never been to California before. Our only exploration of the West Coast consisted of two trips to Seattle, to visit Kenny when he was stationed there while in the air force. There were several places I wanted to visit in the Golden State, but we decided to make San Diego our first stop.

We planned to stay at one of our Wyndham time-share resorts, and then take a day trip to Los Angeles. For the past several weeks I'd been browsing the internet, searching for points of interest. Whenever we traveled, I liked to check out places to see and find good restaurants beforehand. Garry was an avid seafood lover, and I had to have a good steak or prime rib. I found several promising seafood restaurants and steakhouses close to the resort.

As far as places to see and things to do, I was really looking forward to visiting the San Diego Zoo. Everyone I talked to said we could not go there without checking out the infamous zoo. While in Los Angeles, I definitely wanted to visit Universal Studios Hollywood and get a picture of the Hollywood sign. I'd seen it millions of times on TV and in the movies. I was thrilled to have the opportunity to see it up close and in person.

It was actually way too early to pack for our trip; I know Garry only suggested it to give me something to do. We booked the trip for September 28 through October 5. He told me it was an early birthday present. My birthday was October 10, but the resort didn't have anything available the week of my birthday. I didn't really care when we went, as long as we went together.

I loved traveling with my Pooh. He was my road buddy, and I was his ride-or-die chick. He had a way of making every trip we took, whether we hit the highway or hopped on a plane, a big adventure. Both our jobs were stressful, and as hard as we tried to leave work at work, sometimes it followed us home. Despite our best efforts, sometimes it interfered with our personal private time.

Day in and day out, we handled our business at work and took care of home. We did our best not to let the struggle to do so cause irreparable damage to our relationship. That's why our vacation time was so important to us. It was our escape from all our worries and responsibilities. It didn't matter how far we went or how long we stayed, as long as we were together. As soon as we climbed into the car or walked through the doors of the airport, we shed the pressures of the world like extra skin. Nothing existed but the time and space between us.

We became different people—joyful, hopeful, and expectant. Our time away gave us joy. The excitement of experiencing something new or even revisiting the old and familiar gave us hope. We were joyful and hopeful, and we expected to have a good time. Our good time was like a shot of adrenaline. It recharged us; it was the boost we needed to return to the world and continue to fight the good fight. We were getting close, but we still had miles to go before we could reap the rewards of our labor. Our vacations, our temporary escapes, were the bridge between our present and our future. Those precious stolen hours bridged the gap between what we had and what we wanted.

For the first time in twenty-three years, when we returned from vacation, I wouldn't have a job to return to. I was officially unemployed. It wasn't the first time I'd been put out to pasture, so to speak, but I was younger then. At sixty years old, I no longer had the desire or the energy to start over. I wasn't lazy. It wasn't that I didn't want to work; I just didn't want to put my future in the hands of another heartless corporation, only to have it snatched away again on a whim.

I didn't know how much time I had left, but I wanted to spend whatever time I had doing something that made me happy. If I was going to reinvent myself, I wanted to do it for me—for us, not for anyone else. My husband insisted we were going to be fine. He said God would work it out just like he'd done so many times before. When I looked into my spiritual bank book and reviewed all the deposits God had made, the proof was right there in front of me—proof that he had brought us through over and over again. Yet . . . there was this nagging feeling, like a rash that wouldn't heal. This growing sense of doom, an internal warning that for better or worse, our lives were about to change in ways I would never have imagined. I couldn't shake the feeling that whatever was coming, nothing would ever be the same.

I was really looking forward to this vacation. I was praying that the good time I expected to have would dispel that nagging feeling, if only for a little while.

I had about three weeks to go before I really had to start packing for our trip.

In the meantime, I decided to get started on my to-do list. Friends had warned me if we were going to move, we shouldn't wait until the last minute to start packing.

"You'll be amazed at how much junk you've accumulated," they said. "Start getting rid of it now or you'll just wind up taking it all with you. If you're going to pay professional movers to move you, remember—they charge by the box!"

The plan was to downsize, so taking it with us was definitely not an option. We wanted a ranch-style house; we were both done with stairs. Mom was moving with us, so space would be limited. We needed to get rid of as much as possible. One look at our closets and I knew that was probably the first place to start. My weight had yo-yoed up and down more times than I cared to remember over the last several years.

I was sure I had clothes in at least three to four different sizes in my closet, and no doubt Garry did too.

"What you doing?" I asked when I called him at work.

"Trying to finish up some paperwork so I can get the heck out of here. Why?" he asked.

"Can you start bringing me some boxes home?"

"What do you need boxes for?" he asked.

"If we're going to be ready for this move, I need to start getting rid of about thirty years of junk we've accumulated in this house, and since I'm not working, now would be a good time to start. I know it's going to take time, and I don't want to wait till the last minute. I think I'll give some to Goodwill, and I'll probably have a couple of garage sales. Bottom line, I need to start, and while I'm getting rid of the stuff we don't need, I can pack the stuff we're going to keep. If I do a little bit each day by the time we're ready to go, we'll be all packed up."

"Okay, I can start bringing some home this weekend," he said. "Now let me get off this phone, so I can finish up here and come home."

Standing in front of my closet looking at its contents was overwhelming. Sorting through all of the clothes, shoes, purses, and jewelry proved to be physically and emotionally exhausting. At the back of the closets were all of the clothes I could no longer wear.

The larger sizes depressed me; it was painful to remember that I'd ever let myself get that big. The smaller sizes didn't make me feel any better, since I was reasonably sure I'd never get that small again.

Almost every outfit, purse, pair of shoes, and piece of jewelry had a history that told a story about my past. There was the two-piece gold formal I'd worn to Kevin's wedding. His wedding had been the first big event in my life after finishing my breast-cancer treatment. Looking at it now produced fresh tears of gratitude remembering how I'd been so afraid I wouldn't be around to see my sons grow up, let alone get married. Then there was the elegant red evening suit I'd worn to Juanda's wedding. I'd been so happy for her. I smiled to myself thinking about how much fun we'd had at her reception. The blue formal I'd worn to my mother's wedding. I was her wedding coordinator and her matron of honor, but I felt more like the mother of the bride.

When my hair fell out during my chemo treatments, everyone kept buying me these beautiful scarves to wear. I didn't wear them anymore, but up till now I hadn't been able to part with them. They were a reminder of a very difficult and challenging time in my life, and yet they were also a reminder that I was still here—a survivor. I knew that packing up our house in general would not be easy. There were so many memories in this house in the form of clothes, furniture, pictures, and other household items, every one representing significant periods in our thirty-nine years together. We couldn't take everything, however, and if we were going to embrace our future, we'd have to let go of some of our past.

In the spare bedroom, I made two piles of clothes. One pile for the Goodwill, and the other I would save for garage sales. After a couple of hours, I knew it would take more than the three weeks I had before our trip. Decluttering our house was certainly no fun, but it was definitely necessary, and it did help to pass the time. After that first day, I set aside a couple of hours every morning to sort through our possessions. After the first two weeks, I began to feel like one of those people I saw on TV. *I need someone objective to come in and intervene,* I thought as I looked with frustration at my "keep pile." It was still way too big compared to my "get-rid-of pile."

Before I knew it, it was time to really start packing for our trip. As I hauled the suitcases up from the basement, once again I could feel the excitement bubbling up.

On the night prior to our departure, Kevin came out and spent the night so he could take us to the airport early the next morning. It had become his unofficial duty to transport his globetrotting parents to and from the airport, but he didn't seem to mind. We were grateful and comforted by the knowledge that we could count on him to look after the house while we were away. As much as I appreciated his making himself available to us, I looked forward to the day we could all travel together as a family.

I never slept the night before a trip. My brain refused to shut down, and I repeatedly reviewed my travel checklist. I tossed and turned, wondering if I remembered to pack this or that, or if I set the alarm for the right time, especially if we were flying. The last thing I wanted was for either of us to have a heart attack running through the airport trying to make the plane. With Garry's bad knees, running really wasn't an option anyway. From the time my feet hit the floor in the morning, my heart was pounding and I was a ball of nervous energy. I couldn't seem to settle down until were seated on the plane. Just before we started to roll down the runway, I closed my eyes, took Garry's hand, and asked God for travel mercy.

I opened my eyes as I felt the plane speed down the runway and begin to ascend into the clouds. I looked at Garry and smiled and felt the stress leave my body. In a little over four hours, we would land in San Diego. By the time the flight attendants finished the welcome-aboard/safety speech, my sleepless night caught up with me. I pulled out my tablet and attempted to continue reading the second installment in the Fifty Shades trilogy. After reading the same page for the third time, I gave in and shut down my tablet, closed my eyes, and succumbed to the much-needed sleep that had eluded me the night before.

I woke briefly when they brought the beverage cart around, but soon fell back to sleep. It was relatively quiet on the plane considering it was completely full. I don't know how long I slept the second time I closed my eyes; it seemed like only seconds before I felt Garry nudge me and point out the window. We were approaching the San Diego airport, and suddenly, my fatigue forgotten, I couldn't wait to get on the ground and start our vacation.

While standing outside the airport awaiting transport to pick up our rental car, an abundance of warm California sun blanketed our bodies. It was accompanied by a gentle breeze, preventing it from being uncomfortably hot. I was awed by how bright and lush everything looked. The beautiful trees were tall, standing like pillars with bright-green leaves, and there were beautiful flowers of every hue everywhere. The multicolored buildings were even more beautiful than I imagined from the books I'd read and the pictures I'd seen on TV and in the movies.

Once we retrieved our rental car, we checked our directions we printed out at home and headed for the resort. Our routine was always the same. When we arrived at the resort, we checked in, unpacked, located the nearest Walmart, and went shopping for groceries. The thing I liked most about staying at resorts versus hotels was the full kitchen. It allowed us to prepare some of our meals at the resort and not have to eat out all the time. It was convenient, and it gave us the opportunity to save money for other things.

We bought breakfast food, snacks, and preparations for at least two dinners at the resort. No matter where we went or how long we stayed, Garry always requested the same thing: smothered pork chops and rice with gravy. He didn't care what else I bought to cook, but he had to have that!

"You can have that at home," I teased.

"Yeah, but it doesn't taste the same as your 'vacation pork chops,'" he'd say.

I just shook my head and laughed because I made them the exact same way, whether at home or on vacation.

"What do you want to do tonight?" I asked after we checked out and headed to the parking lot.

"I don't know about you, Kitten, but after we put away the groceries and eat a little something, I just want to cuddle up and watch some TV. I'm beat!" he said.

"Sounds good to me," I said. "I'm tired too."

We ate sandwiches and chips, and then cuddled up in bed with the magazines and maps the resort provided highlighting all the local eating, shopping, and entertainment spots. We turned on the TV, but after about twenty minutes, we weren't watching it, it was watching us—sleep.

We were staying at the WorldMark San Diego resort in Mission Valley. Mission Valley was a quiet little suburban city approximately four and a half miles from Balboa Park, which is comparable to San Francisco's Golden Gate Park, or New York's Central Park. The pretty peach-and-turquoise resort was comprised of several three-story buildings, and we were on the third floor of our building. We had a lovely terrace off the family room, and while sitting out there we could see all the comings and goings up to two blocks away. We checked in on Saturday, and I woke early that Sunday morning before Garry. He'd been so tired the night before; I wanted him to sleep as long as possible. Trying my best not to wake him, I slipped out of bed as quietly as I could and went out onto the terrace.

The sun had not fully emerged from behind the clouds yet, and it was quiet except for the singing birds and the sound of the occasional car on the street below.

I sat there for a long time enjoying the quiet solitude and thanking God for blessing us with this opportunity to spend this time together. I didn't even realize I had closed my eyes, nor did I hear the sliding glass door open when Garry opened it and stepped outside. I felt his gentle kiss on my forehead and turned to him with a smile. His eyes were still cloudy with sleep, and his voice husky.

"You left me," he said, pouting, and kissed me again.

"You were sleeping so soundly I didn't want to wake you. I know how tired you were, and we don't have to be any place at any specific time, so I let you sleep. That's one of the benefits of being on vacation."

"I woke up and you were gone, and it was cold in the bed," he said, sounding like a little boy.

"Please," I said, laughing. "You generate enough heat to warm three beds. You couldn't possibly have been cold."

"Come back to bed," he said in that husky voice while nuzzling my neck.

"Aren't you hungry?" I asked, enjoying the nuzzling.

"Yes, I am," he said, his voice deeper and softer.

"I meant breakfast," I said, laughing.

"Hmm, so did I," he said in his sexiest voice.

Before I could reply again, he stood and took my hand, leading me back inside. I figured I better follow him before we were reported by our neighbors for indecent exposure. A couple of hours later we finally got up and got dressed. By then I was hungry, so we decided to check out one of the local eateries recommended by the resort.

By the time we located the infamous restaurant and walked to it from the parking spot, it took thirty minutes to find. I thought I would faint from hunger. I silently prayed the place would live up to its hype. According to their ad, they had an extensive selection of pancakes, waffles, and French toast, among other things. The customer reviews we checked out online praised them for their excellent service and generous portions. The best part was they served breakfast all day, which was great because it was already well past lunch.

We browsed the menu online and we'd already decided what we wanted. I was looking forward to their cinnamon pecan French toast, and Garry had decided on catfish and grits with hash browns. We hoped they tasted as good as they looked in the pictures. When we walked through the doors, my face fell and my heart sank. It was nothing like I imagined from its ad. It looked like a little hole in the wall, and I was afraid we'd made a huge mistake.

Don't judge a book by its cover, I thought to myself. I stole a glance at Garry to see his reaction, but he didn't seem to be fazed by its appearance. Maybe we'd be pleasantly surprised . . . I hoped. A sign just inside the entrance said to seat ourselves, so we chose a table and sat down. There were only a couple other tables occupied, and I sincerely hoped that was because we were in between the lunch and dinner crowd, and not a result of the food. Seemingly out of thin air, a waiter appeared bringing glasses of water and menus.

"Hi, folks, how are you doing today?" he asked.

"Hungry!" we said in unison.

"Is this your first time here?" he asked.

"Yes," I replied. "We saw your ad in the packet supplied by our resort and decided to check you out."

"Well, welcome. My name is John. I'll be your server, and I hope you won't be disappointed."

From your lips to God's ear, I thought.

"Do you need a few minutes to look over the menu?" he asked.

"No," I said. "We already checked the menu out online and we both know what we want."

John took our order and disappeared again. When he walked away, Garry turned to me and flashed a knowing smile. Patting my hand, he said, "Don't worry, Kitten, we both read the reviews and we both chose this place. If it's not good, it's not your fault."

"How do you do that all the time?" I asked.

"Do what?" he asked.

"Read my mind," I answered.

"Oh, I don't know," he said, grinning. "Maybe it has something to do with the fact that I've known you all your life."

"Just about," I said, laughing. "People are always teasing you about stealing me from the cradle."

Just as he was about to respond with a snappy retort, the smell of my cinnamon French toast permeated the air around our table. We looked up just as John, our server, placed a huge platter in front of me. The piping-hot French toast had to be at least two inches thick. You could smell cinnamon and butter drenched in warm maple syrup.

Sprinkled on the top of the toast were huge pieces of pecans, and surrounding the two massive pieces of sourdough bread were four slices of thick, smoked bacon, which looked more like ham slices.

My mouth was watering, and as if to emphasize my hunger, my stomach rumbled loudly. I laughed to myself as I imagined it was saying, "Eat, dammit! What are you waiting for?" While we were salivating over my food, John returned again with a platter for Garry. He placed before him two gigantic, perfectly fried catfish filets surrounded by a generous portion of creamy grits drenched in butter and an equally generous portion of hash browns with diced onions and green pepper.

"Can I get you folks anything else?" John asked.

"Yeah," I replied, "two more people to help us eat all this food!"

"We have carryout containers," he said, laughing. "Enjoy your meal."

I was so grateful for our full kitchen back at the resort, which included an oven and a microwave, because as hungry as we were, we were definitely going to need those carryout containers.

After we paid our check and collected our carryout containers, we made that long walk back to our car. The sun was fully emerged by then and the temperature had risen close to ninety degrees. I had eaten less than half the food on my plate, and yet I was still so full I could barely breathe. As soon as Garry opened my car door, I literally fell into the car.

He turned up the air conditioning and asked, "What do you want to do now, Kitten?"

Do? I thought. *I can barely move.* "I don't suppose we could just take a nap . . . right here, right now."

He laughed. "That sounds tempting, but I'm afraid if I close my eyes, I won't be waking up anytime soon. I think we need to try and walk off some of this food."

Walking anywhere was the last thing I wanted to do, but I knew he was right. "You have some place in particular in mind?" I asked.

"I saw a bunch of shops a couple of streets over, and they have parking over there. You feel like a little window-shopping?"

That got my attention. I was always in the mood for shopping. "I think I can manage that," I replied.

He gave me a look that said, *Why am I not surprised?* "Okay," he said, laughing. "Shopping it is!"

For the next two hours, we ducked in and out of quaint little shops sampling homemade fudge and hand-packed ice cream. We browsed through overpriced jewelry stores and boutiques specializing in resort wear designed to divest tourists of all their vacation money. It was too early in the trip to do any real shopping, so I looked but kept my wallet out of sight.

We succeeded in walking off our late breakfast, and now it was no longer my stomach that hurt, but my feet. I noticed Garry's limp had become more pronounced as well.

"I don't know about you, baby, but I'm ready to head back to the resort. I've had enough for today."

He smiled with a look of relief and asked, "Now who's reading whose mind?"

Taking his hand, I smiled. "Come on, old man, let's go home."

Sunday night was almost an exact repeat of the night before. We changed into our jammies and settled down to watch a little TV, but after a couple of hours, once again it was the TV that was watching us.

Weather-wise, Monday was a carbon copy of the last two days. It was warm but not excessively so, and a cool breeze tempered the rays of the ever-present sun. Being a time-share owner could be viewed by some as a blessing and a curse. Anytime you vacationed at one of the resorts, they did their best to try and sell you more time or convince you to upgrade to the latest, greatest version.

The first order of business at check-in was to get you signed up for a presentation. They took about ninety minutes out of your vacation time, but to compensate you, they offered discounted tickets for local attractions and/or gift certificates for dinner at local participating restaurants.

Over the years Garry and I had devised a system. We checked out the list of available gifts and discounts to see which ones we were interested in. Then we made a pact. We had already paid off our original time-share, and we weren't interested in buying any more. Our only interest was in the gifts. We agreed no matter what they offered, our answer would be a firm no. They were always disappointed they couldn't convince us to take advantage of their outstanding offer, but we'd sat through the presentation so they had to cough up the gifts.

On this particular occasion, we chose discount tickets to the San Diego Zoo, Universal Studios Hollywood, and a dinner cruise. Tickets in hand, we laughed all the way back to our unit.

"Whew, you had me worried there for a minute, old man. I thought you were about to cave in back there."

He laughed and shook his head. "Naw, she was working so hard I didn't want to be too harsh. I had to let her think she was winning me over, and then let her down easy."

"Oh, you're good," I said, laughing and shaking my head. "You're bad—but good!"

I wanted to see the ocean, so after a quick lunch we drove to the beach and spent the rest of the afternoon there. By the time we changed and headed out, the sun had decided to take a siesta behind the clouds. As a result, when we arrived at the beach, the sky looked grey and the ocean looked murky and ominous. Far off in the distance we could barely make out the skyscrapers that dotted the San Diego skyline.

"It looks like it's going to pour down raining any minute," I said, disappointed.

Garry looked up at the sky and shook his head at the dreary skyline. "I don't know, Kitten, do you want to bail and come back another day?"

"Naw," I answered. "We've come all the way out here, let's stay for a while. Maybe it will clear up."

As we walked hand in hand barefoot in the wet sand along the shore, the theme of *Jaws* came to mind. I watched all the children with their parents, and couples young and old frolicking in the vast ocean, and wondered what lurked beneath the surface of all that murky water.

For years I'd dreamed of seeing the Pacific Ocean up close and personal. In the movies it was always depicted as this never-ending body of crystal-clear blue water. On this particular day as we stood on the shore littered with seaweed, it was anything but clear and far from blue. It looked more like a big, grey blanket.

I didn't know if I'd ever get back out to the coast again, so I really wanted to take advantage of this opportunity. I wanted to run out and splash around in the water like everyone else. I wanted to tell everybody back home I'd taken a dip in the ocean, but I couldn't shake that irrational fear of the unknown. I knew it was silly. I was standing in water up to my ankles, but I just couldn't make myself go any farther.

Garry seemed to sense my unease, and he didn't press me to go any farther into the ocean. We stood there together, the water surging and swirling around our ankles, and the look in his eyes told me everything I needed to know. If this was as far as I wanted to go, it was all right with him.

Grateful for his silent understanding, I continued to stand there, content to be right where I was with him by my side. *I'm here*, I thought, *I can see the ocean. I've seen it with my own eyes, and that's enough.* We spent the rest of the afternoon walking up and down the beach searching for seashells, or just sitting talking and enjoying the sound of the waves and the gentle breeze.

We had eaten a light lunch and we were both starting to get hungry again, so we decided to head back to the resort. In the car driving back, I asked Garry what he wanted to do for dinner.

"If you're not too tired, you know what I want," he said, grinning.

"Yeah, I know," I said, laughing. I made his "vacation" pork chops, and after we ate, we planned out the rest of the week.

The next thing on our list of things to see was the San Diego Zoo. We planned to get up early, have a light breakfast, and spend the day checking out the inhabitants. I was really looking forward to seeing the infamous panda bears. The sun was up and out early the next morning, bringing with it intense heat. When we arrived at the zoo, it felt like it was at least a hundred degrees outside, and there was little to no shade to shelter us from the piercing sunshine.

It was fairly early in the morning, but after about an hour we were already looking like we'd been out there all day. Garry's bald head was glistening despite the fact he was wearing a hat, and any curls I had when we left the resort had long since disappeared. We weren't the only ones suffering from the effects of the extremely hot day. Everywhere we looked, adults and children alike were guzzling very expensive water and any other liquids they could consume, as well as desperately searching for the practically nonexistent shade. Despite the heat, we were all excited to see the animals, though it was very clear they could not care less about seeing us.

If they weren't sleeping, they were hiding in their cages trying to escape from the piercing sun and ever-present heat. They weren't the least bit interested in posing for the pictures we mere humans-turned-paparazzi were tripping over each other to take. In fact, the only animals that seemed eager to show off for their guests were the polar bears and the hippopotamuses. Of course, that probably had something to do with the fact that they were swimming around in their own pools. It was so hot outside, just watching them made me want to jump in and join them.

The San Diego Zoo is enormous! I honestly don't believe it's possible to see the entire zoo in one day. You definitely want to go in cooler weather. Between the heat and all the walking, I was ready to go after a couple of hours, but after traveling all that way to see it, I didn't want to punk out.

We hung in there for another couple of hours, but we both caved in soon after that. I could tell all the walking was doing a job on Garry's knee, and the heat had taken a toll on both of us.

"I don't know about you, baby, but I've had enough," I said.

He looked at me with a look of extreme gratitude, and I had to laugh. It was obvious from the expression on his face he had not wanted to be the first to throw in the towel.

"I was hoping you'd say that," he said. "I didn't want to cut your day short. There's so much left to see, but my knee is killing me."

"I could tell," I said. "I've had about enough. My feet are killing me. The sun is giving me a headache, and the heat is making it hard for me to breathe. This reminds me of the first time we took the kids to Disney. We should have come out here at night."

"I agree," he said. "Let's get out of here!"

The plan had been to go out to dinner after the zoo, but we were so exhausted we decided to take a short nap first. We slept like two five-year-olds who'd skipped their afternoon nap. We woke up at 1:00 a.m., ate a quick sandwich, and went back to sleep. After a quick breakfast, the next morning we headed to Los Angeles for our day trip to Universal Studios Hollywood. I had my camera out and ready to capture a picture of the infamous Hollywood sign as we entered the city. It looked a lot more majestic on TV and in the movies than it did in person.

Once we arrived at Universal Studios, I soon realized if you've seen one theme park . . . you've seen them all. Seeing all the props and special effects used to make all the cool movies we'd paid big bucks to see, and still watched over and over again, was a little disillusioning. They seemed so corny. Seeing the shark from the infamous *Jaws* movies made me laugh and wonder how I could ever have been afraid to go in the water after seeing the movie. It did, however, give us a new appreciation for the skill and artistry of the special-effects technicians and the magic of cinematography.

I got a kick out of seeing the lot where they filmed *Desperate Housewives*. Although the houses on Wisteria Lane didn't look as grand on the lot as they did on my TV. Perhaps if I'd caught a glimpse of Gabrielle Solis and that fine husband of hers, or Susan Meyer, or

Lynette Scavo, it would have been more believable. All in all, we had a good day. It wasn't as hot in LA as it had been in San Diego, so we were able to walk around and enjoy all the sights and the food and all the movie theme music blasting everywhere. There were rides and plenty of places to sit and take a break when we got tired of walking.

We left satisfied that we had gotten our money's worth, and as we headed back to the resort, we found that the LA traffic more than lived up to its reputation. When we arrived back in San Diego, we picked up some takeout and some wine. We sat on the balcony, sipped our wine, and listened to the music coming from the local sports bar up the street. Afterward, we vegged out in front of the TV again, where we fell asleep happily exhausted.

♦

DESPITE THE FATIGUE I felt after our visit to the zoo the day before, I woke up very early Thursday morning to the soft purring of my Pooh lying next to me. He was out, and I thought to myself, *I could use a few more winks too.* But my mind was already racing, and I knew going back to sleep would be impossible. Garry looked so peaceful I didn't want to disturb his rest, so I slipped out of bed and went to sit out on the terrace.

While watching the sun make its grand entrance, my mind began to wander, and I started thinking beyond our last two days in San Diego. For the first time in twenty-three years, when we returned home from this vacation, I wouldn't be returning to work. No more last-day-of-vacation depression. No more stressing about returning to my little cubicle and all the work that had piled up while I was away. I wouldn't lose any sleep on our first night back home wondering what went wrong and how many fires I would have to put out. This time when we returned home, I would simply resume decluttering and downsizing our belongings in preparation for our impending move.

I was so busy thinking about the thirty years of memories I had to sift through and somehow bring myself to part with, I didn't hear Garry join me on the terrace.

"What's with this habit you have of abandoning me, woman?" he asked, leaning down and kissing the top of my head.

I smiled as he sat down beside me and kissed his cheek. "I didn't abandon you, baby, I would never do that. You were sleeping so peacefully, I didn't want to disturb you."

"Ah, but don't you know by now," he said, pulling me onto his lap, "when you leave my side, you take my peace with you."

It was such a beautiful and endearing thing to say, it touched me to my core. Much to my surprise, my eyes began to cloud with unshed tears. I snuggled closer, laying my head on his shoulder.

"I'm sorry," I said. "I never thought of it that way, but I know exactly how you feel. I sleep like a stone when you're lying next to me, because I feel loved and safe; but when you're gone, our bed seems so cold and I feel so alone."

As if nothing else needed to be said, we sat there in silence for a long time enjoying each other and the warmth of the early-morning sun. I was grateful I didn't have to go back to work, but my Pooh, on the other hand, did have to return to work. So, I decided we would spend the last two days of our vacation chillaxing. It would be awhile before we could get away again, so I wanted him to soak up all the R&R he could.

We spent all day watching TV, snacking, and discussing our plans for the future. Clad in our PJs, we talked about everything from what we would do to the house to get it ready to go on the market, how much we thought we would be able to sell it for, to where we wanted to move to and how we were going to get there. We made reservations for dinner at a nearby steakhouse for later that evening, and we didn't even get dressed until thirty minutes before we had to leave for the restaurant.

"You know we could have stayed in tonight," I said after we were seated and handed our menus. "We could have picked up some takeout so you could have stayed in and gotten some more rest."

"We've been resting all day, Kitten. Besides, you didn't really think I was going to take you home without getting you a San Diego steak dinner, did you?"

I smiled, thinking to myself how well he knew me. Out of all the good food we had tasted since we arrived in San Diego, I really was looking forward to enjoying a good steak dinner. It was a vacation tradition. Garry got his seafood, and I got my steak! We ordered appetizers and a cocktail, and since I already knew what I wanted for my entrée, we went ahead and ordered that too.

"Are you enjoying your steak, Kitten?" he asked a few minutes after our waiter brought out our meal.

"Yes, thank you," I said, smiling, while I sat there chewing on an amazing ribeye with all the trimmings. "But tomorrow," I said between bites, "we do absolutely nothing, but pack!"

"Okay, babe, but not until late tomorrow," he said, grinning. "I know we have to go back home, but I don't want to face that reality until I absolutely have to."

The sad little look on his face made me laugh, but I knew exactly how he felt.

Even though I didn't have to go back to work, I wasn't exactly looking forward to the project waiting for me at home. On the one hand, it was a little exciting because it was a reminder that we were getting closer to our goal of getting out of Illinois and the cold weather. But truth be told, I wished I could wiggle my nose like Samantha on *Bewitched* and have the whole thing done.

On Friday we slept late, and when we did wake up, we spent the day in bed with the laptop browsing rental websites. We'd decided we didn't want to buy another house when we moved to Houston. Garry said at our age, he didn't want the responsibility or the headaches.

"I don't want to get saddled with another thirty-year or even fifteen-year mortgage. If something happens to me, I don't want you, or the kids for that matter, to have to worry about trying to sell another house, especially if, God forbid, something happens to both of us. If we rent and something happens, it will be a lot less traumatic to just break the lease if necessary and move on."

At first, we were torn between renting an apartment or a house big enough for all of us. After checking out several of both, we discovered we could rent a house with more square footage for the same amount or less than an apartment, so we started focusing in on rental houses. We both agreed it would have to be a ranch. I'd had it with stairs—we both had—and Mom had severe arthritis, so stairs were not a viable option for her either. We needed everything on one level.

We looked at several houses in various neighborhoods close to Juanda. We made a list of the ones we really liked. The plan was to take a trip to Houston when it got closer to our move time to check out the prospects in person and narrow down our choices.

Even though we didn't really do anything or go anywhere all day, our last day at the resort seemed to move in double time. Before we knew it, it was time to start packing and preparing for our early Saturday-morning departure. On the drive to the airport, we were both pretty quiet. We were lost in our own private thoughts, both torn between wanting to go home so we could move forward, but at the same time not wanting the peace and relaxation of our vacation to end. Even the return flight home seemed shorter. Kevin picked us up from the airport when we arrived back in Chi-Town, and in less than thirty minutes we were back home immersed in our daily routine as if we'd never been away. The only evidence of our departure was our suitcases waiting to be unpacked.

CHAPTER NINE

January 2013

SINCE THE TRIP TO San Diego was an early birthday present from Garry, when my actual birthday arrived, I wasn't expecting anything else from him. I should have known better. Garry came home on October 10 with a card, balloons, and a bottle of J'adore by Christian Dior.

I'd mentioned to him while watching a TV commercial that I wanted to try the fragrance. I didn't think at the time he'd even been paying attention. He always teased me about being the mushy, corny, hopeless romantic in the family. I don't know, maybe after all those years together I'd started to rub off on him. Reflecting back, though, I'd like to think he was just a mushy, corny, hopeless romantic in hiding.

I was more than satisfied and pleasantly surprised with the additional gifts, but it turned out he wasn't finished. Since my birthday fell on a Wednesday, he informed me he was taking me out to dinner and a movie on the weekend. It was just another in a long list of special birthdays I will treasure, made even more special because it was my last birthday with him.

At the end of October, Garry scheduled his second knee-replacement surgery for February 12, 2013. He originally wanted to have it in January so he'd have plenty of time to rehab before our anniversary. His company was conducting some major project in January that he had to be there to oversee, so he pushed it back to February.

"It'll be okay, Kitten," he said when I complained he wasn't giving himself enough time. "Come on, Kitten, remember, this is the second go-around. I got this. I should rehab much faster this time."

"The key word in that sentence, Garry Carter, is *should*," I said, shaking my head with doubt. "I don't care if it is the second time around, three months is just that—three months—and I'm just afraid it's not enough time! You promised me a dance at our anniversary party, and I just wanna make sure you're ready."

"I promised you more than just a dance," he said, winking seductively. "I'll be ready, you just make sure you're ready," he said, flashing me a wicked grin.

"Promises, promises," I said, laughing. My husband was a very stubborn man. I knew there was no changing his mind once it was made up.

I decided to let it go for now, but deep down I was still worried. All I could do was pray that he *would* rehab faster the second time around. I just had to trust God that the surgery and subsequent recovery would go well. I really wanted that dance and anything else that came with it. More than anything, I just wanted my Pooh to be healthy again and pain free.

The next couple of months flew by. With great sadness I bid farewell to summer and embraced the colors of fall, while at the same time dreading the return of the brutal winter wind referred to as the "Hawk." Visitors to the infamous Windy City are always saying what a beautiful city it is. I have to admit to a sense of pride for my city. It possesses some spectacular architecture, the cuisine is extensive and unparalleled, and it's literally a melting pot for all ethnicities and cultures.

The spring and summers are great, the fall is beautiful, but as far as I'm concerned, the winters leave a lot to be desired. The winters are not fit for anything but viewing from indoors. Between the mountains of snow and the subzero temps, I couldn't get away fast enough.

Once Halloween came and went, 2012 was basically a wrap! One minute we were getting ready for Thanksgiving and putting up Christmas lights, and then in the blink of an eye, we were breaking out the bubbly preparing to ring in the New Year. I was still basking in the joy of my new kitchen. Even though it wouldn't be mine for long, I still couldn't help smiling every time I walked into it. I admired the refurbished cabinets, rubbed my hands over my new countertops, polished my shiny new stainless-steel appliances, and marveled over my sixteen-inch ceramic tile. It was a new year, and it was our turn to host the first marriage-ministry meeting of the year. I was looking forward to showing off my new kitchen, but I was also looking forward to getting together with all our members.

It had been a rough year for a lot of us. There had been a lot of illness among us, and many were dealing with attacks on their finances, their families, and their marriages. It was time for us to come together and remind ourselves who was in control. We needed to conduct some spiritual warfare. I wanted us to give God the glory for how he'd already blessed us, to intercede on behalf of those who were dealing with a number of challenges, and thank him in advance for what by faith he would do to restore and renew us. I especially wanted the prayer warriors to lift up Garry and seek God's grace and mercy for his surgery.

When everyone arrived, they were all in agreement that our contractor had done a phenomenal job with our kitchen remodel. Everyone assumed we had purchased new cabinets, and couldn't believe we had just dressed up the old ones. The wives were oohing and aahing, admiring and complimenting everything from the new countertops to the new tile floor. The husbands, on the other hand, were shooting daggers at Garry and giving him a hard time.

"Man, see what you started!" they said. "Now they're gonna be bugging us to remodel our kitchens!" Everyone laughed, but when I looked at the faces of my fellow wives, I laughed and thought to myself, *Yeah, you brothers are in real trouble!*

Every couple hosting the ministry meeting usually provided some kind of snack and beverage for the group. Since Garry would be having surgery next month, I knew this would be the last meeting we would be attending for a while, so I prepared a special spread. I also wanted to use this opportunity to introduce my new business to the group in the hopes of enlisting their support.

We brought everyone up to date on what trials and tribulations we'd each been dealing with over the last several months. We then had prayer seeking God's healing, deliverance, and peace. As we sat around my dining-room table devouring the mini feast I'd prepared, we began to discuss some of the illnesses the husbands in particular were experiencing and/or recovering from. I informed them of Garry's upcoming surgery and solicited their special prayers for his successful surgery and subsequent recovery.

The mention of Garry's surgery spurred further conversation about the importance of having the love and support of one's spouse when going through a health crisis. Several of the husbands confessed they didn't know how they would have survived their ordeal had it not been for their wives.

I had gone into the kitchen to retrieve the special dessert I had prepared for the group, and upon my return to the dining room, I was shocked and surprised to hear the voice of my own husband speaking.

"I know what you mean," he was saying. "I've had several surgeries over the last ten years. Some of them serious and some of them supposedly minor, but what got me through each of them was the knowledge that my wife was there for me, that she had my back.

"Every time they ask you to count backward from a hundred and you feel consciousness slipping away, you can't help but wonder if you'll wake up, able to count forward again with the one you love. I've been blessed every time so far to wake up. I've been doubly blessed to have my Kitten waiting for me. It's been her tender, loving care that has motivated me each and every time to do whatever I had to do to recover as soon as possible."

He turned then to see me standing there with tears in my eyes, so moved by his public declaration of love and appreciation. You must understand, my husband, by nature, was a very private person. Sure, he told me often in private how much he loved and appreciated me, but to hear him openly praising me in front of our ministry touched my heart more than I can comprehend even now.

It turned into a very emotional moment for all of us. We sat there, each one of us individually reflecting upon the blessings God had bestowed upon us in the form of our spouses. The evening had been a huge spiritual and emotional success. It embodied everything we stood for. Good food and even better fellowship. Couples coming together in spiritual harmony committed and determined to prayerfully defeat the enemy, whose mission was to destroy our marriages and our lives.

We spent the last few minutes of our time together giving God the glory for his wisdom and guidance, and praise and thanks for his grace and mercy. As we stood at our front door and bid each couple farewell, none of us had any idea that for some, it would be the last time they would see Garry alive. Almost a month to the day later . . . he was gone.

Chapter Ten

February 2013

I'VE OFTEN ASKED MYSELF, if I could, would I want to know in advance the date, day, and hour of my death? When I found out I had breast cancer, I thought the answer to that question was yes. I thought I wanted to know so that I'd have time to settle my affairs, tie up loose ends, say my goodbyes, and prepare my family to go on without me.

Of course, I know now, I would not want to know. I wouldn't want to know because I know I'd spend too much time trying to take care of all those *details*.

I'm afraid I'd be so focused on dying, I wouldn't have time to enjoy whatever life I had left to live. Looking back, I'm glad I didn't know in advance when my husband was going to die. In the days leading up to his surgery and subsequent medical leave, we spent a lot of time together. We took time to do some of the things we knew we wouldn't be able to do immediately after his surgery.

We went to dinner and out to the movies. We finally went and filled out the necessary paperwork and applied for the passports we would need for our trip to Puerto Vallarta. Since we still couldn't decide whether to have our anniversary dinner at a hall or at our home, we visited a couple of halls to check pricing and availability.

We also priced several caterers. It was not only a cold winter, but it was showing signs of being a long, cold winter. Garry would be returning to work in late March, and since those brutal winds would definitely still be hanging around, he needed some heavier work shirts.

Even though he insisted the shirts he had were just fine, I knew otherwise and drug him kicking and screaming to the mall. He hated shopping, especially for himself.

He grumbled and fussed the whole time about wasting money, but I managed to get him to purchase three flannel shirts and three knit shirts. Despite all his complaining, when he tried them on at home, I could tell he liked them. They fit perfectly, and he looked really nice in them. Looking back, I'm grateful I didn't know then he'd never get to wear them.

We spent a lot of time cuddling—our favorite pastime—while we binged on our favorite TV shows and had long conversations about our upcoming anniversary.

"You know I could skip the whole dinner thing and just go straight to Puerto Vallarta," he said, kissing me on my forehead as I lounged on the couch next to him. When he saw the look on my face he started grinning. "I know, I know," he said. "You and your sister want to make a big deal out of this fortieth anniversary business."

I didn't say a word, just looked at him again with raised eyebrows.

"I mean, uh, I know it *is* a big deal," he stammered, moving back as if to get beyond my reach. "I'm just saying, all I really want to do is be with you, baby." It was all I could do not to laugh out loud at his failed attempt to pull his foot out of his mouth.

When I still didn't respond, he opened his mouth to try again, but I put my finger to his lips and shook my head. "I'd quit now if I were you," I said, trying to keep a straight face. "Or your knee won't be the only thing you're going to need surgery on."

Turning down the TV, I turned to him and said, "Garry Carter, we *agreed* our fortieth anniversary was a momentous occasion we were going to share—share being the operative word—with our family and friends. It's only one day—not even a whole day, four to six hours—to create some special memories that will last a life time. When it's over, you'll have me all to yourself for a whole week in Puerto Vallarta."

To demonstrate that as far as I was concerned the discussion was over, I turned the sound back up and resumed watching our program.

"Well all right, Miss Thang," he mumbled under his breath. "I guess you told me!"

Smiling to myself, I nodded my head and said out loud, "Believe that!"

◆

Friday, February 8, 2013

GARRY CAME HOME FROM work to begin what was supposed to have been his six-to-eight-week medical leave. When he walked through the door, I noticed he'd brought home his laptop.

"What's that for?" I asked.

He pretended not to know what I was referring to, but the look on my face told him: I knew he knew exactly what I was talking about.

"You better not be planning on doing any work for the next six to eight weeks," I said angrily. "As of this minute, Mister, you are on medical leave. I don't want you doing anything but focusing on getting through this surgery and your rehab. They've got plenty of people at that job to handle things while you're gone. They've known about this surgery for months, and if they don't have anybody . . . well, that's just too freaking bad!"

Just thinking about him trying to work from home made my blood boil! For once, I wanted him to think of himself. I knew from experience they didn't care about him. If he didn't make it through the surgery, or he didn't have a successful recovery, they'd replace him in a heartbeat and keep it moving. I loved him! I cared what happened to him! I could never replace him! Just once, I wanted him to be selfish and put himself first.

At 5:30 a.m. on Tuesday, February 12, we headed to St. James Hospital in Chicago Heights, where Garry was scheduled to have his surgery. After checking in at the admissions office, we were escorted upstairs to the outpatient surgery wing. We'd been here so many times before, I knew the drill by heart.

A nurse came in and took his vitals, collected some blood, and presented him with a mountain of paperwork to sign. She then left him to rest and wait until another nurse came to take him to surgery. He was particularly quiet, and I had to wonder if he was apprehensive about the surgery. I knew he hadn't slept well last night; I heard him get up more than once and go downstairs. Just as I would decide to go down and check on him, he'd return and lie back down. After forty years of marriage, I knew better than to ask what was wrong, because I knew he wouldn't answer. He'd simply give me that look and say, "Nothin', babe. I'm fine."

While Garry was busy with the nurse, I'd clicked on *The Today Show* on the TV, but neither of us was watching it. Garry's eyes were closed, but I knew he wasn't asleep. I was sitting in the recliner chair next to his hospital bed, and he was holding my hand. Every few minutes he would raise his hand and kiss mine, squeezing it as if to reassure me. I couldn't help but wonder who he was trying to reassure, me or him.

We stayed there for the better part of an hour, silently waiting. Neither of us felt compelled to speak. At times like these, words were unnecessary. My mere presence spoke volumes. Garry knew how much I loved him. He knew how much I wanted him to be healthy and whole again. He knew that I would be there when he came out of surgery and through every step of his rehab. I'd always been there before, and this time would be no different.

My only prayer was that this would be the last time we'd ever have to see the inside of this room, or any room in this hospital again. I was so looking forward to getting past all this. I couldn't wait to celebrate our anniversary and take our trip to Puerto Vallarta. I couldn't wait to feel Garry's arms around me as we danced together at our anniversary dinner, and I was truly looking forward to all the dances we would share after that.

My eyes were getting heavy, and I was just about to give in to the sleep that threatened to overtake me, when the nurse came to escort Garry to surgery. I walked by his side holding his hand, teasing him to behave and not give the nurses a hard time. When we arrived at the double doors leading to the operating room, I leaned down and kissed his cheek.

"Sorry, baby, I can't go any farther," I said, winking. "Now you can take a nap. When you wake up, I'll be waiting." I blew him another kiss as the nurse wheeled him through the doors and out of my sight.

As I walked back to the surgical waiting area, I silently acknowledged a slight uneasiness. I'd been through this so many times before, but for some reason, this time I was more nervous than usual. Sitting in the waiting room, I found it hard to concentrate on the book I'd brought to read. I watched the computerized board that showed the patient's progress during surgery, and the time seemed to move at a snail's pace. We had to be there so early that morning I hadn't had time to eat anything. My stomach was telling me it desperately needed food, but I felt like I was chained to my chair, my eyes glued to that progress board.

I knew I would pay dearly for ignoring my stomach's rumbling, my punishment a severe headache, but with the exception of a few trips to the restroom, I just couldn't bring myself to leave that waiting room. Just when I thought I would explode, the phone rang and the nurse in charge of the waiting room called my name. As I approached the desk, she smiled.

"Mr. Carter is out of surgery and in recovery," she said. "The doctor will be out to talk to you in a few minutes."

"Thank you," I said, and expelled a breath I hadn't realized I'd been holding.

About five minutes later, which seemed like an hour, the doctor appeared in the doorway and beckoned me into the family-consult room. He looked tired to me, and I must have looked worried to him. Placing his hand on my shoulder, he gave me a tired smile.

"He's fine, Mrs. Carter," he said pulling off his surgical cap and wiping his brow. "Everything is fine. The surgery went well; he's awake and alert. He should be out of recovery within the next thirty minutes or so, and then they'll take him to a room upstairs."

"No complications?" I asked.

"None that we've detected so far," he answered. "All his vitals are strong, and of course you know he's already asking when he can go home." He flashed me another tired smile, and I just shook my head and laughed.

"Thank you, Doctor," I said. "No offense, but I hope this is our last meeting."

With a nod and a smile of understanding he squeezed my hand, and then he was gone.

Relieved, I sat back down and waited for them to call me again, to tell me he was out of recovery. When they did, I stepped out into the hall just as they were wheeling him toward the elevator to take him to his room. I couldn't believe my eyes. He was sitting up on the gurney laughing and joking with the nurse. She must have asked about me, because just then he turned and smiled at me. "That's her, the little blond cutie over there."

"Okay, what's going on here?" I asked as they approached. "You didn't have no surgery, not looking like that," I said.

"I did too," he said. "You wanna see my scar?" he asked, pulling back the blanket covering his leg.

I shook my head and laughed. "You must be on some really good drugs then, 'cause you look a whole lot better than you did the last time we were here. I hope your rehab goes as well as the surgery."

By the time we got him upstairs and settled in his room, some of his bravado had disappeared. I suspected whatever pain meds they gave him in the recovery room were starting to wear off. I knew he had to be totally exhausted; after all, we'd been there since five thirty that morning. I stayed with him until the night nurse came in to update his vitals and give him some more pain medication.

"I don't know about you, baby, but I'm beat, and you should get some rest. I'm going to go home now, but I'll be back first thing in the morning."

"Don't want you to go!" he said, but his eyes were already closing.

Smiling, I kissed him on his forehead and then on the lips. "I know, baby, but trust me, whatever she gave you, in a few minutes you won't even know I'm gone."

By the time I made it from his bed to the door, he was out. I stood there for a few minutes and sent up a prayer of thanks. Then, wishing I could take some of his drugs home with me, I headed for the elevator. As tired as I was, I knew it would be a long time before I could fall asleep. I hated sleeping alone.

♦

WHEN I GOT HOME I set the alarm, made myself a sandwich, and went upstairs to our bedroom. I turned on the TV and watched the news while I ate the sandwich. After the news went off I turned off the TV, but I was unable to succumb to the exhaustion that should have knocked me out the minute my head hit the pillow.

It was too quiet in the house. There was no warm body to snuggle up to . . . no soft purring in my ear. There was nothing to drown out the pops and groans of the furnace kicking on and off, and nothing to silence the creaking sounds of the house shifting and resettling on its foundation. I knew it was irrational fear that made me hear footsteps on the stairs—especially since I knew I'd put the alarm on—yet every time I closed my eyes, I heard them just the same.

I missed the warmth and security of my Pooh lying next to me. I tossed and turned for several hours until finally God must have had mercy on me and put me out of my misery. I didn't remember drifting off or even realize I'd been asleep until the bright sunlight peeking through the blinds assaulted my eyelids. Shielding my eyes from the piercing winter sun, I lay there feeling groggy and disoriented. I glanced at my phone to check the time, and was shocked to see it was already after 8:00 a.m. Visiting hours at the hospital had already begun. I needed to get moving, but my whole body felt like it had lead weights attached to it. After a few more minutes of trying to shake loose the cobwebs, I finally managed to drag myself out of bed and into the shower.

I emerged from the shower feeling mentally refreshed, but my body was still weary from lack of sleep. I dressed as quickly as possible and headed back to the hospital. I hoped to be there by the time the doctor made his rounds so I could hear from him directly about Garry's progress. When I walked into Garry's room, my Spidey senses went on red alert. There was something very different about the man I left here last night and the man I was looking at now.

My Pooh was a dark-skinned brother. I lovingly referred to him as my chocolate-covered honey. As impossible as it might seem, he was looking very pale. I was disturbed by the sight, but I assumed despite the pain medication they were giving him, the trauma to his body resulting from the surgery was finally kicking in. Gone was the grinning, joking Garry from yesterday; he was replaced by a more somber version who appeared to be either in pain or some other kind of distress.

He made a valiant effort to perk up and disguise his discomfort when I walked through the door, but I could tell it took a great deal of effort. He greeted me with a weak smile when I leaned down to kiss him.

"What's up, old man?" I asked. "You don't look so hot."

"I didn't sleep well last night. I guess I'm just tired, plus, I was missing you," he said, looking like a little lost puppy.

"Aw, I'm sorry, baby, you know I would have stayed if I could have. Maybe then I would have gotten some sleep too!" I said, kissing him again. "You know how much I hate sleeping alone."

He smiled again, stroking my arm, but I still had a feeling there was more to his pallor than just lack of sleep.

"Have you been up walking yet?" I asked.

"Yes, they actually got me up last night after you left."

"Really?" I said, surprised. "Wow, I thought you were down for the count when I left."

"I was, but they came in at shift change, took my vitals again, and made me get up and walk up and down the hall a couple of times. They said it was doctor's orders. I was so tired I thought I'd go right back to sleep, but I couldn't."

"I'm really surprised the pain pills didn't knock you out. Have you eaten this morning?" I asked.

"They brought me some breakfast, but I don't have much of an appetite. I just wanna go home," he said.

And here we go, I thought, *the battle begins.* "Well, you know the drill," I said. "You have to eat and show them you can keep some food down. Then you have to have a bowel movement, so they know everything is working like it's supposed to. Until you do that, you're not going anywhere."

He didn't acknowledge what I said, but I knew he heard me, and I didn't bother to press the issue. *You can ignore me all you want to,* I thought. *The doctor will come in and tell you the same darn thing! I'm not going to waste my breath arguing with you. I'll just wait for the doctor. He's getting paid big bucks to tell you what you don't want to hear,* I said to myself, *and he has the last word!*

"Why don't we take a stroll around the nurse's station?" I asked. "Maybe you can work up an appetite for lunch." I didn't give him a chance to say no, I just got his walker and brought it over to the bed and started moving furniture out of the way to clear a path to the door. It took him a while to get to his feet and start moving, but eventually we made it to the door and out into the hall.

Just as we were finishing up our second turn around the nurse's station, we saw the doctor coming down the hall, headed for Garry's room. He was looking at Garry's chart when we came through the door. He waited till Garry was settled on the side of the bed, and then began to examine him. He checked his breathing, his pulse, and his blood pressure.

"Your vitals are okay, but you're looking a little pale," he said. (*Okay so it wasn't just me,* I thought.) "How do you feel, are the pain meds working?" he asked. "I see you didn't eat much of your breakfast either," he added, before Garry could answer.

"I'm not really in any pain, I'm just tired. I can't sleep in here."

The doctor and I exchanged looks and smiled, knowing that was his subtle way of hinting he wanted to go home.

"Well, you know the drill, Garry. This is not your first rodeo," he said, smiling. "You have to eat, and you have to have a bowel movement. Providing you don't spike a fever or experience any other complications in the next couple of days, you should be out of here by . . . Thursday or Friday."

You only had to look at his face to know that was definitely *not* what he wanted to hear! *You go, Doc!* I said internally. I didn't dare look at Garry, because I knew I wouldn't be able to hide my satisfaction. The doctor had just confirmed everything I'd already told him. *This isn't my first rodeo either!* I thought smugly.

Garry was very quiet after the doctor left. I knew he was stewing about what the doctor had said, and since it mirrored what I'd already told him, he probably felt like we were ganging up on him. Thursday was Valentine's Day, and as much as I wanted him home, I figured we'd have plenty of Valentine's Days to share in the future. Right now, it was more important that he stay in the hospital for as long as it was necessary to ensure he was 100 percent ready to move forward with his rehab.

Shortly after his lunch arrived, Kevin and Jillian arrived for a visit. I was trying to coax him into eating some of the food on his tray when they walked in. There wasn't really a whole lot to eat. It was his first full day after surgery, and he was on a soft diet. His tray consisted of tea, broth, Jell-O, and sherbet. He ate a couple of spoonfuls of the broth, a couple of bites of Jell-O, and promised to eat the sherbet later.

Kevin hugged him, and Jillian kissed him on the cheek.

"How are you doing, Dad, you feeling okay?" Kevin asked.

"I'm fine," he answered. He obviously had not sounded convincing to either Kevin or Jillian, as they both looked at me with raised eyebrows.

"Your dad is already bugging the doctor about going home," I said. "You know how he is."

"Dad, you need to chill, once you leave here. I know you don't wanna have to come back."

"Yeah," Jillian piped in. "You need to give yourself time to heal, and give them a chance to make sure they didn't make any mistakes. If you have any complications, it will be a lot easier for them to take care of you if you're already here."

I appreciated their support, but I also knew they were wasting their breath. My husband hated hospitals. On some level he knew we were right, but bottom line, he didn't care. He just wanted out, and the sooner the better. The kids had to go to work, so after another thirty minutes or so they prepared to leave.

"You behave yourself, old man," Kevin said, hugging him again. "I'll be back out to see you this weekend when you come home."

After Jillian said goodbye, I walked them out to the elevator.

"What's really going on with him, Mom?" Kevin asked. "He doesn't look so good."

"I know," I said. "He says he's just tired because he can't sleep in here, but I have a feeling it's more than that. He should be hungry, he hasn't really eaten anything since Monday night, but he says he doesn't have an appetite. I don't understand. He was so upbeat and full of energy yesterday after the surgery, and now he's pale and lethargic. It's like he's everything I expected him to be yesterday today, and vice versa."

"What does the doctor say?" he asked.

"The doctor said all his vitals are good, the surgery went well, but he seemed to be a little concerned as well. Which I'm sure is the reason he's not rushing to release him."

"Well, keep me posted. Let me know if I need to come back before the weekend."

I promised to do just that, and kissed them goodbye.

When I returned to Garry's room, I was relieved to see he had fallen asleep. I knew he needed to rest, and if he was resting he wouldn't be obsessing about going home, at least for a little while. For the second day in a row, I'd left my house early without eating, and once again my stomach was expressing its displeasure at being neglected. I decided to take advantage of Garry's nap and run down to the cafeteria for a bite to eat.

In the cafeteria I ordered a burger and requested it to go. I wanted to get back to Garry, if possible, before he woke up, so he wouldn't think I had abandoned him. When I returned, thankfully he was still asleep. He slept for nearly two hours.

"You're still here," he said when he opened his eyes and saw me sitting next to his bed.

"Of course I am," I said, caressing his face. "You didn't think I'd leave you, did you?"

Stretching and yawning, he gave me a sheepish grin. "I wouldn't blame you if you did," he said. "I know I'm a pain in the butt."

"True," I said, laughing. "But I've never left you before, and I'm not going anywhere now—you're stuck with me!" I lay down on the bed next to him, laid my head on his chest, and snuggled as close as I could get. He put his arms around me and kissed me on the forehead.

"I'm a lucky man," he said.

"And don't you ever forget it!" I responded, smiling and snuggling even closer. We stayed that way until the nurse came in with his dinner tray.

His dinner tray was only marginally better than the lunch tray. This time he had chicken noodle soup instead of broth, but the rest was the same. Gone was the hope that his appetite would improve. Poor baby, given the fare provided by the hospital, it was no wonder he had no desire to eat. I didn't want him leaving the hospital one minute before he was ready, but I would be happy to take him home so I could give him some real food.

He didn't eat any more at dinner than he had earlier in the day. I understood the food wasn't great, but I couldn't get him to understand that not eating was counterproductive. If he really wanted to go home, he needed to eat!

"You need to eat, baby, you're going to need all your strength for your rehab when you get home."

"I know," he said. "I'll do better tomorrow."

I sure hope so, I thought. "Okay, I'm going to hold you to that," I said. "Believe it or not, I want you to come home too, so I can take care of you."

When the nurse returned to retrieve Garry's dinner tray, the look on her face told me she was as disappointed as I at his lack of appetite. "So you're not a fan of our food, huh? Are you sure you don't want to hang on to your sherbet at least?"

Garry shook his head, and she gave me a look. I shrugged my shoulders and threw up my hands, indicating that I'd already tried.

"Okay," she said. "If you get hungry later, let me know and we'll get you a snack."

After she left, I got him up to walk again. "Come on, baby, let's take another stroll around the nurse's station before I go. Maybe the exercise will help you sleep better tonight."

I could tell he really didn't feel like going. For a second he looked like he wanted to say so, and just as quickly he seemed to remember his promise to do better. Going very slowly, we managed to circle the nurse's station three times. He was perspiring profusely by the time we returned to his room. I could tell what a toll the walk had taken on him. My prayer was that his reward for his efforts would be a much-needed good night's sleep.

He got back in the bed and we watched TV until visiting hours were over. He could barely keep his eyes open by the time I prepared to leave, and I hoped that was a sign that my prayer would be answered.

"I'm going to go now, baby," I said, kissing him. "I'll be back in the morning. Hopefully, the doctor will release you tomorrow."

He squeezed my hand, and kissing me, said, "Be careful going home, baby. Did you leave some lights on?"

"I will, and I did," I answered. His eyes were closing again, so I blew him another kiss on my way out the door and headed for the elevator.

When I made it to my car, I got in, laid my head back, and closed my eyes for a few minutes. I was tired and hungry. I dreaded going back to my house alone again, and I definitely didn't feel like cooking. The burger I ate earlier was a distant memory, so I stopped at my favorite Chinese food restaurant and picked up some dinner. I ordered my usual pepper steak and ate it while watching TV. I'd eaten less than half before the stress of the day caught up with me. One minute I was watching *Law and Order: SVU,* and the next the weather man was previewing the forecast for Valentine's Day.

I wanted nothing more than to crawl into bed and dissolve into mindless slumber, but I already knew tonight would be a repeat of the night before. As soon as I got into bed, I was wide awake. It wasn't just the night noises that kept me up this time. I was conflicted. Part of me wanted Garry home as much as he wanted to be home. I wanted to take care of him the way no doctor or nurse could. I wanted to shower him with TLC, cook his favorite food, and help him with his rehab. But something was nagging at me; something was wrong! Knowing how stubborn Garry was, I was afraid if they released him before he was absolutely ready, and something happened . . . the chances of getting him to willingly return to the hospital were slim to none.

Like the night before, I tossed and turned until at some point, I must have passed out from sheer mental and physical exhaustion. It wasn't the sunlight that woke me the next morning. An annoying persistent buzzing penetrated the recesses of my sleep-addled brain, hell bent on dragging me back to consciousness. The more I tried to ignore it, the louder it seemed to get.

It took a few minutes before I realized the sound came from the vibrating phone on my nightstand. Reaching out from the cocoon of my bedcovers, I blindly stabbed at the offending nuisance, almost knocking it to the floor in the process.

"Hello," I said groggily after finally managing to push the talk button. "HELLO!" I repeated loudly, irritated when there was no immediate answer on the other end.

"You still asleep?" the voice on the other end asked.

"Not anymore," I answered with more than a little sarcasm.

Then suddenly, still struggling to free myself from the remaining cobwebs in my head, recognition dawned. I sat straight up in the bed, finally fully awake.

"Baby, what's wrong? Are you okay?" I asked. I glanced at my alarm clock and saw that it was just 7:00 a.m.

"I'm fine," he answered. "The doctor said I can go home today."

He doesn't sound fine, I thought. News like that should have had him jumping up and down, or at least sounding like he was jumping up and down. Instead, he sounded annoyed.

"Can you come and get me?" he asked.

"No," I said, laughing, "I'm afraid you're just going to have to take a cab. Hello? I was only kidding," I said when he didn't respond. "Are you sure you're okay?"

"Yeah, I'm fine, Kitten. I just want to get the hell outta here."

"Okay," I said. "Has the doctor signed you out yet?"

"No, he's supposed to sign the paperwork and give me my prescriptions when he comes for his rounds."

"All right, I'll get dressed and come now. I'll just wait with you until you're paroled."

I waited for a witty comeback, but there was dead silence on the phone. "Nothing?" I asked. Still no response. "Okay, you're not laughing at my jokes," I said. "Something is definitely wrong, and when I get there, you are going to tell me what it is!"

Both concerned and a little angry, I didn't wait for him to respond. I just hung up the phone. I sat there for a few more minutes trying to figure out what was wrong with my husband. He was finally getting what he wanted, so why didn't he sound happy about it?

I really expected him to be there another day at least, considering his condition yesterday. So what had happened overnight or early this morning to convince the doctor he was ready to go home? I didn't know, but I was sure as hell gonna find out!

When I arrived at the hospital forty-five minutes later, Garry was sitting on the side of the bed in his shirt and underwear. Gone was the hospital gown, and some of the pallor from the past couple of days. He was attempting to put on his pants.

"You look like you could use a little help," I said as I came through the door.

"More than a little, I'm afraid," he said. He had some nifty little tools that he'd been given when he had his first surgery last year, and I had brought them with me.

"Well, first of all, why don't you sit in the chair; it's lower than the bed, so it should make it a little easier to put those pants on. This might help too," I said. I gave him the thing that looked like an oversized pair of tongs. It was designed to help him put on pants and socks.

"Wow, Kitten, I forgot all about these. Where did you find them?"

"In the basement where I put them last year, after you went back to work."

"Good looking out, babe," he said, smiling.

"You know I got you," I said, winking. I knew from last time it was important for him to do as much as he could on his own, so I stood back and let him put his pants and socks on. The shoes were a little harder to negotiate, so I sat on the floor and helped him put them on, and then tied them up. After he was fully dressed, I suggested he lie down and rest until the doctor arrived with his paperwork.

"I don't want to lie down, I'm ready to go!" he said.

"Okay, suit yourself!" I said. I knew there was no point in arguing with him. So we sat and waited . . . and waited . . . and waited! I had arrived at the hospital a little after 8:00 a.m., and it was a little after 3:00 p.m. before the nurse finally wheeled him down to the entrance and helped me get him in the car. I knew he was livid, but he obviously decided going home was more important than being mad, because I was the only one who knew he was about to blow.

When we pulled out of the parking lot, he laid his head back and closed his eyes. I could tell he was more tired than angry, which he wouldn't have been if he'd rested like I told him to. I also knew he would never give me the satisfaction of saying I told you so. So, I kept my thoughts and comments to myself. My main objective was to do all I could to get him healthy and back on his feet. My need to get my husband back was more important than my need to be right.

CHAPTER ELEVEN

GETTING GARRY OUT OF the car and into the house all by myself was more of a challenge than I anticipated. His height along with his inability to bend his right knee made it very difficult to get out of the car. We let the seat back and down as far as it would go, and he still had a hard time. By the time he finally got out, we were both sweating like we'd just finished a 10K run.

Once in the house, the next hurdle was getting up the stairs to our bedroom. Thank God, there were only six stairs up to the bedrooms. He took his time, leaning on me for support. When we made it to the top of the stairs, we rested before taking the last few steps into the bedroom. We were both breathing hard, and when we finally made it into our room, we both collapsed on our bed looking and feeling like we'd just completed a decathlon.

When I finally found the energy to move, I got up and brought Garry his walker so he could get around the room and to and from the bathroom by himself. While I went to fix him something to eat, he washed up and put on clean sweats and a T-shirt. When I returned with some chicken soup and a sandwich, he was sitting up in bed looking slightly better than when I'd left him.

For the first week after surgery, Garry would rehab at home with the help of a special physical-therapy machine provided by the hospital through his insurance. Just as I came back downstairs to make myself a sandwich, the doorbell rang. When I answered the door, it was the man from the medical-supply company come to deliver the machine. He set it up in the family room and gave me the instructions for Garry's daily exercise regimen.

"Do you need me to give him a demonstration, Mrs. Carter?" he asked.

"I don't believe so," I answered. "I remember what to do from last year, and I'm sure he does too."

"Well, here's my card. If you have any questions or need any assistance at all, please call."

"I will, and thank you," I said as I walked him to the door.

The first thing I noticed when I returned to our bedroom was that Garry had barely touched the food I'd brought him. "Was there something wrong with the food?" I asked.

"No, Kitten, I guess I'm just not hungry. Why don't you wrap it up and I'll eat it later."

"Are you sure?" I asked. "You barely touched your breakfast, and you need to keep your strength up."

Ignoring my statement, he asked who was at the door.

"It was the guy bringing your machine. Do you want to go downstairs and get in an hour of PT?" I asked. "Afterward, you can do a couple of laps."

Last year when he came home he'd been a man on a mission. He was exercising like a maniac, determined to get back on his feet as soon as possible. I remember warning him to slow down, afraid he would overdo it. Now at the mere suggestion that he begin his rehab, he was looking at me like I'd lost my last mind.

"Maybe later," he said, sounding unenthusiastic.

"You know what the doctor said—" I began, but before I could finish, he snapped at me.

"I know what the doctor said," he yelled. "I know what I'm supposed to do . . . I just don't feel like it right now. Okay?"

The sting of his words was like a slap across my face. I stepped back away from the bed in shock. I opened my mouth to say something and closed it immediately. Turning on my heels, I left the bedroom as fast as I could. "Help me, Lord," I mumbled under my breath. *I have to remember he's probably in terrible pain,* I thought on my way back down the stairs. Acknowledging that fact, however, did little to ease the pain of his outburst. I busied myself getting everything set up for him when he was finally ready to begin his rehab. I moved furniture out of the way, giving him a clear path for his walker, and I found and put everything he would need at his fingertips when he came down to exercise. In the meantime, I left him alone, knowing when he was ready, he *would* come down.

It was important that he move around and do his physical therapy. Blood clots were a very real and serious complication of knee- and hip-replacement surgery. The doctor had put him on a blood thinner; still, it was crucial that he move. I would just have to toughen up because hurt feelings or no, if he didn't come down those stairs on his own . . . I would go up there and get him!

After I finished setting up everything, I decided to watch some TV. I was just getting into a program when I heard him call out to me. "Kitten!" he called out from upstairs. I got up and headed for the stairs to see what he wanted. Walking into the kitchen, I saw him standing at the top of the stairs holding on to his walker with a sheepish grin on his face. I walked up the stairs to meet him, measuring his mood.

"I'm sorry I snapped at you," he said, leaning down and kissing me on my forehead. "I was tired and hurting, but I shouldn't have taken it out on you."

Damn right, I thought. "It's okay, baby, I didn't mean to push. I just want you to do what you need to so you can get better. You owe me a dance, remember?" I said, smiling.

"Well, I guess I'd better get busy, huh?"

I walked back down with his walker and stood at the bottom and watched him maneuver down the stairs one at a time. It took him a while, and by the time he got to the bottom, he was breathing hard and sweating.

"Do you need to take a break and sit for a minute?" I asked.

"No, I'm gonna do a lap, and then I'll get on the machine. I'll do another lap after that, and that will be it for today."

"Okay, well, let me get out of your way."

He took off through the living room, dining room, and back into the kitchen. Our house had an L-shaped floor plan, which allowed him to make a complete circle. He looked really tired after the lap, and I wondered if he'd make it through a whole session on the PT machine.

After a few minutes, I could tell he'd expended all his energy. Once again he was breathing hard and sweating.

"Maybe you should rest, baby. I'll fix you something to eat, and you can try again later. Or maybe just get a fresh start in the morning."

"Okay," he said, "but don't fix too much. I'm really not hungry."

I didn't want to aggravate him again, so I resisted the urge to remind him that he needed to eat to keep up his strength. *Maybe his appetite will return by tomorrow,* I thought. *I sure hope so.*

Since we were already downstairs, I brought him the reheated soup and a fresh sandwich in the family room. He looked at the food when I set it down in front of him, and I could already tell he thought it was too much.

"Just eat what you can," I said, reading his thoughts.

"I'll do my best," he said, giving me another sheepish grin. He ate the majority of the soup, but barely touched the sandwich. I was very concerned about his lack of appetite, but I refrained from making an issue of it. *Tomorrow,* I thought to myself. *Things will be better tomorrow.*

We watched TV for a little while longer, until I realized that he was nodding off.

"I think you've had enough for today. Why don't we go upstairs? Hopefully you'll sleep better in your own bed."

Fifteen minutes later he was in bed, eyes wide open. "I don't know what happened," he said. "A few minutes ago I couldn't keep my eyes open, now I'm wide awake."

"I know," I said, laughing. "Been there, done that! It's been that way ever since you went into the hospital. I'll just turn on the TV, you'll drift off eventually."

I woke up at 3:00 a.m. My eyes just popped open, and I lay there trying to figure out what caused me to wake up. I could feel Garry beside me, and after a few minutes I could tell he was awake too. I wanted to say something, but I knew he needed his rest, so I kept quiet hoping he'd drift off again. After about twenty minutes or so I realized he'd obviously been awake a lot longer than I thought. I began to wonder if he'd even slept at all.

Still I remained quiet, wondering what was wrong and why he couldn't sleep. He obviously became aware that I was awake too; maybe he could feel my concern and the subsequent tension in my body. He reached over and grabbed my hand, bringing it to his lips. Kissing it gently, he then squeezed it and said, "I'm okay, Kitten, go back to sleep."

Friday, February 15, 2013

AS WORRIED AS I was, I was even more exhausted. The last few days of stressing and intermittent sleep had taken its toll. I didn't remember falling asleep again, but the next time I opened my eyes, it was 7:00 a.m. A tiny sliver of sunlight was streaming through the blinds, shining right into my eyes. As I lay there trying to focus, the first thing I was consciously aware of was the sound of retching. While I tried to wrap my brain around the sound of vomiting and determine the source, I noticed Garry was no longer in the bed beside me. It was not easy for him to get in and out of the bed, so I wondered how he had done so without me hearing or feeling him. I could only conclude that I had really been knocked out. I got up immediately and went to find him.

I found him in our bathroom standing over the toilet. It was full of a green, slimy substance—bile, I suspected. The pallor I'd seen in the hospital had returned; so too had that nagging feeling that something was different this time. Something was definitely wrong! There had been no pallor, no loss of appetite, no apathy about his rehab last year. He had even more motivation this year to do everything in his power to get better as soon as possible, so what was the problem? Was it physical, mental, or a combination of both?

"Baby, what's wrong?" I asked as I wet a washcloth and began wiping his forehead.

"Sick to my stomach," he said breathlessly in between gagging.

"Well, it couldn't have been anything you ate," I said, laughing nervously.

My weak attempt at humor was lost on him. He finally stopped retching, but he looked weak and unsteady as if he'd keel over any second.

I flushed the toilet and put the seat down. "Here, sit down, baby."

When he sat down, I put some toothpaste on his toothbrush and handed it to him. He brushed his teeth and rinsed his mouth out, and then I helped him back to bed. Many people have an upset stomach and nausea after surgery. This is often because of the anesthesia, pain, pain medication, or simply the stress of surgery. I finally realized that's what Garry was experiencing. I knew I would have to ease up on him about eating. As much as I knew he needed the nourishment, pushing him to eat now would only increase his physical distress. Now that I knew what was wrong, I could relax a little and accept that he would eat when he was ready.

"Do you feel a little better now that you got that off your stomach?" I asked.

He was shaking his head yes, but his face told a different story.

"Hmm, you don't look convincing, but I'll take your word for now. Is that why you couldn't sleep last night?"

"I guess," he said. "My stomach was roiling, but I couldn't throw up, and I couldn't go to the bathroom either. I was miserable."

"Why didn't you wake me up?" I asked.

"What for? There was nothing you could do. There was no point in both of us being awake."

"But I woke up anyway."

"I know," he said. "I'm sorry."

"You don't have to be sorry, silly. That's what I'm here for, to help. To take care of you. Promise me the next time, you'll wake me up. Even if I can't help, at least you won't be alone. Promise?"

"Okay, Kitten, I promise."

"Since you can't eat anything too heavy, how about some tea and toast? I can also make you some Jell-O."

"Real Jell-O, with fruit in it?" he asked, smiling.

"Absolutely," I said, smiling back.

While I was making the tea, my phone rang.

"Hello," I said, answering it.

"Hey, sis, how's my brother doing?" It was Donna calling to check on Garry.

"Not as well as I would like," I said. "He had a rough night. He didn't sleep well, and he has an upset stomach and nausea; from the anesthesia, I believe. I was just about to make him some tea and toast. He's barely eaten anything since before the surgery. I hope he'll be better soon. What's up?"

"Well, I was calling to invite you to my red party tomorrow night, but I guess you won't be able to come."

"What's a red party?" I asked.

"Well, it's actually a Valentine's Day party, so I want everyone to wear red."

"Oh, okay," I said, laughing. "Sounds like fun, but yeah, I'm afraid I won't be able to make it this year. I don't want to leave my Pooh home alone, and he's not ready to go out yet. I'm hoping to get him back up today for some rehab. I'd like to contribute something to the party, though, since I can't be there. Since you've got this red theme going on, how about I make some of my red-velvet cupcakes?"

"That sounds wonderful, but are you sure you have the time?"

"Of course, it will give me something to do while Garry is doing his rehab, and make me feel like I'm a part of the party."

"Wonderful, I'll have Karl come over and pick them up, and he can check on Garry in person."

"Okay, I'll call you tomorrow when they're ready."

By the time I hung up the phone, I'd finished making the tea and toast, so I put it on a tray and took it upstairs.

"Who's downstairs?" he asked when I sat it down on the nightstand beside him.

"Nobody," I answered. "Why do you ask?"

"I thought I heard voices."

"Oh, you did," I said. "I was on the phone with Donna. She called to check on you and to invite us to a party she's having tomorrow night. She called it a red party. It's for Valentine's Day. I told her we wouldn't be able to make it."

"You mean I can't make it," he said. "There's no reason why you can't go."

"Yeah right, like I'm going to leave you here by yourself. You haven't been out of the hospital two days! I can miss one party. Besides, if I'm gonna be with anybody for Valentine's Day, it's gonna be you."

"It's not gonna be any fun cooped up in here with me," he said.

"Well, it won't be any fun being there without you, so the subject is closed."

He sipped on the tea, but I noticed while we were talking, he barely touched the toast. I was still concerned that he wasn't eating, but I knew obsessing about it wouldn't help either of us, so I let it slide.

"Are you feeling up to exercising?" I asked. He was supposed to do it three times a day, and he'd already missed his morning session.

"I guess," he said unenthusiastically.

"Good," I said, ignoring his lackluster reply. "I'll go and set up the machine for you."

I left the room before he could object. Before I got the machine ready for him, I set out eggs and butter for my cupcakes. I didn't have to worry about cooking a big dinner, so by the time he started his last session for the day, I'd be ready to make and bake the cupcakes.

He was taking so long coming downstairs, I was afraid he was gonna punk out on me. Just as I was about to go up and check on him, he appeared at the top of the stairs. I went up and retrieved his walker again and waited at the bottom of the stairs for him. When he made it down, he did one lap and then went into the family room to get on the machine. While he did his reps, I made his Jell-O. I hoped I could get him to eat a little soup later, but if he only ate the Jell-O I'd be happy with that.

As I busied myself in the kitchen making the Jell-O, I watched his progress on the machine. I noticed right away that his energy level was very low. He seemed to be struggling with each rep. I didn't know if it was because he was in pain, or because he wasn't eating.

"Are you okay, babe?" I asked. "You seem to be having a hard time. Are you in pain, or just tired?"

"I'm not in pain, I'm sore . . . but more than anything, I'm just tired. I thought it would be so much easier the second time around." He sounded weary, and I felt helpless.

"Is there anything I can do?" I asked. "Anything I can get for you?"

"Right now the only thing I need is for you to come here," he said, patting the couch beside him. I sat down beside him and took his hand in mine.

"I want to help, but I don't know what to do," I said. "Tell me what to do."

Giving me a tired smile, he looked at me for a long time, and then finally said, "You're already doing it, Kitten. You're here!"

Those words meant so much to me. I dropped my head so he wouldn't see the tears pooling in my eyes. He took his finger and lifted my chin so he could look into my eyes, and wiped away a tear that had escaped down my cheek.

"I know you don't think that's enough . . . I know you love me, and even if I don't always show it, I really appreciate everything you do. I don't know why I can't seem to get it together this time, but I will, and having you here to help me through it makes all the difference. You have to stop worrying, I'm gonna be okay. We're gonna be okay."

From your lips to God's ear, I thought.

We stayed there for a while just holding on to each other. It was starting to get dark outside, and I realized neither of us had eaten since earlier in the day.

"You think you could eat some soup now?" I asked. "Your Jell-O won't be ready for a while."

"I'll try," he said, "but not a lot."

"I guess there's no point in asking if you want a sandwich with that," I said, smiling.

"I'm sorry, Kitten. I'll be doing good if I can eat the soup."

"It's okay," I said, laughing, "but I had to try."

I went into the kitchen to prepare the soup and made myself a sandwich while I was at it. After we ate, Garry said he wanted to lie down, so I helped him back upstairs. I was pleased that he managed to eat most of the soup, so I was hopeful his condition was improving.

After getting him settled in bed, I went downstairs to get him some juice. When I came back up with the juice, his eyes were closing. I sat the juice down on the nightstand, intending to tiptoe out of the room and let him sleep, but as I turned to leave he grabbed hold of my shirt and pulled me down on the bed beside him.

I squealed, surprised, and laughing said, "Hey, I thought you were tired!"

"I am," he said, grinning. "But I'm also lonely. Stay with me for a while."

"Okay," I said, smiling. "I'll stay for a little while, but I have to make some red-velvet cupcakes for Donna's party."

Lying down next to him, I snuggled up close and stayed with him till he drifted off to sleep. While he slept I made the cupcakes and my cream-cheese frosting. I checked on the Jell-O, and decided to make omelets for dinner. I was sure he was getting tired of soup. The omelets, full of protein, would be filling but hopefully not too heavy on his stomach.

I was pulling the cupcakes out of the oven when he called my name. I looked up to see him standing at the top of the stairs. "Hey you, how was your nap?"

"Not long enough," he said, "but better than nothing. I was thinking I'd try and get on the machine again."

"Okay," I said as I started up the stairs to get his walker. "So I was wondering, how do you feel about omelets for dinner?"

"Sounds good, I guess, as long as it's not soup!"

I laughed out loud.

"What's so funny?" he asked.

"I was just thinking you were probably getting really tired of soup."

He smiled as he made his way down the stairs. "You think you know me, huh?"

"And don't you forget it!" I said, laughing again.

While I prepared the ingredients for the omelets, I kept an eye on Garry in the family room. He was making a valiant effort, but once again he seemed to be struggling with the exercises. I couldn't tell if it was because he was weak from lack of nutrition, if he was in pain, or if he was just plain tired. In addition to having trouble with the physical aspects of his rehab, he seemed to be struggling mentally; he seemed distracted. It was if he knew what he needed to do, but his heart just wasn't in it. I was as disturbed by his lack of focus as I was his lack of appetite.

Everything we'd been working toward was within reach. It was almost over, we were almost to the finish line, but he seemed unable or reluctant to take those last few steps. My gut was screaming something was wrong. There was definitely something off, but I just couldn't put my finger on it. I didn't know how to help him; all I could do was pray and hope God would turn it around.

I was whisking the eggs and about to add the vegetables to our omelets when I glanced up again and noticed Garry had stopped exercising. He was just sitting there staring into space. I froze for a few seconds, the hair on the back of my neck standing up. As if I had an alarm system embedded in my brain, the sight of him sitting there so still set it off. That annoying sound in my head was even louder than the sound my home alarm made when it was activated.

"Hey you, are you okay?"

At first he didn't answer; he seemed not to have heard me. The noise in my head escalated. I stopped what I was doing and walked into the family room. Standing directly in front of him, I asked him again. "Babe, are you okay?" I believe it was not my voice, but the sight of me standing in front of him that finally brought him back from wherever he had gone.

He seemed surprised to see me standing there. Looking confused he said, "I'm sorry, Kitten, did you say something?"

"I asked if you were okay. You checked out for a minute, and when I asked if you were okay, you didn't answer me. I was a little concerned."

"Oh, I'm sorry, I guess I did drift off. I'm okay, just tired. I think I'm done for the day."

I wasn't happy about that, but I decided not to argue with him. "Okay, well, let me go and whip up these omelets. I hope you're at least a little hungry."

He didn't really answer me, but I chose to ignore that as well. When I finished the omelets, I brought everything into the family room. We ate in relative silence, both lost in our own private thoughts. I had no idea what he was thinking about, but I was consumed with questions about what was going on with him. I was worried about his lack of exercise and overall movement. Even though he was on a blood thinner, I knew that blood clots were a very real danger after this kind of surgery. I tried to convince myself that I was being paranoid, but I wasn't having much success with that.

After we finished eating, Garry watched TV while I frosted the cupcakes and packed them up for Karl to pick up. By the time I finished, the Jell-O was ready. Garry had eaten pretty much all of his omelet, which was encouraging.

"Babe, your Jell-O is ready. Do you have room for some?"

"I'll try a little, but not too much," he said.

I dished up a small portion for him and brought it into the family room. "Here you go," I said, sitting down beside him. I sat there in silence for a few minutes while he ate it.

"Hmm, this is really good, Kitten, thanks."

"You're welcome," I said, smiling, pleased that he liked it and that it appeared he was going to eat all of it. Despite my pleasure, I still couldn't shake that nagging feeling that something was wrong.

"Garry, is everything all right with you? I know you're tired and I understand that, but it seems more than that . . . you seem distracted and unfocused. You're not keeping something from me, are you?"

"Like what?" he asked.

"The doctor told me the surgery went well, and you looked great when you first came out of recovery, better than you did last year. Your lack of appetite and focus really have me worried. Did the doctor tell you something you're not telling me?"

Putting his arms around me, he pulled me close to him and kissed me on my forehead. "You worry too much, Kitten, I'm fine. Yeah, I'm having a little harder time bouncing back this year, but it's nothing serious. I'll be okay."

I wanted so much to believe that, but his words didn't have the comforting effect he probably hoped. I knew that pushing him was a waste of time, so I decided to let it go for now. Maybe I *was* being paranoid. He was, after all, another year older. Maybe it really did just boil down to his body not bouncing back as fast this time around. God, I hoped that was all it was.

He watched TV for a little while longer while I cleaned up the kitchen. I was going to sit and watch with him when I was done, but I noticed he was nodding. "Okay, big guy, looks like it's time for you to turn in. The TV is watching you instead of the other way around."

He looked up with blurry eyes and smiled. "I guess you're right," he said, yawning.

I wanted to be encouraged by the fact that he'd eaten pretty good that night, but my joy was short lived. I woke up hours later to the sound of retching and realized he was throwing up again. Standing in the doorway of our bathroom, I looked at him, shaking my head.

"Babe, you do realize you should be past all this by now, right? You barely eat, and what you do eat, you can't seem to keep down. So you're weak, you can't focus, and you're not doing your exercises. That's dangerous, and you know that!"

"Baby, you worry too much!" he said, sounding annoyed. "I keep telling you I'll be okay, but you worrying and stressing yourself out is not going to make that happen any faster. Please just go back to bed . . . okay?"

"Well, you ignoring the problem is not going to make it go away either!" I said, stomping back to the bedroom.

Tears of frustration welling up in my eyes, I was angry at his total disregard for my concern, but more than anything, I was really scared that my concern was warranted. I tried to lie down and calm myself so that I could get some sleep, but I already knew between the anger and the fear, that wasn't going to happen.

The retching had ceased, but Garry stayed in the bathroom a long time afterward. So long that I started to get up and go check on him. Before I could move to do so, he finally came out of the bathroom, hobbled over to the bed, and got in. I was still angry, and so despite my relief, I refused to open my eyes or acknowledge his presence. We both lay there in silence, until he finally reached over and took my hand. When I didn't pull away, he pulled me into his arms. He didn't say anything, he just held me. I listened to the night sounds of the house and the steady beat of his heart. I don't know exactly when, but eventually, I drifted into a fitful sleep.

◆

EARLY THE NEXT MORNING, I woke suddenly from a terrible dream I could only partially recall, consumed by an unnamable fear—a fear momentarily replaced by the joy I felt at seeing, for once, Garry seeming to be sleeping peacefully. I didn't know how long he'd been asleep, but I was grateful for however long. I lay there unmoving, not wanting to disturb him, and prayed silently: "Lord, please let this be a better day; please let this be the beginning of his recovery!"

I would like to say that my prayers were answered, but if you're this far along in my story, you already know that was not the case. The next few days were exactly like the ones preceding them. His appetite didn't increase, although he did continue to make an effort to eat. His desire and ability to exercise didn't improve, and I continued to worry. My last ray of hope came on February 21. It was the day he was scheduled to go for his first outpatient physical-therapy consult. He would meet with the therapist and discuss the plan and the schedule for the remainder of his rehab. The therapist would put him through a few exercises to evaluate his progress since the surgery and tailor the rest of his plan accordingly.

I drove him to his appointment and felt my hope slipping away. Just the process of getting him out of the house, into the car, and into the rehab facility seemed to exhaust all his energy. His mood left a lot to be desired as well. He was highly agitated, and I could tell he wasn't looking forward to this office visit. I had to wonder if it was the exercise he was not looking forward to, or having the therapist confirm what I'd been telling him: something wasn't right. I sat in the waiting room trying desperately to hang on to the last vestiges of hope, that he'd either get better or allow me to take him back to the hospital so they could determine why he wasn't better. Forty-five minutes later, I looked up from the magazine I hadn't been reading, to see my hopes circle the drain.

Garry was barely walking toward me, drenched in perspiration, followed closely by the physical therapist. He assisted Garry to a chair, which he literally collapsed into. Then he turned toward me, and the look he gave me chilled me to the bone. The look in his eyes confirmed what I already knew. I wasn't the overreacting, worry-too-much, paranoid, concerned wife Garry tried to make me out to be. I should have been comforted by the knowledge that I wasn't crazy, and I wasn't alone in my concern. I should have felt vindicated by the knowledge that a bona fide medical professional agreed with my layman's assessment that something wasn't right. Instead, I was filled with a mind-numbing dread that the words about to come out of the therapist's mouth were far worse than I imagined.

"Mrs. Carter," he said, looking from Garry to me. "I don't want to alarm you (*Too late*, I thought), but I'm very concerned about Mr. Carter. He wasn't able to do even the easiest of his exercises. As you can see, he is sweating profusely, and he seems really weak and unfocused. He said he's not in pain, just tired; but it seems like much more than just fatigue."

I nodded at the therapist, keeping my eyes on Garry. He had laid his head back and closed his eyes. He was still sweating, and he seemed to be having difficulty breathing.

"I know he's weak," I said. "He can't seem to keep any food down, and he hasn't had any energy to do his exercises. I keep trying to get him to go back to the hospital, but he keeps telling me he's just tired, and he'll be all right."

"Well, in my opinion, he's definitely not all right."

"I agree," I said. "Maybe you can convince him." I prayed the look in my eyes telegraphed my desire for his help.

Apparently my silent message was received. Approaching Garry, he said, "Mr. Carter, I'm inclined to agree with your wife. You're nine days out from surgery, and I think you should be doing much better by now. I really think you should get checked out by your doctor."

It took all my self-control not to look at him so he wouldn't see the *I told you so* I knew was written all over my face. I held my breath waiting for his response, desperately hoping the therapist had succeeded where I had failed. You would think after forty years of marriage I would know better. If stubbornness were money, my husband would be filthy rich.

"I keep telling my wife, and now I'm telling you: I'm tired . . . I just want to go home and lie down. I'll be fine."

The edge in his voice made it very clear we were wasting our time, and as far as he was concerned, the subject was closed. The therapist handed me his schedule and helped me get him to the parking lot and into the car. He gave me a sympathetic look that said he was sorry, and I thanked him for trying.

I drove him home that afternoon, and despite my concern for his condition, I still had no idea that was the last time I'd drive him anywhere. We argued again that night. I begged, I pleaded, I got angry, I apologized, I cried . . . but nothing changed. I went to bed that night but didn't sleep. I lay awake throughout the night, and despite my absolute certainty that something was wrong, I had no idea that would be the last time I would lie next to him.

Sometime very early that morning, I woke realizing I had succumbed to sheer exhaustion and finally drifted off. Garry was awake, and I wondered if he had slept at all.

"Did you get any sleep?" I asked.

"Not much," he answered. "I already know what you're going to say—" he started, but I interrupted him before he could finish.

"Then don't make me say it. Do you really think I want to keep nagging you about this? I love you, and I just want you to get well. I can't explain why I'm so worried, but I am. I'm not just worried—I'm scared! I don't want anything to happen to you, I don't want to lose you. Why can't you understand that?"

"Baby, I'm not going anywhere. You're not going to lose me."

"Don't you dare tell me you're just tired, you're fine! You've been telling me that for the last ten days, and you're not any better! Don't you want to have our happily forever after? Why can't you just humor me? I'd like nothing better in this world than to be wrong. I'd welcome the opportunity to hear you say, 'See, I told you I was fine.'"

I'd been trying so hard to hold them back, but my tears had a mind of their own and they were streaming down my cheeks with complete abandon. I got up and walked toward the bathroom intending to wash my face. Before I made it to the door, he called my name and I turned to look at him. He looked at me for a long time, and finally he said, "Come here."

I walked over to the bed, and he pulled me down into his arms and held me close, wiping away my tears with his hand. "I'm sorry I've been such a bad patient, and I've caused you so much stress. I'll make you a deal: if I'm not feeling better by this evening, you can take me to urgent care."

"Why do we have to wait till this evening?" I asked, exasperated. "Why can't we just go now?"

"Babe, I don't feel like going and sitting forever in the ER. Besides, I'm sure I'll be okay. I'll try and eat something light, and maybe I'll be able to take a nap. If I don't feel better when I wake up, I promise I'll go. Okay?"

He made me a promise, and I was going to make sure he kept it. I lay there for a few minutes longer just letting him hold me. That annoying alarm was ringing in my head again, and I just wanted to hold on to that moment a little longer. I kept telling myself, *It's going to be okay now. Either he's gonna feel better, or I'm getting him the hell outta here.* I thought, *Either way, Arlita . . . it's going to be okay now.* I had to keep telling myself that until I believed it. I finally got up and started toward the door. He had drifted off, and I decided to go fix him a light breakfast.

I tried to move as lightly and slowly as possible so I wouldn't disturb him. I thought I had succeeded, but just as I reached the door, he called out to me.

"Kitten."

I turned at the door. "Yeah?" I answered.

"I love you," he said, smiling. "No matter what happens, you're going to be fine. I know that . . . I need you to know that."

The alarm in my head got louder. My throat felt tight, and I could feel tears building up behind my eyes again. It took me a minute or two to find my voice.

"You're going to be fine too, 'cause if you're not better later, I'm hauling your butt outta here." I pasted a smile on my face I didn't feel. "You promised," I said, trying to sound stern.

He smiled again, and I blew him a kiss before heading downstairs to the kitchen.

It would be months later before my mind would allow my heart to remember those last few hours. Before I could acknowledge my regret that I didn't walk back over to that bed and kiss him and hold him and tell him I loved him . . . but you see, I had no idea that in a little less than eight hours, he would be gone!

CHAPTER TWELVE

February 28, 2013

AFTER INITIATING THE PROCESS for me to receive Garry's life insurance from his job and assisting with the funeral arrangements, Kenny flew back to Atlanta so he could drive back with April and the children to attend the services. It had only been eight months since I'd last seen my grandbabies. As they came through the door with a chorus of "Hi, Grandma," I could tell they hadn't fully grasped the gravity of the circumstances surrounding their visit.

After conception, it takes nine long months to bring a child into this world. But once they make their grand entrance and utter that very first ear-piercing cry . . . time seems to move at warp speed. One minute you're tenderly and very carefully supporting their tiny little heads cradled in your arms, feeding and changing them, checking them every few minutes while they sleep to make sure they're still breathing, and just marveling in awe at this little human you created. Then in a blink of an eye they're walking, talking, and letting go of your hand, fearlessly claiming their independence, impatient to make their own way into the world.

That moment you feel them slipping away can be both exhilarating and frightening for both parents and grandparents. It's the reason you don't want to miss a second of their lives, that transition from dependence to independence. It's what made it so hard for me to be so far away from my grandchildren. They grew and changed so fast, and each time I saw them, I felt like I'd missed so much. I didn't know what Kenny and April had told them, how much they had explained about this sudden road trip, but it broke my heart to think of how they would react when they fully understood: their beloved Papa was gone.

McKenzie was the oldest of Kenny's three children. Of the three, she had spent more time with Garry, and judging from the sadness in her eyes and the way she hugged me, I suspected she felt and understood more than her siblings. Londyn, the middle child, adored her Papa, and though she'd had less time with him, I sensed a keen awareness of his absence. Even so, I felt it had not completely registered that she would not see him again.

Both girls had been to the house several times before, and I knew they considered it their second home. They knew every inch of the house from the upstairs to the basement. Aside from a little surprise at the recent changes to the kitchen, which they highly approved of, they didn't seem to register anything out of the norm except the absence of their grandfather.

When I looked at my youngest grandchild, Mason, my eyes filled with tears and a sharp pain pierced my heart. He'd had exactly four days with his Papa. Ninety-six hours . . . not even that much if you subtracted the time he slept. The thought that he would grow up perhaps never knowing how much Garry loved him produced pain and a profound sadness that nearly took my breath away.

I watched him in his father's arms and wondered if he remembered the giant of a man who, upon seeing him for the very first time, had lifted him up into his arms, held him tight, and in a voice thick with emotion told him he was his grandfather. I wondered if he would remember sharing his grandfather's Arnold Palmer, or falling asleep on his broad shoulders. I wondered if he would remember pressing his little forehead up against Garry's and kissing him on his nose, or tickling each other and laughing so hard they both could barely breathe.

I was blinded by my tears as I remembered all those special moments from our vacation last year, memories I would carry in my heart for the rest of my life. Mason was so young, and I wondered if even after only eight months, he would remember. I knew it would be up to us to show him the pictures and tell him the stories. It would be up to us to keep his grandfather's memory alive, to let him know and never forget he lived and he had loved him very much.

This was Mason's first visit to our house. It was unfamiliar, uncharted territory, and as he squirmed in his father's arms, I could see the curiosity in his eyes. As he strained to get down, to be free, I could sense the first craving for independence. It was obvious his desire to explore was overriding any fear of the unknown. I knew it was just a matter of time before he would conquer this unfamiliar territory and, like his sisters, make this his home as well.

As soon as his little feet hit the floor, he was in hot pursuit of his sisters and his cousins David and Noah. The determined look on his face said he wasn't going to let stairs or any other barrier deter him from joining them. As I looked around the room at the other adults, I smiled through my tears, realizing I wasn't the only one whose heart was beating double time fearing the worst.

Five years ago, Garry finished off the basement, turning it into his "man cave," which he happily shared with his grandsons. All the other children were down there playing video games. Mason, having discerned their location, headed for the basement steps like a rocket shot out of a cannon, his short little legs, much to my amazement, propelling him faster than I would ever have imagined.

As if of one mind and one body, collectively we leaned toward him mentally willing him to slow down, fearing he would take a header down the basement steps.

I couldn't help but laugh out loud when he reached the steps, realizing we'd all underestimated the advanced mind of this industrious little boy. When he reached the top step, he hesitated for only a second and then turned around and proceeded to descend the stairs backward on his hands and knees. Oblivious to our concern, he laughed with glee all the way down, reveling in his freedom and anticipating his reunion with the older children. Releasing the breath I'd been holding, I shook my head.

"I swear, every one of my grandbabies has negotiated those stairs the exact same way!" Looking at Kenny, I laughed. "You and your brother learned to go up and down stairs the same way as well. Must be hereditary."

It was good to have the distraction of my children and grandchildren, to laugh even if just for a minute. I wanted to shield them from this all-consuming sorrow, this emptiness that threatened to crush me, for a long as possible. It was hard, though. I seemed to always be on the verge of tears, and I couldn't seem to hold on to a single clear train of thought to save my life.

Kenny, April, and Juanda were going through all the food my neighbors and the church had dropped off to piece together a meal for all of us. I was sitting at my new kitchen island contemplating sleeping arrangements and feeling like a guest in my own kitchen, when the arms of my eldest grandson circled me from behind.

"You okay, Grandma?" Noah asked in a soft but surprisingly grown-up voice.

Seeing my eldest grandchild standing next to me, looking just like his father and grandfather, brought back memories and a fresh wave of tears.

"I'm okay, baby," I answered, trying to sound like I was okay. "Are you guys getting hungry?"

"A little," he said, leaning his head on my shoulder.

Noah, Kevin's only child, had the longest and closest relationship with Garry. I could already tell he was going to be tall like his father and grandfather. He was growing up so fast, but it seemed like only yesterday we were sitting in the waiting room of South Suburban Hospital awaiting his arrival. I remembered in vivid detail receiving that phone call from Kevin: "Mom, it's time, we're headed to the hospital."

We rushed over to meet them, and we took turns pacing and talking and doing our best to comfort and reassure them both while we waited.

After a long wait, he finally arrived via C-section. It had been a traumatic day for everyone, and we were so glad we had been there to support Kevin and Toya. I remembered crying with relief and joy, and thinking with awe, *My baby is having a baby!* The whole experience was surreal and brought back memories of the night Kevin had been born, also via C-section.

Garry had been laid off since November of 2003, and Noah was born the following March. It turned out to be a blessing for everyone. Since he was still not working, he took care of Noah and he was able to bond with his first grandchild from the very beginning. They became inseparable, and looking at him now, I knew Noah was feeling the loss more acutely than any of the other grandchildren. He hadn't cried, at least not in front of me. Like his dad, I suspected he was trying to be strong for me and his younger cousins.

I had no doubt looking at the sadness in his eyes, the quiet way he moved around the house—this house he was so familiar with, this house that was so filled with the presence of his grandfather—when he finally let go and let the tears fall . . . that was a river that would take a long time to run dry.

All the other children came filing back upstairs, having noticed Noah's absence. There were only five of them, but with all the noise they were making, everyone talking at once, it sounded like three times that many. Watching them once again, my mind attempted to focus on sleeping arrangements. Just as the thought entered my mind, the doorbell rang.

It was another member of the church with more food, followed by Donna and Karl. After hugs and kisses were exchanged, once again the noise level in my kitchen escalated and my concentration was broken again. After we all ate, the kids retreated back to the basement to their video games. The conversation turned to memories of Garry, and there were tears and laughter as we recalled our fondest memories of him.

"Is everything set for Saturday, sis?" Donna asked.

"Yes, the obituary is done and it's being printed up. Reverend Powell came over to talk to me about the eulogy. My cousin is coming over to the house while we're at the service to watch the house and receive more food donations, and Joyce will set everything up once she arrives. The boys are going to the funeral home in the morning for one final check…"

I could hear myself reciting all the little details, but I hadn't realized I was crying again until I felt Donna's arms around me.

"It's okay, sis," she said. "I can see you have everything under control."

Really? I thought to myself. *Then why do I feel so out of control?*

"I'm taking her shopping in the morning to buy something to wear," Juanda chimed in. "I'm *not* letting her wear black; I think she should wear something bright. My brother would want that."

"Yes, I agree," Donna said. "I have a surprise for you, sis. When you return from shopping, I want you to call me. I've arranged for a friend of mine to come here to the house and give you a relaxing foot massage and a pedicure. She'll even give you a facial, put on lashes, and do your nails if you want. I want you to look and feel pretty for Garry's homegoing. Are you okay with that?"

Smiling through my tears, I nodded my head. "Yes, thank you, sis. Garry always said I was his best step...he wouldn't expect anything less."

Looking around the room, she said, "You know, you have a full house. Where is everybody going to sleep?"

I looked up at her and laughed. "I've been trying to figure that out all day!"

"Well, I think I have a solution," she said. "Why don't Kenny and his family come to my house? Kenny, April, and Mason can sleep in the guest room, and the girls can sleep on the pullout in my office."

"Oh, sis, you're sure it wouldn't be an imposition?"

"Absolutely not!" she said. "We'd love to have them. I'll talk to Kenny and April. It will be fine."

Kenny and April were okay with staying with Donna. "You're sure we won't be imposing?" he asked.

"Of course not, we'll have a great time."

The girls were ecstatic about spending the night with Aunt Donna. She promised to make them her special hot chocolate with marshmallows, and they were sold.

That being settled, Donna and Karl went home to get everything ready for their guests, and Kenny and April promised to come later closer to the kids' bedtime. We spent the rest of the evening talking quietly and watching the children bond. I was sitting on the couch in the family room alone thinking about trying to get through the next couple of days, when Mason waddled into the room. There were pictures on the end table next to me. Mason seemed instantly drawn to the pictures, one in particular of me and Garry. I watched him approach the table focusing on that picture. I watched him looking at the picture, wondering if he recognized the two people in it.

"Do you know who that is, baby?" I asked.

Looking up at me, a huge smile broke out on his face. He pointed to me, and then pointed to me in the picture.

Smiling, I asked again, "Who is that? Do you know who that is, Mason?"

"Gama," he said in his cute little toddler voice.

"That's right, baby, that's me, Grandma."

I could feel the tears building just beneath my eyelids. I wanted to ask, but I was afraid of my reaction if I didn't get the answer I desired. As if he'd read my mind, he looked at the picture again. He seemed to be studying it, and he suddenly looked up again with another bright smile. There was a twinkle in his eyes like he suddenly remembered something important. Pointing to the picture again he looked at me and smiled.

"Papa!" he said, pointing at Garry.

My breath caught in my throat. I wasn't sure I'd heard him right. I was afraid I'd heard what I wanted to hear.

I picked him up in my lap, and then I picked up the picture and pointed to Garry. "Do you know who that is, Mason?"

He looked at the picture again and then looked back at me. There was no mistaking it this time. He smiled at me and said, as clear as a bell, "Papa."

I couldn't hold the tears back anymore, but this time they weren't tears of sadness—they were tears of pure joy. I hugged my beautiful little grandson tightly to my chest.

"I love you, little man. Yes, baby, that's your Papa," I said smiling, "and he loved you, so very much!"

My last thought that night before I succumbed to sheer exhaustion was, *Thank you Lord! He does remember! He remembers you, Garry, and I'm going to do everything in my power to make sure he never forgets!*

Chapter Thirteen

March 1, 2013

I WOKE UP THE next morning before everyone else and went down to the family room. It was so quiet in the house, if I didn't know any better I'd swear I was home alone. I curled up on the chaise and closed my eyes. I felt more exhausted than I had before I went to bed last night. I felt like I'd been running all night. I didn't need a therapist to tell me I was running from reality.

His sweaters were still folded up on top of his armoire. His toothbrush and his razor were still in a cup on the sink; his bathrobe still hung on the hook on the back of the door. My mind was still trying to register the fact that he was gone. He wasn't in his man cave, he wasn't in our bedroom, he wasn't at work, he wasn't anywhere . . . and yet my heart refused to acknowledge what everyone else seemed to have already accepted: he was gone, and he wasn't coming back!

I should be going to the funeral home this morning with the boys, I thought. *I should be there to see that everything is all right. I want him to look as natural as possible. If tomorrow is the last time my grandbabies will ever see their Papa, I want him to look as if he's just sleeping. If I had my way they wouldn't see him at all. I don't really want them to remember him lying in a casket. I'd prefer them to remember their Papa wearing his sunglasses day and night, inside and out throughout our entire vacation last year because he lost his regular glasses, but played it off like he was just cool like that. I want them to remember the Papa who drove a little too fast up and down the hills of Villa Rica, Georgia, to make them feel like they were on a roller coaster. I want them to remember the Papa who spent the whole day with them at the pool, and then took them to Golden Corral so they could eat anything and everything they wanted. I want them to remember him alive, laughing, loving, and spoiling them rotten.*

That's what I want, I thought. But I know as young as they are, like the rest of us, they need closure. So, I should be there . . . but I just can't do it! It's going to be hard enough seeing him tomorrow, to face reality. I'm already dreading seeing him again still and lifeless. I can't stand the thought of seeing them close that casket, knowing that I'll never see him again. I know once I do, my heart will no longer be able to deny what my mind is struggling to accept. That part of my life is over forever.

"How long have you been up? Did you get any sleep, Ma?"

Startled, I opened my eyes to see Kevin standing in front of me, looking like he hadn't slept any better than I had.

"A little bit, but I'm still tired."

"Ma, why don't you go back to bed for a little while?" he asked.

"Wouldn't do any good; I won't be able to sleep, so I might as well stay up. I need to do something. I guess I should fix the boys some breakfast."

"You need to rest; they can fix themselves some cereal."

How could I tell my baby? How could I make him understand resting wasn't something I'd be doing for a long time?

"Well, I still need to get up and get moving. Your auntie wants to take me shopping. I don't really feel like going, but I do need something to wear tomorrow. Are you sure you and Kenny don't need me to go with you?" I felt the need to ask the question, but to be honest I was hoping the answer would be no.

"We got this, Ma, Ty called and said the programs are done and Dad will be ready to view around noon. You go with Auntie and pick out something pretty. You'll have enough to deal with tomorrow."

I stood up and he took me in his arms, giving me a big bear hug, and kissed me on my forehead. He didn't know—couldn't know—that was exactly the kind of thing his father would have done. Standing there in the circle of his arms, I could feel the tears building behind my eyelids. When he released me, I went upstairs as fast as I could. The last thing I wanted to do was break down in front of him again.

When I walked back into my bedroom, Juanda was emerging from the bathroom.

"Hey you, where did you disappear to? Did I wake you up with my snoring?"

"No, sweetie," I answered, smiling. "I got up so I wouldn't wake you with all my tossing and turning. I went downstairs and got on the chaise. I tried to go back to sleep, but no such luck. I was thinking that maybe I should be going to the funeral home with the boys, but Kevin said they have everything under control. He said I didn't need to put myself through that."

"He's absolutely right, sis, you don't need to go through that. But you do need to get out of this house for a while. Have you had breakfast yet?"

"No, I'm really not hungry."

"Why don't I fix you some breakfast while you get dressed?"

"Why don't *you* stop worrying about me?" I said, laughing. "I'm not hungry right now, but I'll make you a deal—we can get some lunch while we're out."

"Deal," she said. "But I don't wanna hear any of this 'I'm not hungry' business later on. You need to eat something!"

"Yes ma'am," I said as I walked into the bathroom. "I promise to eat something later." I mumbled under my breath, "You so bossy."

"I heard that!" she said, laughing.

When I came out of the bathroom, she was already dressed and catching up on some work emails.

"Is there any place in particular you want to go to look for an outfit?" she asked.

"I saw a commercial yesterday advertising a sale at K&G. I thought we could start there. It's in Orland, and there are plenty of places nearby where we can get lunch afterward."

"Sounds good to me, I'll be downstairs when you're ready."

I sat on the bed after she left and tried to summon the energy to get dressed, comb my hair, and put on some makeup. All I really wanted to do was lie down on my bed and pull the covers up over my head. I wanted to stop the clock, or turn it back. I wanted to be anywhere else but here—getting ready to go buy an outfit to wear to my husband's funeral. The last thing I wanted to do was buy an outfit that I'd probably never wear again after tomorrow. It would be a constant reminder of the worst day of my life, and I was pretty sure I was never, ever going to want to see it . . . much less wear it again.

By the time I pulled myself together and walked back downstairs to the kitchen, Kenny, April, and the kids were coming through the front door. After exchanging kisses and hugs, Kenny reiterated what Kevin had already told me. "We can handle this, Mommy, you go with Auntie. Get out of this house for a while. We'll take care of Dad."

Since I didn't seem to have any other choice, we left and headed to the store. After looking at several outfits, none of which appealed to me, I finally settled on a red-and-black pantsuit I found on clearance. I hadn't realized that I'd lost weight over the past several months. The suit was a little big on me, but since it was on clearance and it was the only one they had left, it would have to do.

After purchasing the suit we went to Kohl's and I bought a pair of four-inch red patent peep-toe pumps. If I had one vice, it was my love of shoes, especially heels. They were my absolute weakness. If there was anything that could lift my spirits even a little bit, it was a new pair of shoes. Walking back to the car after leaving Kohl's, I was reminded of my promise to eat something, so I asked Juanda what she had a taste for. Looking at the grin on her face, I knew I had just wasted my breath asking the question.

"Okay," I said, laughing. "Ariston's it is."

Ariston's on the corner of 175th and Kedzie in Hazel Crest was a must-stop whenever she visited Chicago. She complained all the time about not being able to get a *real* Maxwell Street Polish in Houston, and they had the best in town. My favorite was their Italian beef sandwich. I ordered one with fries, but I was only able to eat half, and I only ate that so I wouldn't have to hear her fuss at me for the rest of the day.

When we returned home, I called Donna to let her know I was back and in for the rest of the evening. "Okay, sis, we'll be over later. Prepare to be pampered!" Kevin and Kenny assured me that everything was in order for tomorrow. The only snag was that the local honor guard would not be available for the service due to a prior commitment at the same time.

"It's okay, Mommy," Kenny said. "They provided us with a flag for the service, and I will present it to you myself."

I wasn't upset that they wouldn't be there, but I knew it was important to Kenny that his dad be honored for his military service. "Are you sure you're okay doing it yourself?" I asked.

"Absolutely," he replied. "If I could do it for all those other soldiers . . . I can certainly do it for my dad."

Everything seemed to be in order for Garry's homegoing—everything except me. There were several people scheduled to speak at the service, including me. Just thinking about getting up in front of all those people attempting to express my feelings—to tell them, especially my children and grandchildren, what he meant to me, to convey the extent of my loss—made my insides seize up. I knew what I wanted to say—what I must say— but the thought of opening my mouth and actually saying the words scared me to death.

I wanted to stand before them with dignity and composure and say farewell to a man who had been a huge part of my life for fifty years, and I knew I would be anything but composed. All I could do was pray and ask God to give me the peace and the strength to get through it without breaking down. Up until the night he died, I didn't have any woulda, coulda, shoulda regrets. I believed that I had both told and showed my husband often how much I loved him . . . how much he meant to me. If I was wrong, if I had failed to do that in any way, this was my last chance. For I believed with all my heart he was up there watching and listening, and I didn't want to mess it up.

I needed to get my mind off tomorrow, at least for a little while, and reduce some of the acid steadily building up in my stomach. Whenever I got worked up like this, there was only one thing that calmed me down. There was only one place I could escape from my stress and focus on something that gave me both joy and peace.

While the children played and the adults were busy talking, I slipped into the kitchen and began taking eggs and butter from the refrigerator. Then I began to measure out flour and sugar. My grandbabies were the first to notice when I pulled out and plugged in my mixer.

"Ooooh, Grandma, are you getting ready to bake something?"

"Yes," I said, smiling. "I think I'll bake a cake. What do you think about that?" I asked.

"I think that sounds great!" Juanda said, walking into the kitchen.

"Hmmm, did I hear you say cake, Ma? What kind of cake?" Kevin asked, yelling from the family room.

"I'm thinking about my lemon supreme pound cake," I answered. When I looked up from my measuring, I couldn't help but laugh at all the grinning faces gathered around me. *Yes*, I thought to myself as I felt the acid in my stomach begin to dissolve, *this is exactly what I needed!*

Just as I took my cake out of the oven and set it on a rack to cool, the doorbell rang. It was Donna and her friend. Donna had promised some pampering, and judging by all the equipment the young lady had brought with her, she seemed prepared to do just that. After introductions were made, I placed a piece of foil over the cake.

"Okay," I said to Kevin and the kids, "this cake has to cool before I can put the glaze on it. I'll do that when these ladies are done with me. I'm going to trust all of you not to touch it until I get back down here. I *can* trust you. *Right?*"

They all mumbled a halfhearted yes, but when I didn't move, they all said in unison, "Okay, okay, we won't touch it!"

We all laughed, and then the ladies and I headed upstairs to my bedroom. As I sat in my recliner chair, the very talented young lady proceeded to give me what had to be the best pedicure I'd ever had. It became obvious after a few minutes that my two sisters were trying to do their best to take my mind off tomorrow. They were both talking a mile a minute about everything under the sun. Everything except what was going to take place in the morning.

"Do you want me to do your nails too?" she asked. Apparently I had spaced out, because I didn't hear her.

"Sis, do you want her to do your nails?"

I sat there staring at all of them, and finally it registered that they were talking to me. "Oh, I'm sorry," I said. "I guess I must have zoned out. What did you say?"

"She asked if you wanted your nails done," Juanda said.

I looked over at Donna since she was footing the bill, and she nodded yes. "Of course," she said. "She needs to be together from head to toe!"

When she finished my nails, on a whim I decided to let her put on some lashes. I had them put on once before for a vacation. They looked really nice for as long as they lasted. I never had any luck putting them on myself. I could only manage to get one of them on straight. I thought the expense frivolous unless it was a really special occasion. I figured nothing could be more special than this, and since my big sis was treating, I thought why not.

While she applied the lashes, they talked and I listened. I even tried to contribute to the conversation, but I found it hard to concentrate. My mind kept moving forward to tomorrow morning. Looking in the mirror, I saw my face. I didn't feel as though I looked any different. They said the lashes looked really nice, and that they highlighted my eyes. What I saw were tired eyes that revealed a lack of sleep and the shedding of too many tears. The woman in the mirror didn't look different to me, but I knew she was—in every way possible. I knew she would never be the same. In the blink of an eye, her whole world had changed forever. I sat at my dressing table oblivious to the conversation in the background. I looked at the woman in the mirror, and a sad revelation washed over me. The woman who used to sit here no longer existed, and no amount of makeup could ever bring her back.

"Sis, did you hear what I said?"

I looked in the mirror again at Juanda standing behind me, wondering how long she'd been standing there. "No, I guess I must have zoned out again," I replied. "What did you say?"

"I said the natives are getting restless down there. Girl, they are literally hovering around that cake!"

"Well, I guess I'd better get down there," I said, laughing. "If I don't put that glaze on it soon, there won't be anything to glaze!"

I smiled to myself a few minutes later standing in my kitchen, when I realized aside from Juanda and Donna, no one even noticed my lashes; they were too focused on the cake. The kids were all talking at once boasting who was going to get the first and biggest piece. Kev was teasing me about taking too long to make the glaze, and how I should just cut the darn cake already! Despite the distractions, I was trying to concentrate on what I was doing. It would be a shame to mess up the cake now, I thought, after making them wait so long. Standing in my new kitchen, surrounded by my children and grandchildren and my two awesome sisters, reminded me of happier days. I thought about all the holidays we had shared in this very kitchen—well, the old kitchen anyway. I thought about how much Garry would have enjoyed this moment. He always claimed not to like sweets. I could hear him now, saying, "I don't eat sweets!" knowing full well he would have been first in line with the children jockeying for the first piece of cake.

No sooner had that thought entered my head, I was abruptly reminded of the reason we were all here tonight. That all-too-familiar sadness engulfed me, and once again my thoughts turned to the coming morning. In the morning I would get up and get dressed. In the morning the funeral director would arrive at nine thirty to take us to the church. In the morning we would walk into the church and say goodbye to our beloved.

We would see him for the last time and each in our own way try and make peace with that finality. For the very last time I would look upon my husband's face and kiss him goodbye, and when they closed the lid on his casket, I would be forced to close the door on that chapter of my life—forever!

CHAPTER FOURTEEN

March 2, 2013

WHEN I WENT BACK to bed that morning, I never anticipated going back to sleep. I fully expected I would lie staring up at the ceiling waiting for the alarm to go off. Whether from sheer exhaustion or a desperate desire to escape, the second my head hit the pillow, I closed my eyes and the world disappeared.

An annoying piercing sound that seemed to be coming from very far away finally penetrated my brain. I opened my eyes, and after a few minutes realized it was the alarm buzzing on my nightstand. As I turned it off, I was conscious of the eerie silence in the room and the fact that I was alone. I lay there quietly listening for the sound of running water, but heard nothing. It was then I noticed the dress Juanda planned to wear to the service was no longer hanging on the closet door.

Thinking that I'd overslept, I looked at my phone in a panic and was relieved to see that I had not. *She must have gotten up early*, I thought. I slowly sat up and swung my legs around to the floor and willed my body to get up. My legs, like my heart, felt like lead. When I finally summoned the energy to stand, I walked over to my bedroom door and opened it just a crack. I could hear mumbled voices coming from down in the kitchen. Apparently I was the last to rise. The last hope I had that this was all just some horrible nightmare disappeared. I took a deep breath, walked into my bathroom, and turned on the shower.

Twenty minutes later when I walked back into my bedroom, Juanda was sitting on the bed fully dressed. Her eyes were moist and I could tell she had been crying.

"I'm not going to ask how you're doing," she said. "I know that would be a stupid question. Is there anything I can get for you? Anything I can do for you, sis?"

I could tell she was barely holding it together, and I was far from okay myself. I sat down on the bed and hugged her.

"Can you make this day go away?" was all I could manage.

I didn't expect an answer; we both knew the answer. We just held each other for as long as we dared, and then she stood up.

"I'm going to go check on things downstairs. Kevin went to pick up Momma, everyone else is here. Just yell if you need anything."

I sat there for a few minutes longer fighting the urge to cry, and then I finally got up and got dressed. When I finished dressing, combing my hair, and applying makeup, I stood in front of my full-length mirror and wondered what Garry would think about my outfit. He always liked me in red.

"I don't know if I'm your best step today, baby, but under the circumstances, this is the best I can do."

Taking one last look at my reflection in the mirror, I grabbed my purse and went downstairs to join my family. Everyone was so subdued; the atmosphere was so different from the boisterous chatter of the night before. Even the children seemed to be deep in their own personal thoughts. Kenny looked up when he saw me coming down the stairs and came to meet me giving me a warm hug.

"You look really nice, Mommy," he said.

Kevin, ever the comedian, managed to lighten the mood at least for a few minutes. He shook his head in mock disgust at Kenny's comment and said to no one in particular, "Suck-up!"

Kenny rolled his eyes and said, "Forget you, man!" Everyone else laughed.

Jillian gave me a hug and told me I looked nice as well. "I spoke to Ty, Ma, the car is on its way."

"Thanks, baby," I said, walking into the living room. I walked over to the bay window and stood there looking out on my street. The sky was an awesome clear blue, and the sun was so bright it was almost blinding. Were it not for the barren trees and the snow on the ground, one might believe it was as warm out as the sun was bright.

I was under no such illusion. I'd lived in Illinois all my life. It was March, and I knew without a doubt it was as cold outside as I felt on the inside. I closed my eyes and my mind traveled back to the day we moved into this house. Garry was driving the U-Haul and I followed in our car with our two boys and our lab, Sarge. We arrived at our "dream house," and as soon as Garry backed the truck into the driveway and opened its door, neighbors showed up to help us move in. Among those who came to help was a scrawny little boy with a huge smile. He eased up to Kenny and said, "Hi, my name is Shawn." Kenny introduced himself, and then Sarge, and from that moment on the three of them were fast and inseparable friends.

As if watching a video, the visions in my mind's eye sped up, cataloging all the events and wonderful memories we'd made over the last thirty years. I was so absorbed in my trip down memory lane I jumped, startled, when I felt a hand on my shoulder.

"I'm sorry, Ma, I didn't mean to scare you." I turned to see Kevin standing behind me. "The car is here," he said. "It's time to leave."

The acid in my stomach began to boil and bubble and my knees suddenly felt weak. *This is it*, I thought. *Lord, please give me strength.* Everyone started putting on coats and filing out the door to the car.

When I stepped out on the porch, I noticed some of my neighbors in their cars. They were lined up forming a caravan to follow us to the church. I looked at them and smiled in gratitude for their support. *They're all here for you, baby,* I thought as I stepped into the car. The church was less than ten minutes from the house via car, but this morning it seemed to take forever to cover that short distance.

I was standing in the small fellowship room provided by the grief ministry talking to some of Garry's coworkers, when out the corner of my eye, I saw Rev. Powell stick his head in the door and say something to Kevin. Seconds later Kevin walked over to me.

"Ma, it's time. Reverend Powell says we need to start the service soon. Are you ready to see Dad now?"

Inside I was screaming, *No!* But in my heart I knew if I didn't, I would regret it for the rest of my life. An announcement was made that the service would begin soon and anyone who had not yet viewed the body should do so now. Once the casket was closed, it would not be reopened.

My boys and I, along with the rest of the family, lined up behind Rev. Powell and we were escorted into the sanctuary. Supported on either side by Kevin and Kenny, I approached the casket, and the closer I got the faster my heart beat. I had not seen him since that night in the hospital. Lying there in the same suit he'd worn when we renewed our vows, he looked handsome even in death.

My initial relief at how well he looked quickly faded as reality set in. *This is it,* I thought. *This is the last time I will ever look upon your face.* His face became more and more blurred as my eyes filled with tears. I took a deep breath and reached out my hand to caress his cheek. I bent to kiss his forehead, and at the touch of his cold, stiff skin my heart shattered yet again. Suddenly I felt the ground disappear beneath my feet, and with superhuman effort, I resisted the urge to cry out.

"It's okay, we got you, Ma," I heard Kevin say in the distance.

I closed my eyes, wanting to succumb to the darkness, but Kenny's voice pulled me back into the light: "Come on, Mommy, come and sit down." Holding me firmly by my elbow, he steered me away from the casket. "Come on, Mommy," he said. "You can do this."

No I can't! I thought. But a voice deep within said, *Yes you can!* I took my seat and dried my eyes. "Get it together, Arlita," I said to myself and echoed my inner voice. "You can do this!"

Those late to arrive filed past the casket and then past the front pews where we were seated to offer their condolences. Finally the casket was closed and draped with the flag. For the next forty minutes I bore my grief in stoic silence, determined not to cry again. I did okay when Juanda read the obituary, and the soloist sang Garry's favorite song, "Your Will Is What's Best for Me." It was when Kenny performed his honor-guard duties my resolve faltered and I came close to letting go and giving in to the full extent of my sorrow. Watching my son expertly fold that flag and walk slowly over to me . . . standing before me and in a voice thick with emotion utter those words I had heard so many times before on TV and in the movies . . . was almost my undoing.

The entire time Kenny was in the air force, I had stayed on my knees and prayed I would never get that knock on the door. I prayed I would never hear those words: "On behalf of a grateful nation." I prayed I would never receive that flag, and now here I was doing just that. My only consolation was that Garry had not died in the line of duty thousands of miles away in some foreign land. Still, as I sat there holding that flag, I identified with every mother, father, sister, brother, wife, and child who'd ever received one. I felt their pain just as I felt the palpable pain all over my son's face, standing before me now. With tears streaming down my face, I hugged that flag, and just for a few minutes I gave in to all the pain and grief it symbolized.

I listened to one after another speak about my husband. I listened to them tell us what kind of brother, mentor, and friend he had been. I listened to my boys tell us what kind of father he had been, and finally it was my turn to tell everyone what kind of husband he had been. As I approached the podium, hoping no one noticed now much my hands were shaking, Kevin and Kenny followed and stood on either side of me. Standing close like two centurions, I was grateful for their presence, and their strength.

My mouth was so dry at first I was afraid I wouldn't be able to get the words out, but I looked over at the casket and imagined I could hear Garry say, "You got this, Kitten!" As I looked around the congregation, it might have appeared that I was looking at our family and friends, but truth be told, I couldn't see anyone. I was aware of their bodies in front of me, but their faces were invisible.

With a shaky voice that got stronger as I went on, I told them how we met and how he came to earn the nickname "Pooh Bear." That story got quite a few laughs and lightened the mood for everyone. I told them despite his physical absence in my life, he would always be with me. I would see him every time I looked into the eyes of my sons, or heard the laughter of my grandchildren, or watched the many young men he mentored grow and flourish. I told them looking out into the congregation today at all of them, I was reminded of his kindness, his generosity, and his willingness to extend his hand and his heart to anyone in need, especially the children.

"The very last thing Garry told me just before he went in to have this last surgery was how much he couldn't wait for it to be over with. He couldn't wait for the rehab to be over. He said the one thing he wanted more than anything in this world was to dance with me on our anniversary. We would have celebrated our fortieth wedding anniversary this coming June."

With tears that I could no longer hold back, I told them that I believed in my heart one day we would meet again, and one day we would have that dance.

Walking back to the pew I felt a strange calm come over me, and as I took my seat I glanced briefly at the closed casket. I felt his love reach out to me, and in my spirit I heard him say, "You did good, Kitten!" I listened to Rev. Powell give the eulogy, and for a brief time ... I was at peace.

Chapter Fifteen

W HEN REV. POWELL FINISHED the eulogy, just before he gave the benediction, he made an announcement. "Due to a prior engagement, the fellowship hall is unavailable for the repast. The Carters have asked me to inform you that the repast will be held at their home immediately following the service. You will find the address on the back of the program. Due to the limited space, please limit your attendance to immediate family and close friends."

Following the benediction, we exited the sanctuary the same way we entered—lined up behind Rev. Powell. Preceding us was the casket being carried by the pallbearers, who consisted of friends of Kevin and Kenny. Between community-league football and eight years of high school football, at any given time you could find at least half of the football team in my home. There was no official community center in our neighborhood, but unofficially our home was definitely considered the "center" of Marycrest.

To these young men Garry was "Coach Carter," he was "Pops"; he was their mentor, their friend, and a surrogate father. They loved him, and they had all come back today to show their love and say goodbye. Since it had been Garry's wish to be cremated, there would be no trip to the cemetery, no gravesite service. For that I was extremely grateful. This had been hard, but I had no doubt whatsoever that would have been far worse!

While waiting for all of the family to reassemble, I stood in the vestibule and talked with some of my former coworkers. They were already seated by the time the service started, so I was not aware of their presence until afterward. I hadn't seen many of them since our last day of work six months prior, and I was extremely moved by their attendance.

"I'm so touched that you came today," I said. "I know what Reverend Powell said, but you've come a long way and you're more than welcome to come to the house. It might be a little crowded, but we'll make room."

"Ma, the limo is here," Kevin said. "Are you ready to go back to the house?"

"Yes," I said. "I'm ready to get out of these clothes."

The limo took us back to the house, and when we walked in the door I couldn't believe how many people were already there and how much food had arrived while we were at the church. As I looked around and greeted everyone, I thought to myself, *There might not be a lot of room, but at least no one will starve.*

As soon as I could, I excused myself and escaped upstairs to my bedroom. I sat down on the bed and kicked off my shoes, then tried to summon the energy to get back up and take off my clothes. Juanda walked in a few minutes later and found me still sitting staring at the floor.

"Sis, are you okay?" she asked.

"Yes and no," I answered. "I've been running on empty all day."

"Why don't you lie down for a little bit?"

"I'd love to do just that, but I can't. There are a lot of people down there who came a long way to be with me, with us. I can hold out a little longer. I probably should try and eat a little something, though; I'm feeling a little light headed. I'm going to change into something more comfortable. Would you check and make sure everything is okay down there? I'll be down soon."

"Are you sure, sis? Everyone would understand if you needed to rest."

"I'm sure," I said, smiling. "I'm okay."

By the time I came downstairs again, the house truly was bursting at the seams. Most of the family members were in the living room, along with some members of the church from the marriage ministry. Joyce was taking care of the food and everything was running like a well-oiled machine. My extended family was holding court in the kitchen, mostly the young folks. Coworkers and friends were spread out in the family room. All the children were down in the basement, and it sounded like there were at least a hundred of them. The front door was constantly opening and closing with more people coming and going. I went from room to room trying to spend a little time with each group, and I could feel my body grow wearier with each passing minute.

I was standing in the middle of the kitchen trying to decide which way to go next, when Joyce came over to me and gave me a hug.

"I want you to come and sit down," she said.

Juanda said, "You haven't eaten anything, and I'm going to rectify that right now. I have a seat waiting for you, so come and sit and I'll fix you a plate."

I smiled a tired smile and did what I was told. The food looked and smelled really good, and judging from the way everyone was putting it away, I had no doubt it tasted good too. Maybe I'd be able to taste it later, but right now I couldn't taste a thing. I ate out of necessity, but not out of any real desire for anything on my plate. I couldn't even finish it all, a fact Joyce wasn't happy about.

"I guess I wasn't as hungry as I thought I was," I said. "I promise to try and eat something else later—really, I promise!"

"You better," she said, looking like she didn't believe me.

"Don't worry, that other bossy woman is still here, and she will make sure I eat."

"Did I hear somebody say my name?" Juanda said as she walked into the living room.

"See?" I said to Joyce, laughing. "I didn't even mention her name and she knew I was talking about her."

"Yes, I knew you were talking about me," she said. "Don't worry, Joyce, I'll get her to eat."

"I rest my case," I said, and we all laughed.

I didn't know when we'd all see each other again, so I asked the boys to take some pictures with our cousins from Atlanta and Detroit. It had been a long day for all of us, and they were getting ready to go back to their respective hotels to get some rest before traveling back home later this evening and tomorrow.

"I'm so glad you were able to come," I said, standing at the door as we said our goodbyes. "You don't know how much it means to me to have your support today. Now look, we need to stay in touch. We can't let the next time we see each other be the result of another funeral."

They all agreed, and as hugs and kisses were exchanged, they all promised to keep in touch.

About an hour or so later, the last of my coworkers and church family had left, leaving only my immediate and extended family. They were still hanging out in the kitchen, which had always been the "hub" of the house. I walked into the kitchen just in time to hear a conversation between Candyman and Jaleel about the newly redesigned kitchen.

"I didn't say I didn't like it, I just said it's not 'our' kitchen; it's not the kitchen we grew up in."

"I know," Jaleel responded. "I walked in and I thought I was in the wrong house!"

"You were," Kevin replied. "This ain't your house, fool, you live down the street, remember?"

I smiled as I took a seat at the island. *Oh, it's on now*, I thought, laughing. A warm feeling came over me as I thought to myself, *This is what I missed. I missed my babies and their camaraderie.* I looked around the room at all my boys, and my heart filled to overflowing. I could feel the sting of fresh tears behind my eyes and willed myself not to cry. I knew from past experience this was just the beginning of a back-and-forth between them that would likely last well into the night.

Sure enough, after they finished trading opinions and barbs about all the changes to their "childhood" home, the conversation switched to their memories over the years of Garry, or "Pops," as they called him. I laughed at their recollections that became more embellished with each telling, and I was shocked at some I'd never heard of. What surprised and comforted me the most was how emotional some of them got the more they remembered. Shawn, who'd been my adopted baby for the longest, was sitting at the island with me.

"I'm really going to miss Pops, Ma," he said, leaning over and hugging me.

"I know, baby," I said, no longer able to keep the tears from falling. "We're all going to miss him. The best way to keep him alive, to honor his memory, is to make him proud. You've got your whole life ahead of you. Remember everything he taught you, and don't waste a second of it."

For a while I forgot how tired I was as I sat there and listened to the boys reminiscing about the "good old days," but soon the fatigue I was feeling earlier caught up with me. I could hardly keep my eyes open. As much as I hated the thought of going up to my room to my empty bed, I didn't think I could last much longer. Apparently Kevin had been watching me and noticed I was running out of steam.

"Ma, you look like you're about to keel over," he said. "It's been a long day. Why don't you go to bed?"

"I think I will," I said. "I'm about done."

"Do you want us to leave?" the boys all asked as I got up and walked toward the stairs.

"Nope," I answered. "I'm going to take one of those magic pills the doctor gave me. In a few minutes, I won't even know you're here."

"We promise to keep the noise down," they said as I collected hugs and kisses on my way up the stairs.

I walked into my bedroom and collapsed on my bed. The full weight of the day overwhelmed me. Finally alone, the tears began to fall, and I lacked the energy to try and restrain them. I fell back on the bed and let them flow freely. I resisted the need to close my eyes for as long as I could, not wanting to see the vision I knew would come as soon as I did. I didn't want to see the vision of my husband lying in that casket. I didn't want to see him again still and forever silent. I didn't want to think of the days, weeks, months, and years ahead. I didn't want to think about all the plans we made that would never come to pass. I couldn't stand to think about life without him!

Turns out I didn't need the magic pill after all. Eventually the tears dried up and I lost the battle to keep my eyes open. God must have taken pity on me. I don't remember closing my eyes, but I know I did, because hours later I woke squinting from the sun coming through the blinds. I was fully dressed and lying on top of the covers. Any other time I would have laughed at myself, but today I could find no humor in my situation. I lay there for a few minutes, wanting nothing more than to undress, crawl under the covers, and retreat from the world, but Kenny and the kids were going home very early tomorrow morning. Today would be my last day with them for I didn't know how long, and I didn't want to waste it.

Juanda was leaving this afternoon. I wanted to spend as much time as possible with all of them. Reluctantly, despite the lingering fatigue I still felt, I drug myself from the bed, undressed, and headed to the shower. Thirty minutes later, I emerged from my room and found everyone in the kitchen eating breakfast. I wasn't really hungry, but I hadn't eaten much the day before so I nibbled on toast and bacon and enjoyed the banter between my children and grandchildren.

"You probably won't have to cook for a month, sis; there is still so much food left over from yesterday."

"Yeah, I am so grateful for the way the church, my neighbors, and family showed up and showed out. Everybody really came through, but I doubt I'll eat any more of it past today. You two should take some of this food with you," I said to Kenny and April. "I know you're not going to feel like cooking after your long drive tomorrow. Please, please take some of that cake. Lord knows I don't need that around here."

"Don't take it all!" Kevin said, and we all laughed. My oldest child had unfortunately inherited his sweet tooth from me. I knew as far as he was concerned they could take all the food they wanted, but he would fight them for the sweets!

"We'll take a look at what's in there, Mommy, and see what we can take off your hands—especially the cake!" he said, winking at me.

I laughed, knowing he had said that last part just to annoy his brother. It was a quiet day; just a couple of neighbors dropped by to check on us. I spent the rest of the day cuddling with my grandbabies, especially Kenny's kids, trying to get all the kisses and hugs I could. McKenzie seemed extremely quiet and subdued, and I wondered if she was having a delayed reaction to yesterday.

"Come sit with me, baby girl," I said. "How are you doing? You're missing your Papa, huh?"

She nodded her head and I could see the water collecting in her eyes. Putting my arms around her, I held her close, rocking back and forth.

"I know, baby, it's okay," I said. "We all miss him." I put a finger to her heart and said, "You know he'll always be with you. Right here in your heart. He'll be watching over you, and he's gonna be so proud because I know you're going to grow up and become a beautiful, intelligent, talented young woman. He'll be up there in heaven bragging to the angels, 'That's my grandbaby. That's my Kenzie bear!'"

"What about you, Grandma?"

"What about me baby?"

"Is Papa going to be watching over you too?"

My heart felt constricted, and I could feel tears begin to build up in my own eyes. God, would I never stop crying?

"Yes, baby, Papa will be watching over me too."

"I don't want to leave you here." She said it so low, at first I couldn't make out what she said.

"What did you say, sweetie?"

There was no missing the tears in her eyes this time when she looked up and said it again. "I don't want to leave you here. I don't want to leave you here alone without Papa . . . you should come home with us."

"Oh, baby," I said, hugging her close again. "Truth be told, I don't want to stay here alone without Papa either, but I'm afraid I have to, at least for a while. I won't be completely alone, though, your uncle Kevin and Noah will be around sometimes, and they'll look after me."

She looked at me with an *I'm not convinced* look and tried to smile. "I miss you, Grandma. It always seems so long before I see you again."

"I know, sweetie, but I'll make you a promise: since I'm not working anymore, I don't have to wait to take vacation. I've got some things around here I need to take care of, but I'm going to come for a visit real soon."

"When?" she asked.

I laughed out loud, not expecting her to pin me down right that minute. "Tell you what, I'll come while you're on your summer break." Pulling up the calendar on my phone, I said, "How about July? I'll come for a whole week. I don't know the exact week right this minute, but as soon as I decide . . . you'll be the first to know. Will that work for you?"

"Okay," she said reluctantly. "You'll stay a whole week?"

"Absolutely," I said. "Seven whole days!"

She hugged me again, and then she was off to join her siblings.

As if they had planned it themselves, I had more one-on-one private moments with the rest of my babies. Mason was too young to really understand what was going on, but even he seemed extra affectionate, as if he sensed my need to be close to him. He climbed up on the couch with me, and we played until we both fell asleep. I woke up first and watched him sleeping next to me, wishing with all my heart his grandfather could see him right now . . . to see how much he'd grown in just eight months. No doubt if he were here, Mason would be in his arms sleeping peacefully on his shoulder. I tried not to think about the clock winding down. I tried not to think about how in just a few more hours, they would all be on the road headed back to Atlanta.

For a few minutes, I thought about how nice it would be to pack a bag and go with them, to put this all behind me and escape to Atlanta. But I knew I couldn't do it. I couldn't just walk away; it wasn't that easy. I had things to do, I couldn't just run away, but I would keep my promise to McKenzie. No matter where I was in the process, I would take the time to go and spend a week with them in July.

Everybody was feeling it. You could feel it in the room as we ate our last meal together. Kenny went to bed early since he would be doing the driving, and the kids stayed up a little longer with their cousins, knowing it would probably be a long time before they saw them again. Juanda had left hours ago, securing a promise from me to spend a few days with her later in the month.

"There's not much you can do until you get the check from the insurance company, sis. You need a change of scenery, even if it's only temporary. Come spend a few days with me, just to clear your head. I'm going to need to move from the place I'm in now, and you can help me look for a new one." I promised to consider it, and I would keep that promise too.

I finally went and lay down, but I couldn't sleep. I set the alarm for 3:00 a.m., the time Kenny and the kids were scheduled to leave. He wanted to leave that early so they would arrive in Atlanta while it was still light outside. I wanted to get up and see them off. I didn't realize I had drifted off to sleep until I heard Mason's voice. He was crying, probably unhappy about having his sleep disturbed. I got up and headed downstairs. Everyone else was already crowded around the front door. Kevin helped Kenny load up the car, and I sat on the bench in the foyer and hugged and kissed April and the kids. I thought I would get through it without breaking down again, but just as McKenzie walked out the door, she turned around and came back. She hugged me like she would never let me go. In a trembling voice, she asked if I was sure I didn't want to go home with them.

I hugged her back just as fiercely. "I can't come with you right now sweetie, but I promise . . . I promise I will be there in July just like we talked about. Just as soon as I set a date, I will call you and let you know."

Reluctantly, I let her go, and stepping out on the porch, I kissed my son. "Drive safely, baby. Call me when you get home, okay?"

"I will, Mommy. You get back in the house now; it's cold out here."

Despite the cold, I stood on the porch and watched them drive off. I stood there watching until their taillights disappeared. I stood there, tears running down my cheeks, and remembered just a few days ago watching the ambulance disappear down the same street, trying to convince myself that even though there were no sirens . . . there was still hope. Finally, the cold penetrated my bones as all the heat drained from my body—just like the night eight days ago when I arrived at the hospital—and all the hope drained from my heart.

CHAPTER SIXTEEN

J UANDA HAD BEEN RIGHT about my need for a change of scenery, a time out from my grief. My time with her was truly a gift from God. It was not only a chance to bond with her, but helping her look for a new place provided an opportunity for me to focus on something other than my very uncertain future. Since I was still planning to relocate to Houston, and we were considering sharing a place, it gave us a chance to consider renting versus buying, as well as viewing properties suitable for the three of us. In addition, her constant encouragement gave me the much-needed confidence in my ability to return home and handle my business.

"Sis, I know my brother spoiled you, he always took care of everything, but I believe you know more than you realize, and what you don't know you'll learn. Garry believed in you. You just need to believe in yourself. He always said you were his best step, not because of the way you looked, but because of who you are . . . who you were to him. He didn't just love you, he admired you. He was tough, but you were his softer side and he was your strength—but that doesn't mean you don't have strength of your own. You know what they say about us: Women are like tea bags. We don't know how strong we are until we are dropped in hot water. You've been thrust into a 'sink or swim' situation, and I have no doubt you're going to swim like a champ! I'm not saying it will be easy—I'm sure at times it's going to get really hard—but between your faith and your family, I know you will weather this storm."

I hung on to those words all the way back to Chicago, and by the time the plane landed at Midway . . . I almost believed them.

Prior to leaving for Houston, Kevin and Jillian invited me to go with them to Vegas for four days. Her mother and sister were going too. Jillian's mother had been comped the rooms at the hotel we would be staying at, so all I would have to pay for was my airfare. They were leaving April 1, just one day after my return from Houston. I would barely have time to unpack and repack again. I'd only been to Vegas once with Garry, and part of me didn't mind going there again, yet still I hesitated.

"You're not working, Ma, you don't have to rush to make any major decisions. You don't really have any excuse for not going. Whatever you decide, whatever you have to do, will be here when you get back. We're only going to be gone four days."

I knew he was right, and yet in my heart, all I could think was . . . my husband had only been gone a month. How could I go on vacation? My life was a mess, I had no idea what the future held for me, so how could I go traipsing around Vegas?

As if he'd read my mind, Kevin came and sat next to me. "Look, Ma, I know what you're thinking, but there's no law that says you have to sit up in this house and be alone and miserable. Dad is gone, but you're still here, and I know without a doubt he would not want you to shut yourself off from the world. He would want you to live! I get that you're grieving—we all are—but that doesn't mean you can't take a few days to enjoy yourself. Don't think of it as a vacation. If it helps, think of it as therapy." He hugged me and said, "Come on, come with us. We want you to go, and I know you can afford it!"

"All right, all right," I said. "I'll go!"

Later that evening, I called Juanda to give her my itinerary and told her about the kids' invitation. If I didn't know any better, I'd swear Kevin had called her and prepped her on what to say.

"Of course you should go, sis. My nephew is right; it's not a sin for you to enjoy yourself for a few days just because my brother is gone. You know as well as I do Garry wouldn't want you to sit up in that house alone and miserable. Come out here, spend some time with me, then go to Vegas and enjoy some time with your son. He probably needs you to go as much as you need to go. Whatever you think you need to do, it will be right there waiting for you when you get back. Besides, it's not like you can't afford it."

Wow, did you guys have a script? I thought to myself, laughing.

I guess it's settled, I thought when I hung up the phone. Just before I left for Houston, I gave Jillian the money to book my flight to Vegas. She purchased all our tickets at the same time so we'd all be on the same flight. While I was in Houston, I did a little shopping, and when I returned, I packed some of the new items to take to Vegas.

The last time I'd been on a plane with my son was our second trip to Orlando. Kevin was nine years old, and he was not thrilled at all about flying. As excited as he was about going to Disney World, he was absolutely miserable on that plane. Now some twenty-nine years later he sat in the aisle seat across from me. I watched his face as we taxied down the runway about to take off. Like that little nine-year-old boy, he was gripping the armrest so hard I thought he'd pull them right out of their sockets. I wouldn't say he was scared, but it was obvious he was extremely uncomfortable. When I first started flying, takeoffs and landings were always the worst part for me too. Once we were in the air, I could tell from the look on his face that all he wanted was to be back on the ground.

I tried to take a nap on the plane, but every time I closed my eyes, all I could think about was what was waiting for me when I returned home. I couldn't shake the feeling that I had no business being on the plane in the first place. I needed to find out what my options were with regard to the house. I needed to decide if I was actually going to relocate and when. Aside from the mortgage payment, I needed to determine what, if any, bills needed my immediate attention and how much money would be required to pay them. I knew that the kids said there's no rush, but I felt restless and unsettled. Reality was setting in, and the facts were, I had no idea what I was facing or how I was going to get through it. But I knew I had no choice but to figure it out—sooner rather than later.

By the time the plane landed and we took the shuttle to the hotel, the sun was already setting. The streets overflowed with tourists and vendors like it was the middle of the day. After registering and getting our key cards, we went to our respective rooms and settled in. While I was unpacking my suitcase, my stomach reminded me that I hadn't eaten all day. As if on cue my phone rang.

"Ma, what are you doing? Are you hungry?"

"Yes, as a matter of fact, I am."

"We're going to go to the buffet in the hotel. You wanna come with?"

"Yep, that sounds like a plan."

"Good. We're right down the hall; we'll meet you by the elevator in about five minutes and we'll all go down together."

The fatigue that had been building over the last two days was catching up with me. As hungry as I was, I was equally as tired. I looked longingly at the bed just before leaving to meet the kids.

"I'll be back soon," I said to the room, just before walking out the door.

Chapter Seventeen

WE MET AT THE elevators as planned and went down together to the buffet. Once confronted with all the menu choices, I realized I was actually more tired than hungry, but I forced myself to eat something anyway. I tried to keep up my end of the conversation after we filled our plates and found a table, but I grew wearier with every forkful of food I put in my mouth. Between the lack of sleep over the last couple of days, my feelings of guilt for being there, and my inability to stop obsessing about my future or lack thereof, I could barely keep my eyes open.

It also didn't help that the conversation inevitably turned to remembrances of Garry, which only served to fuel my guilt.

"Earth to Mama. Where did you go, lady?" Jillian asked.

It took a minute for me to refocus. "I'm sorry, did I space out?"

"Yes, you did. You look really tired, Ma. Why don't you go on up to your room and get some sleep?"

"I don't have the desire or the energy to argue with you," I said with a tired smile. Standing up on weak legs, I kissed them both. "I'll see you two in the morning."

Winding my way back through the hotel casino, I found the elevators and headed to my room. I thought about taking a long, hot shower, but I was too exhausted. I peeled off my clothes, climbed into bed, and I was asleep minutes after my head hit the pillow. I slept like a brick despite all the noise coming from the street below. They called New York the City That Never Sleeps, but I believed that title could just as easily belong to Vegas.

I woke up first with my ears to the sound of splashing water, laughter, and loud music. I opened my eyes to near pitch-black darkness, feeling groggy and disoriented. It took me several minutes to figure out where I was. The windows of my room were covered with those marvelous blackout drapes, and because of the darkness and the noise, I assumed it was still the middle of the night.

I stumbled to the bathroom, and when I returned, before I crawled back into bed, I decided to take a peek outside. The sunlight assaulted my eyes, nearly blinding me. In shock, I looked at the clock on the nightstand, thinking with all the activity outside, instead of the middle of the night, it must be the middle of the day. I was surprised to discover it was only seven o'clock in the morning.

Heading back to bed, I crawled in and pulled the covers over my head. My last waking thought was that the people making all that noise were out of their minds. Two hours later I woke again, this time to the sound of my telephone ringing. Groping around with closed eyes, I finally managed to answer it.

"Hello," I said in a voice still thick with sleep.

"Ma, are you still asleep?"

"I'm awake now," I said, still struggling to open my eyes.

I could hear Kevin laughing and telling Jillian, "Yeah, she's out of it. I was calling to see if you wanted to go and get some breakfast, but if you're still tired, go back to sleep."

"What time is it?" I asked.

"It's a little after nine o'clock."

"Are you ready to go right this minute?" I said, trying to untangle myself from the covers.

"No, we're still getting dressed."

My first thought was *Yes, I could stay in this bed all day*. I had barely eaten anything yesterday, and now my stomach was reminding me of that.

"No, I'm getting up," I said, sitting up and swinging my legs over the side of the bed. "Where are you going?"

"There's a Denny's up the street within walking distance. We thought we'd go there."

"Okay, give me about forty-five minutes or so, and I'll come down to your room."

"Okay, sounds good," he said and hung up.

Not wanting to keep everybody waiting on me, I showered and dressed as quickly as I could. When I went down the hall to Kevin's room, they were still getting ready. I stretched out across their bed and fought the urge to go back to sleep while I waited for them. Fortunately, when we arrived at the restaurant about thirty minutes later, we didn't have to wait long for a table. By now my stomach was really sending me signals that a meal was long overdue. After eating breakfast, the gnawing in my belly ceased and the fog in my brain finally lifted.

Instead of going back to the hotel, we decided to walk off all the food we consumed. We walked to the Venetian and browsed through the shops. While there, we sampled some gelato and other delicacies. Everything you could think of, they had it: gourmet taffy apples, giant candy bars, jewelry, designer handbags, etc.

We came upon a kiosk with designer handbags and matching wallets. I looked at all the styles they offered, and there was one in particular that caught my eye. It was a beautiful black bag with sliver trim. I looked at several bags in all different styles, shapes, and colors, but I kept coming back to that one bag.

"You gonna stare at that bag all day, Ma, or are you gonna buy it?"

"Naw, I was just looking at it. I'm not doing any shopping."

"Why not?" Kevin asked.

"How about because I'm not working, I'm on unemployment. I don't have any business doing any frivolous shopping. Besides, I don't need a new purse."

"But you want that one … right? You act like you're some welfare queen or something. You're collecting unemployment, so what? You worked all your life, and while you were working, they deducted from your check so other people could collect unemployment. You're not taking food out of anybody else's mouth because you treat yourself to a new purse!"

Just as I was about to reply, a sales lady walked over to us. "That's one of our most popular styles. Can I wrap it up for you? We have the matching wallet too."

Shaking my head, I was about to say no, but before I could get the word out of my mouth, Kevin said, "Yes, she'll take it, and the wallet too!"

He was right. I did want the purse, and figuring it was pointless arguing with him, I asked her how much for the purse and the wallet.

"One hundred and ten dollars," she answered, smiling.

"Come on, Ma," Kevin said as I reached into my purse to get my wallet. "I saw that same purse in a shop back at the hotel for a lot less." He took me by the arm and started leading me away.

"Wait, I can give them both to you for seventy," the sales lady said, watching her sale walk away.

Out the corner of my eye, I saw a wicked smile form on Kevin's lips as he turned around and nodded ever so slightly at me. Laughing to myself, I squeezed his hand and whispered, "Good looking-out, son!" as I handed her my credit card.

Chapter Eighteen

AFTER PAYING FOR MY purse, we continued to browse around the Venetian, checking out a few more shops and purchasing tickets for a show. When we emerged back onto the strip, we soon realized both the sun and the temperature were a lot hotter than when we first left the hotel that morning. We walked up and down the strip for a couple of hours and then found an outdoor restaurant where we had lunch.

By the time we finished lunch, between the food and the heat I was totally exhausted again and ready for a nap. We headed back to the hotel, and when I returned to my room, I did just that. I slept hard for a couple of hours, and probably would have slept longer had it not been for the sound of my phone ringing.

"Hello," I answered, trying to shake the cobwebs from my brain.

"Ma, you still asleep?"

"I was, I'm up now," I said, smiling. "What's up?"

"We're thinking about hitting the strip again and finding someplace for dinner. Do you want to go with, or are you staying in?"

"Are you ready to go right this minute?"

"Nope, just making plans."

"Okay, if I have time to shower and change, I'll hang out with you."

"Cool. Yeah, you have time. You don't have to get fancy either, and wear some comfortable shoes."

"Okay, buzz me when you are close to being ready to leave."

About an hour later, we were out on the strip and I was amazed at the hordes of people meandering up and down the street. I was especially in awe of the number of children out. My first thought was *Why aren't they in school?* Then I wondered why anyone would bring their children, especially young children, to Vegas. If we were in Orlando, it would be perfectly normal to see this many children out and about, but I would never have imagined Vegas as a place that would appeal to children. I'd always thought of it as more of an adult town. As we strolled in and around the various casinos, I was intrigued by the number of people sitting glued to the rows and rows of slot machines. I wondered how many people were spending their precious vacation time staring at the screens on those machines, mindlessly pulling down those handles and hoping for that big win that would change their lives. I also wondered how many of them were local residents throwing away their hard-earned paychecks hoping the same thing.

I'd never been into gambling, and I wasn't about to start then. Giving in to a whim and buying a purse was one thing, but throwing money down the drain at a slot machine was completely out of the question. I was grieving, but I wasn't out of my mind. It did occur to me fleetingly that one lucky pull on a slot machine could be the answer to all my problems, but I didn't believe in luck. Luck was for people who had no faith—and no hope. I lost my job, my husband, and I'd temporarily lost some of my confidence, but one thing I hadn't lost was my faith, and I certainly had not lost hope!

We walked around for a while longer taking in all the sights and sounds, and then started looking in earnest for a restaurant for dinner. It took a while before we found one that didn't have at least an hour wait. By the time we found one and were seated, I was both exhausted and famished. Even at that late hour it seemed like there were three times as many people on the street as when we first left the hotel. Feeling full and tired, I was struggling to keep up with the kids. I felt like a little kid trying not to get separated from my parents. When we finally arrived back at the hotel, I could hardly keep my eyes open in the elevator.

Once we reached our floor, my legs felt like lead as I trudged down the hall to my room. Even though I was bone tired, I felt tight all over and decided to take a hot shower, thinking that would help me sleep. Standing in the bathroom afterward, drying off with the luxurious bath towel provided by the hotel, I realized the shower had the exact opposite effect. Suddenly I was wide awake and thinking about the last time I was in Vegas.

We hadn't stayed on the strip. We stayed at one of the resorts in our time-share. It was a beautiful place . . . quiet, cozy, and far away from the hustle and bustle of the strip. It offered all the comforts of home minus the stress and responsibilities of home and work. There was nothing but peace there. We spent long, lazy days cuddled up on the ample sectional sofa watching movies, laughing, talking, dreaming out loud, and planning a future we'd never have, although we didn't know that at the time. We only ventured out from the resort to do some grocery shopping, a little sightseeing, shopping, and one night for dinner and a show. Each time we left, it seemed we couldn't wait to get back to our little haven. It was so quiet it almost felt like we were the only ones there, though the cars in the parking lot assured us we were not.

I recalled with a smile even as tears ran unchecked down my cheeks how we must have looked so happy, because every time we went into the lobby, the people at the desk kept asking if we were on our honeymoon. I suppose it also had something to do with the fact that they'd barely seen us since we checked in.

I don't know how long I lay there reminiscing and crying, but I woke the next morning on top of the covers still wrapped up in that incredibly soft, thick towel, the tears having dried up on my face. I rolled over on my back staring up at the ceiling I could barely see, thinking about the empty house I would have to go back to in another forty-eight hours, and fought off another onslaught of tears.

CHAPTER NINETEEN

FORTUNATELY KEVIN CALLED AND inadvertently broke up my pity party. "Hey, you okay?" he asked, sounding alarmed.

"I'm fine, baby, why?" I answered.

"I don't know, you sound funny. Have you been crying?"

Busted! I thought to myself. "I'm okay. What are you all up to today?" I said in an attempt to change the subject.

"Jillian and her sister want to go shopping at some outlet mall they heard about. You want to go?"

"I'm going to call my friend Lorraine and see if we can hook up while I'm here, hopefully sometime today. I'll let you know after I talk with her. What time are you planning to go to the mall?"

"It won't be until later this morning. We are still trying to figure out how we're going to get there." Since we were staying on the strip we hadn't bothered to rent a car, so we had to walk everywhere or rely on public transportation.

"Okay, I'll call Lorraine and get back to you." Lorraine had to work, so we agreed she'd pick me up at the hotel later that evening and we'd have dinner.

Since I had all that time to kill, I decided to go to the outlet mall with the kids. They discovered there was a bus we could take right outside the hotel in the same area where we caught the shuttle to and from the airport. After a light breakfast, we walked to the bus stop and headed to the mall. I enjoyed browsing the shops, but I managed to exercise supernatural willpower and not buy anything. It helped that the stores were mostly high end, and what they called a sale I considered regular price. I wanted to get some souvenirs for my grandbabies and my mom, and I was determined I wasn't spending any money on anything else.

I made it back in plenty of time to shower and change before meeting Lorraine. I hadn't seen my friend since she got married and moved to Vegas. I missed her, and I was really looking forward to seeing her and catching up. A lot had happened since the last time I saw her. My whole world had been turned upside down. We talked on the phone, texted, and emailed, but I wanted to see with my own eyes that she was healthy and happy. I was happy for her; I just wished she wasn't so far away.

We had a very pleasant dinner. The food was great, and the conversation was better. She brought me up to date on her move and her marriage. Lorraine was a good listener; she listened and didn't interrupt when I poured out my heart about Garry's death and my feelings about everything. She didn't judge or try and tell me how I should feel or how long I should feel it. She assured me that she had no doubt that I was strong enough to get through it. She encouraged me to take my time through the grieving process and not to let anyone make me feel like I had to rush through it. After dinner, she took me to see her new home. It was beautiful, and I was relieved to see that she was really happy. On the way back to the hotel, we promised to keep in touch, and I promised to try and get back out there to see her soon. Even as I said the words, I hoped and prayed that I would be financially able to keep that promise.

Between walking all morning in the extremely hot Vegas sun at the outdoor mall, rushing back to shower and change, and dinner with Lorraine, I was physically spent but not sleepy. When I returned to my room, I crawled up in the middle of the bed, remote in hand with the intention of watching TV, in the hopes it would lull me to sleep.

Ten minutes into the movie, I found my mind strayed to the last week of Garry's life. Talking about it at dinner brought it to the forefront of my mind. Every day since his death I had vigorously avoided going there. I avoided revisiting those frustratingly emotional days and the guilt associated with them. The intense feelings of despair and guilt that I had not done enough, said enough, insisted enough that he return to the hospital. I believed with all my heart, had I been successful in getting him to do so, he would be alive today.

I closed my eyes tightly and tried to block out the images swirling around in my head. I tried unsuccessfully to block out the pain in my heart, to dispel all the what-ifs. I recalled what Lorraine said about grieving, and I realized if I ever had any hope at all of moving past— surviving my pain and grief—I had to first face it. I felt that I had let Garry down, and by extension let my children down. I'd lost a husband. I knew that I would never be able to replace him in my heart, but as cold as it might sound, the reality was, if God was willing, at some point in the future he might bless me with another mate.

I had absolutely no doubt, however, that there would never be a replacement for my son's father. No man would ever replace the larger-than-life man they loved and worshipped. How could I ever forgive myself for taking him away from them?

As I sat there contemplating that, the words of my doctor came back to me. When I was diagnosed with breast cancer, she'd spoken words to me that I'd never forgotten. She looked at me with a very serious expression and said, "I have at my disposal the latest and best medicine, and the most advanced medical technology. If you research me, you'll find that I rank at the very top of my field in this state—in this country. Let me be clear, though: If *you* do not have the will to live, the desire to fight this disease with everything in you, none of that is worth the price of a cup of coffee."

Was that it? Was that the problem? Had Garry simply lost the will to live? Did he lack the desire to fight? If so, why? How? If not for himself, how could he not want to live for me . . . for us, for his children and grandchildren? I sat there staring at the TV screen, blinded by my tears, seeing nothing, hearing nothing, and wishing with all my heart I could feel nothing. Unfortunately, all I could do was feel. The pain in my chest filled up the room and made it hard to breathe. As much as I hated the thought of returning to my empty house and my empty bed . . . I was ready to go home.

Chapter Twenty

I T WAS TIME FOR me to go home and deal with reality. It was time to try and pick up the broken pieces of my life and see what I could salvage. I don't know how long I sat there crying or when I finally succumbed to sleep, but I woke the next morning, remote still in hand, to the voice of the local weatherman forecasting another blistering day. I closed my eyes, hoping to escape back into oblivion, but the sound of my phone signaling my morning wakeup call dashed those hopes.

"Morning, son. What are you guys up to this morning?"

"We're going to hang out in the hotel today, have some breakfast and check out the souvenir shop . . . just chill until it's time to go to that show tonight."

"Sounds like a plan. I want to get some souvenirs too. Are you all up and dressed already?"

"Nope, we're feeling lazy this morning. How was your friend?"

"She's doing great; we had a really nice dinner. It was good catching up. After dinner she took me to see her house. She seems really happy."

"We should be up and ready to go down in about an hour. Does that work for you?"

"Yep, I can do that." I was about to hang up, when I heard him say, "Ma." There was silence for a moment as if he was trying to collect his thoughts. "Yes, son, what is it?"

"I know you don't believe it now, but you'll be happy again."

Moved by his intuitiveness, and holding back a fresh batch of tears, I said, "From your lips to God's ear, baby."

"See you in about an hour," he said and hung up.

He was right. I didn't believe it then, but I prayed he'd spoken a prophetic word that would one day come true.

After we finished breakfast, we went to the souvenir shop in the hotel and I looked for T-shirts for the boys. I thought about my grandsons with a mixture of love and profound sadness. I remembered the day their fathers, my sons, lost their grandfather and how it forever changed our entire family. Now they'd lost their grandfather, and my sons their father. The two most significant and revered men in their lives were gone, a wealth of love, wisdom, and guidance gone too soon. With sadness and more than a little fear, I wondered if I had what it took to fill that void in their lives.

I thought about all the fishing trips they wouldn't get to go on, the long walks and talks they wouldn't have, and the stories that seemed to get embellished with each passing year they wouldn't get to hear and pass down to their children. I felt that familiar pain in my chest begin to surface and wished there was a magic pill I could take to make it go away. Shaking off the endless tears that threatened to spill from my eyes, I made my selections and went to look for something for the girls and my mom. I found cute little necklaces for them and a pretty toiletry bag set for my mom.

By the time we finished our shopping, it was lunchtime. We ventured outside and grabbed some burgers at a nearby fast-food restaurant, and then returned to the hotel.

We still had plenty of time before the show, so I spent the time repacking my suitcase, leaving out an outfit for that night and one to wear home the following day.

We probably wouldn't get in until late, and checkout was at 11:00 a.m. Our flight wasn't until four, so the plan was to have breakfast, do any last-minute shopping, and hang out in the casino until it was time to take the shuttle back to the airport.

Dressing for the show later that night, I realized I was really looking forward to the show and our last night in Vegas. It wasn't a mainline show—it wasn't Toni Braxton, Celine Dion, or Cirque du Soleil—but it was affordable and entertaining. I'd always had a soft spot for musicals. The singing was very good, and the sets and costumes were pretty good as well. For an hour and a half I sang along, laughed, cheered, and clapped, pretending to be normal. For a brief time I was able to forget about my pain, my nonexistent future, and the endless lonely days and nights that loomed ahead. I was determined to enjoy the night, the show, dinner afterward, and my children. I would eat too much of whatever I wanted to eat, drink a little too much, laugh too loud, and concentrate only on enjoying that night. There would be plenty of time on the plane tomorrow to focus on the rest of my life.

Chapter Twenty-One

I LOVE TO TRAVEL. I did next to none as a child, and I've always been grateful for the blessing to be able to do so as an adult. Even more grateful that we were able to travel with the children and provide them with experiences I never had at their age. The only thing I don't like about traveling is the last day. The day you're forced to acknowledge that all the fun is over. The day you have to go home and return to reality. The day you have to resume your everyday activities. The day you have to return to work, schedules, responsibilities . . . life. All the things you look forward to leaving behind when you go on vacation. I can deal with facing reality, I can deal with having to go home; it's the process of getting there I have a problem with. Once I accept that my vacation is over and going home is inevitable, I just want to be there.

I wanted to skip the whole repacking, getting to the airport, waiting for the plane, getting back home, unpacking, and diving into the chaos. We had to check out of our rooms at 11:00 a.m. that last day, but since our flight wasn't until later that evening, it would be another eleven hours before we finally arrived back home. We checked our luggage at the front desk and then went to breakfast.

The rest of the time was spent hanging out at the casinos until it was time to catch the shuttle back to the airport.

Once at the airport after passing through security, we sat around waiting for the plane. After landing back in Chicago, we had to wait for the driver we hired to take us back to the hotel, where we parked our car, and then make the long drive back home.

It had been a long and exhausting day, which actually turned into a blessing. Usually I started unpacking and simultaneously going through the mail the minute I walked in the door, but not this time. By the time we walked through the door at the house, I barely had enough energy to make it up the stairs to my bedroom. I didn't bother to take my suitcase upstairs, nor did I even look at the mail that had accumulated while we were away. For the first time since Garry died, I peeled off my clothes and climbed into the bed I had avoided for the past several weeks. I was too tired to register the painful emptiness I usually felt just looking at it.

Before I slipped into the much-needed release of sleep, I thought to myself, *The suitcase will still be there in the morning . . . the mail will still be there in the morning . . . any and everything I need to deal with will still be there waiting . . . in the morning.*

I slept like the dead and woke the next morning feeling a little rested, yet surprised to find myself in my bed. Since the day after Garry's funeral, if I slept at all, it was in the recliner chair in our room. We never slept apart intentionally, and after sleeping in our bed with him for the better part of thirty years, I found it hard to sleep without him now. After weeks of tossing, turning, and crying, I finally gave up and stopped trying. Most nights I stayed up watching TV until I passed out in the chair. My inability to sleep was not about being scared to be in my home alone, it was about not being able to face the loneliness and emptiness of that king-size bed—our bed.

Lying there in the early-morning silence, I thought about all the decisions I needed to make regarding my house, my family, and my future. The more I thought, the more I wished I could retreat back into the mind-numbing sleep I'd just emerged from. I didn't have a clue where to begin. We'd made so many plans together, and I didn't want to think about trying to pursue any of them alone. Even more depressing was the thought of making new plans without him. I turned on my side and shut my eyes as tightly as I could in an attempt to stem the flow of those damn never-ending tears. I didn't want to move forward, and yet I was forced to acknowledge that I couldn't go back—nor could I stand still.

It was so quiet in the house, for a minute I thought I was alone. *Had the kids gotten up and out already?* I thought. When I stepped out into the hall on my way downstairs to retrieve my suitcase, I could hear the soft rumble of Kevin snoring. I looked at the clock on the microwave in the kitchen and realized it was still very early.

I drug my suitcase upstairs, trying to make as little noise as possible.

While unpacking, I tried to sort out my thoughts and make a mental checklist. My first priority was to determine exactly how much money I had and how long it would last. We had never planned to retire in Chicago. The older we got, the harder it was to endure the cold winters. I desperately wanted to go to a warmer climate, and since I had to take my mother with me, I believed the warmer climate would be better for her arthritis as well.

Picking up and moving to another state and all that entailed would have been a major undertaking for the both of us, and now I wondered if I was up to tackling it alone. As much as I hated leaving all my friends, I knew I couldn't stay in the house alone. There were simply too many memories, too many reminders of the life I'd had and the one that was now no longer possible.

Even if I could have paid the house off, the taxes and the overall upkeep would eat up my savings and retirement funds in no time. I simply didn't have a choice; one way or another I had to go. I couldn't stay there, and yet I didn't want to give up my house. It would be great if I could manage to keep it in the family, to always have somewhere to come back to even just to visit. As long as I had family and friends in Chicago, I knew occasional visits would always be inevitable. It would be so nice not to have to stay at a hotel every time I came back. I wanted very much to rent the house out to the kids, or even let them buy it, but doing so would depend upon my ability to lower the mortgage payment to an amount they could afford. I was still hoping to work something out with the bank.

Refusing to give up on the hope of keeping the house in the family, I spent the next two and a half months going back and forth with the bank and several mortgage companies. I got dozens of phone calls, emails, and letters a week all promising to lower my interest rate and lower my mortgage payment. No matter how many I talked to, the outcome was always the same.

I wasn't far enough behind in my mortgage payment to qualify for the mortgage-reduction program, and apparently losing my job and my husband wasn't considered enough of a hardship either. I couldn't refinance the loan because I wasn't working, and I didn't have enough debt to qualify for bankruptcy. It was the most annoying and frustrating situation I'd ever experienced. It was no wonder I couldn't sleep at night and I cried all the time.

I felt like I was trapped in a tunnel and there was no way out. If I couldn't hold on to the house, I'd probably end up reverting back to our original plan, which was to sell it. Then I would have to start over somewhere else. The challenge was to stay in the house for as long as possible, while managing to save as much of the insurance money as possible, so I could start over somewhere else.

In the midst of stressing about my future, I was also trying to get acclimated to my present new reality. By the beginning of June, I had a whole new appreciation for my husband and all the things he had taken care of around the house that I had been totally unaware of. Around mid-April I started getting calls reminding me that it was time to get the air conditioner serviced for the coming summer. The dryer went out, and I couldn't remember if we still had an active service contract on it, or who it was with. On top of all that, I discovered the upstairs toilet was leaking and the tile around it was disintegrating.

If Garry were alive, he would have handled all of these things with ease. I was embarrassed to admit I didn't even know where to begin. I kept the house clean; I cooked and took care of my children. I bought groceries and made sure all the utilities stayed on, all while holding down a full-time job. Garry had always taken care of everything else. Now, with shock and more than a little bit of trepidation, I realized it was all on me from here on out.

Juanda was right about my being in a sink-or-swim situation. I felt like I had been unceremoniously dumped into the deep end of the pool, and I couldn't swim. I was trying real hard not to slip into full panic mode as I strove to keep my head above water. I sat on the couch in my family room staring up at Garry's urn, wishing with all my heart I could call him and ask him what to do, who to call, and how to fix all these things that kept cropping up. As I sat there not knowing whether to laugh or cry, I was reminded of something Kenny said in his speech ten years earlier when we renewed our vows for our thirtieth anniversary.

"I'm so proud of my parents for hanging in there together for thirty years. These days couples are lucky if they make it three years. Now that I'm an adult, I know firsthand marriage is not for the faint of heart. It takes hard work, but growing up with my parents, I never saw all that hard work—I just saw two people who were committed to each other. I saw two people who weathered every storm, who got through the good times and the bad times, and made it look easy."

It's what I was thinking about Garry: he made it look so easy. He must have had a system, but I didn't know what it was. Staring at the urn again, I said out loud, "I could use a little help here!"

After sitting there a few more minutes not getting an answer, I got up and walked downstairs to the laundry room. I stood there looking at my nonfunctioning dryer, thinking about how much I hated the thought of having to go to the laundromat.

I stood there cringing in disgust, recalling those days of dragging my kids, dirty clothes, laundry detergent, fabric softener, and rolls of quarters and dimes to the laundromat. It was usually an all-day or evening ordeal, spent vying for machines to wash and feeding an endless stream of dimes to those dryers that never seemed to get the clothes dry. The whole time, all I could think of was all the other things I could be doing in the privacy of my own home.

I vividly remembered the day we were finally able to purchase our own washer and dryer. I was so happy I cried and felt like we had won the lottery. Irrational as it might sound, the mere thought of having to return to the laundromat felt like a giant step backward, like I had somehow failed in life. I stood there staring back and forth between the basket of clothes that seemed to taunt me and the useless dryer that mocked me. Deciding to postpone the laundry for another day, I started to walk out of the laundry room when suddenly something caught my eye. Backpedaling, I stood in front of the dryer to get a closer look.

I laughed at myself imagining I could hear Garry's voice clear as a bell saying, "Kitten, if it was a snake, it would have bit you!" Right there on the front panel of the dryer next to the on/off button was a sticker—a sticker with the name and phone number of the company that last serviced the dryer. Laughing until I began to cry,

I wondered if this was Garry's way of providing the help I'd asked for just a few minutes ago.

For the first time, I looked around the laundry room and noticed writing on the wall in front of me next to the furnace. And there it was, the system I knew he must have had, staring me right in the face . . . hidden in plain sight. The name of the company we purchased the furnace and air conditioner from, along with the phone number and dates of service for both going all the way back to the date we purchased them. There was also a calendar of sorts that told me how often to change the furnace filters and the sizes to buy when our supply ran out. I walked closer to the wall and slowly ran my fingers over all his notes. Smiling through my tears, I said a silent thank-you. *If only everything could be that easy,* I thought as I walked upstairs to call the repair man for the dryer.

CHAPTER TWENTY-TWO

AFTER SCHEDULING AN APPOINTMENT to have the dryer repaired and the air conditioner serviced, I asked my neighbor to come over and look at the toilet. The leak was coming from the hose attached to the toilet connected to the water supply. He told me what size hose I needed to replace it and offered to put it on after I purchased it. While at Home Depot, I also bought new filters and priced some tile to replace the portion damaged by the leak.

Driving home I felt lighter and more confident about my ability to handle things in Garry's absence. Whether intentional or not, he'd left me instructions, and all I had to do was follow them. Like Juanda said, whatever I didn't know, I'd figure it out. Two days later the dryer was fixed, and by the end of the week the air conditioner had been serviced and was all ready for the first signs of summer, which couldn't come fast enough for me.

The toilet was fixed too, but replacing the tile was going to be more involved than I anticipated. It wasn't going to be as simple as replacing just the area around the toilet. Apparently it had been leaking for quite a while, and the subfloor beneath the tile had begun to rot. More than likely I would have to replace the entire floor. That was a project that would have to wait until I had a better idea of what I was going to do about the house.

I felt like I was living two separate lives. In one I strove to adjust to my new identity, my new reality. Literally overnight I had become a single woman responsible to and for myself. I tried to convince myself on a daily basis that I was completely capable of handling that. I concentrated on building my business, I paid my bills—all of them—I bought groceries, I paid for my car and health insurance, I kept up the maintenance on my car; I did all the things every other single woman did. And all the while in what seemed like an alternate universe, I ached physically and mentally for the husband I'd lost. The other half of me was gone, and he was never coming back.

People still referred to me as Mrs. Carter, and that prefix grated on my nerves like chalk on a blackboard. It didn't just irritate, it hurt to my very core like I'd been stabbed in the heart. It was a misnomer, it was inaccurate. I wasn't a "Mrs." anymore. The title felt like a well-loved, well-worn sweater that no longer fit. I needed to purge it, yet I couldn't bear to give it up!

The days bled into weeks as I worked hard to arrive at a place of acceptance. I kept busy perfecting old and creating new cake and cupcake recipes in an effort to expand my product line. I went to lunch or dinner with my girlfriends from church and tried not to whine about how lonely I was. I went to church and pretended it didn't bother me to be there alone, and I prayed day and night for God to release me from the pain that had become my constant companion.

Despite all my efforts to keep my mind and my hands occupied, to fill my days, at the end of the day I had to face the loneliness. It was like an unwelcome visitor appearing as soon as the sun went down. Ever since my return from Vegas, I had managed to at least get in my bed, but I rarely slept. It was the same routine every day.

When I shut the kitchen down for the night, I went up to my bedroom and sat in the recliner chair.

I tried to watch TV until the news came on. I moved from the chair to the bed, but I didn't turn off the TV, hoping the sound would eventually lull me to sleep. I set the timer on the off chance I would fall asleep. Sometimes I would doze off, but as soon as the TV shut off, I'd wake up. I tossed and turned for the rest of the night, finally passing out just before the sun came up. As tired as I was physically and emotionally, I still managed to get up every morning and start all over again. I felt like I was operating on autopilot.

In addition to the pain and the loneliness that consumed me, my frustration with the bank was ever increasing. The stress was beginning to affect me physically. On my last doctor's visit, my blood pressure, which had been under control, was through the roof, and my doctor was concerned about how much weight I'd lost. I wasn't as concerned about the weight loss as I was about the fact that my hair was falling out. I'd kept my hair short ever since it started to grow back after the chemo, making the bald spot on the top of my head even more noticeable.

I had decided to take advantage of the bank's unemployment forbearance program when I returned from Houston, hoping it would buy me some time and stretch my money until I figured out what to do about the house. Since then I had completed and submitted a mountain of paperwork, twice, and still hadn't heard anything about my application. I'd heard countless horror stories about people going through their savings and retirement accounts trying to hold on to homes they ultimately lost anyway. I didn't just want to relocate; I needed to start over … somewhere else. I prayed constantly that somehow I would be able to get out of this with my health, my sanity, and enough money to make a new start.

By mid-June, the stress had become unbearable. My sister's words echoing in my head, I was getting that feeling that once again a change of scenery was in order. Remembering my promise to McKenzie, I decided it was time to plan my trip to Atlanta to spend some time with my grandbabies. Thanks to modern technology, whatever answer the bank was going to give me they could give to me in Atlanta just as easily as here. They could send me an email or call me on my cell phone. There was no reason why I couldn't get away for a while.

Surrounded by my son and my grandbabies, maybe I could finally escape the ever-present pain and loneliness that haunted me. The great thing about being my own boss was that I could decide when I wanted to work and when I didn't. I checked my calendar to see what orders I had coming up, and after I shut down for the day, I sat down at the computer and started checking airfare.

Full of anticipation about getting away for a while, I actually fell into a peaceful sleep that night, slept more than my usual two to three hours, and woke up feeling more rested than I had in months. I couldn't wait to call McKenzie and tell her Grandma was coming!

CHAPTER TWENTY-THREE

"HEY, MOMMY, HOW YOU doing?"

"I'm okay, baby, or at least I will be. How are you and the family doing?"

"We're okay. Like you, we're just taking it one day at a time."

"Where is my oldest grandchild? Is she home?"

"Yeah, she's here, what's up?"

"I made her a promise before you all left after the funeral. I'm calling to let her know I'm about to make good on that promise. I just booked my flight; I'm coming out there for a week the second week in July. I want to tell her myself."

"Okay, I'll get her."

"Hey Grandma."

"Hi, baby girl, how you doing? You been a good girl?"

"Yes ma'am. How are you doing?"

"I'm okay, sweetie, and I'm going to be better real soon. You know why?"

"Why?"

"Because I'm coming out there to see my beautiful grandbabies! I just booked a flight, and I'm coming for a whole week the second week in July."

"Yeah! That's next month!"

"Yes it is, and I can't wait to see you guys!"

"Are you coming to stay?"

I smiled to myself, realizing she hadn't given up on the idea, and sad that I would have to disappoint her. "This time I'm coming for just a week, baby, but I promise from now on I'll be able to visit you all more often." I could hear it in her voice; her initial excitement over my pending visit was tempered with disappointment at the knowledge that my visit wouldn't be permanent.

She was too young to understand how complicated my situation was. I was sure she couldn't comprehend why I couldn't just walk away from the house I'd lived in for the last thirty years. Eventually I would be leaving my home, but I was still a long way from making that move. When I was ready, wherever I ended up I was determined to keep my promise and be more present in their lives.

The time between booking my flight and actually getting on the plane passed by more quickly than I anticipated. Thanks to a barrage of orders, that provided both a financial blessing and a much-needed distraction. As much as I enjoyed baking and as much of a therapeutic blessing it had been since Garry died, all the stress I'd been under and subsequent lack of sleep left me feeling worn out and drained. So much so that at times I had a real hard time focusing on anything other than my baking. I was really looking forward to doing nothing but spending time with my grandbabies.

"I'm glad you're getting away for a while, Mom," Kevin said as he drove me to the airport. "Hopefully you can finally relax and get some much-needed rest."

"I don't know how much rest I'm going to get," I said, smiling. "I'm really looking forward to spending time with Kenny and the kids, though. They are growing up so fast! I can't wait to see how much bigger Mason has gotten since they were here for the funeral. Hopefully he's going to get his height from his grandfather."

"Yeah, I have a feeling those girls are going to be tall too," Kevin said. "Have a good time and try to destress," he said, hugging me after taking my luggage from the car.

"I'll try," I said, smiling and kissing him before heading to the curbside check-in.

♦

I KNEW KENNY WAS picking me up from the airport, but I didn't know the kids were coming with him. As I approached the Southwest baggage-claim area, I was greeted by a chorus of "Grandma, Grandma" from the girls, followed by hugs and kisses. I hadn't seen them in almost four months, but one look at the huge grin on Mason's face told me he remembered me—a fact that brought immense joy to my heart. The girls talked a mile a minute on the drive back home. They brought me up to date on their school year. They were both on the honor roll and had won awards for both their grades and their attendance. I was very proud of them and hoped they would continue to maintain their level of enthusiasm for school as they got older.

A change of scenery was what I was sure I needed to escape the loneliness, to escape the pain as well as my concerns and fears about my future. I thought I could get on that plane and leave all my problems behind me. I was sorely disappointed to discover they had somehow gotten into my suitcase and come along for the ride. The only thing that had changed was my location.

I thoroughly enjoyed my grandchildren. After weeks of being alone in my house with nothing but my thoughts, going through days and days of hearing nothing but the sound of my own voice had taken its toll. Playing games with them, watching TV with them, talking with them, and listening to their banter back and forth was like a salve on an open wound. But when it was time to go to bed and I retreated to the guest room alone, I was overcome with memories of past visits there with Garry.

Unable to sleep, I lay there in the dark and recalled how proud and frightened we'd been when Kenny announced his intent to enlist in the air force. I recalled how grateful we were that the Lord had spared him to return home to us healthy and whole in mind, body, and spirit. I recalled how proud we were when he purchased his first home, pleased that it was far better than our starter home.

Smiling, I recalled Garry sitting on the couch with his granddaughters sitting at his feet, several naked Barbie dolls scattered on the floor beside them. Laughing out loud in the dark, I recalled hearing Garry ask them why none of their dolls had any clothes. He made some joke about not being able to hang out with all those naked women. "You're going to get me in trouble with Grandma." His little joke went completely over their heads, but I got a kick out of it. It literally broke my heart knowing that my grandbabies would never have the opportunity to make more memories with their grandfather. I thought about how proud he would have been of them and all their accomplishments. I thought about the award ceremonies he would miss out on, and all the graduations and weddings he would never attend.

Tears running down my face, I prayed that their limited memories of him would never fade and vowed to always remind them of how much he loved them. He wouldn't be there, so I would have to take care of myself. I would have to do everything in my power to make sure I would be there. I lay there for hours thinking about the future without him, something even after five months I still couldn't imagine.

I woke startled the next morning to the sounds of three little voices all speaking at once. The sound was coming from downstairs, and I could hear April telling them to keep it down.

"You guys are going to wake Grandma," she said. I laughed to myself as they tried to talk lower, an effort that only lasted a few seconds before their voices escalated again. Looking out the window, I saw that the sun was just coming up, and my body was telling me I hadn't had nearly enough sleep.

I had intended to get up and see what everyone was up to, but my body had other ideas. I closed my eyes just for a minute and opened them again an hour later.

When I finally drug my weary body from the bed and headed downstairs, I found them all in the kitchen having breakfast.

"What do you want for breakfast, little lady?" Kenny asked.

"I'll have whatever you're having; you don't have to fix anything special for me," I answered.

"We're having pancakes," McKenzie chimed in.

"And bacon!" Londyn added.

I laughed out loud seeing the look on her face when she said bacon, suddenly remembering her love of bacon. "Well, pancakes and bacon it is!" I said, mimicking the look on her face. I was a bacon lover too and recalled that I hadn't had pancakes or bacon since our vacation the year before.

After breakfast, we talked about what we wanted to do for the next few days. I knew the week would go by too fast, and I wanted to do as much as possible with them while I was there.

"So, what do you guys want to do this week?" I asked.

McKenzie wanted to go to the show, Londyn wanted to go bowling, and Mason just looked from one to the other like he was trying to figure out what the heck we were all talking about. I wanted to do some shopping while I was there, so we decided one day would be devoted to the outlet mall. I was planning to follow through with the plan Garry and I had to take the kids to Disney World next year, so we spent some time going through our time-share catalog deciding which resort we wanted to stay at so I could book the trip when I returned home.

Kenny and the kids weren't the only family I had in Atlanta. I had four cousins on my father's side as well as a cousin on Garry's side and two goddaughters. I wanted to see all of them too while I was in town, so we decided to have a cookout over the weekend. The cookout would allow me to see everyone at the same time. It was important to me that my children and grandchildren get to know their family. Unfortunately, our circle was getting smaller and smaller every day. I didn't know what was next, what the future held for any of us, but I knew the love and support of family would be crucial in getting through whatever life had in store.

CHAPTER TWENTY-FOUR

OVER THE NEXT SEVERAL days, we took the kids to the movies and out to dinner to their favorite restaurant, Golden Corral. I watched them eat to their hearts' content, and once again I was reminded of our last vacation with their grandfather. I remembered the look on their faces when he told them they could have anything they wanted to eat. I remembered . . . and I wondered if they remembered too.

We went bowling, and I was amused by all the trash-talking my granddaughters did and in awe of their ability to back it up. I was so proud of them; they were so good at everything. I was also more than a little embarrassed that they were beating the pants off of me. In the midst of all the activities, we talked about and planned the cookout. We decided to make it a real family affair, inviting my cousins, my two goddaughters, and April's sister and her family.

We also discussed the menu. "I don't care what you all make," April said, "as long as one of you makes some peach cobbler." Kenny looked at me, and then April looked at me and smiled.

Knowing what those looks meant, I laughed. "Well, I guess that's settled. What else do you want me to make besides the peach cobbler?"

We eventually decided I would make a cheesecake, and once the desserts were out of the way, we decided we would provide ribs, chicken, and sausage, and everybody else could provide the side dishes. We called to extend the invitation, and I made note of what everyone was bringing.

I tried really hard to be in the moment and focus on how much fun I was having with the kids. No matter how hard I tried, though, I couldn't stop thinking about my pending application with the bank. I hadn't said much to Kenny and April about what I was going through, and I wondered if they had noticed how distracted I was and that I kept checking my phone. I was hoping to see an email from the bank or receive a call, but every time I checked I was disappointed.

Usually I enjoyed shopping; even if I didn't spend any money, I usually enjoyed just browsing. Other than spending a little money on my grandbabies, I didn't get much enjoyment out of our trip to the mall this time around. I was too distracted and concerned about my financial status to get excited about all the sales. I felt like I was suspended between who I was and who I wanted to be. The only thing that finally calmed me down and managed to take my mind off my troubles was preparing for the cookout. I hadn't seen my cousins for a long time. I was looking forward to seeing them and my goddaughters. I immersed myself in the preparations, and when I finally got the call I'd been waiting for, it caught me completely off guard.

I was down in the kitchen preparing the batter for my cheesecake when I realized I left my phone upstairs. On the way up the stairs to retrieve it, I heard it ringing, and running to catch it, managed to catch it just in time.

"Hello," I said, out of breath from sprinting up the stairs. "Yes, this is Mrs. Carter."

I listened intently, holding my breath as the bank representative introduced herself and informed me she would be handling my case.

She told me I would be receiving a packet of documents outlining everything she was about to tell me, and then she proceeded to tell me about the program. The good news she finally got around to was that I'd been accepted into the program. My mortgage payment was being reduced to an amount I could manage according to my current income for a period of nine months. If I hadn't found employment in that time period, my case would be reevaluated to see if it could be extended or there were other options available at that time.

"When you receive the paperwork, please read it thoroughly and make sure you understand and agree with all the terms. Then sign them, keep a copy for yourself, and return the originals to me. If you have any questions or concerns, please free to call me. My name, phone number, and extension will be on the cover letter."

"Okay, about how long will it be before I receive them, and how long will I have to return them?" I asked. "I'm out of town right now."

"They will be mailed out today. I'd say you should receive them in about three to four days. You'll have seven business days from the date you receive them to get them back to us."

"I'll be back in Chicago in three days, so that should give me plenty of time," I said.

"Do you have any questions now?" she asked.

"No, I think I'll wait till I get the forms and read over them. I'm sure I will have some by then. Thank you for calling with the good news. I think I can really enjoy the rest of my visit now."

"You're welcome, Mrs. Carter."

We both hung up, and I exhaled a temporary sigh of relief. It wasn't the solution I wanted, but it would have to do for now. Paying the lower mortgage payment would buy me some time and enable me to stretch the insurance money a bit farther. Feeling lighter than I had in days, I returned to the kitchen to finish my baking.

"Where did you disappear to, little lady?" Kenny asked when I walked back into the kitchen.

"I went upstairs to get my phone, and I got a call while I was up there."

"Well, judging from the look on your face, it must have been good news."

"It was, sort of. I applied for the unemployment forbearance program at the bank, and I finally got an answer from them stating that I'd been approved. For the next nine months they are reducing my mortgage payment to an amount I can afford to pay based on my current income. If I haven't found a job by then, they'll reevaluate my case and either give me an extension or determine what other options are available at that time."

"Are you looking for a job?"

"No, I'm not, not really. I only applied to give me some time to figure out what I want to do and what other options are available to me. I really want to relocate to Houston like we planned. I want to continue to grow my business, and hopefully have enough money to start over."

He walked over to me and put his arms around me. "It's okay, Mommy, it's all going to work out. I know this is hard, I know it's stressful . . . but I really believe everything is going to be all right. We're here for you, Mommy—me, Kev, and April—and we'll help in any way we can."

"I know you will, baby. I can't tell you how much you and your brother's support means to me. I love you both so much." My eyes getting misty, I joked, "Now, if you don't let me go, I'm never going to get this cheesecake in the oven, or the peach cobbler for that matter. We'll be in big trouble with you-know-who if that happens."

We both laughed, and then he got busy seasoning his ribs and chicken, and I finished my baking.

CHAPTER TWENTY-FIVE

WE WERE UP EARLY the next morning putting the finishing touches on our contributions to the cookout. In addition to my desserts and Kenny's BBQ, April was making mac 'n cheese. Kenny was in and out of the house tending to the grill on the patio while I finished putting the whipped cream and strawberries on the cheesecake and put it back in the refrigerator to chill. I turned on the oven and began putting my cobbler together. A few minutes later, the whole house smelled like peach cobbler.

Getting dressed a couple of hours later, it suddenly occurred to me it had been several hours since I'd obsessed about the fate of my house or my future. Getting that phone call from the bank had been a huge stress reliever. Even though it wasn't the permanent solution I was looking for, at least I knew what I had to look forward to over the next nine months. I had time to work out a more permanent solution. I didn't have to worry about being put out on the street, at least not yet.

The doorbell rang, announcing the arrival of our first guests. As I descended the stairs with a smile on my face, I thought fleetingly, *Is this what peace feels like?* April's sister Neko and her family were the first to arrive. I hadn't seen them in a long time, and the first thing I noticed was how grown up her girls were. They were both as tall as me and looked very mature for their age. It wasn't about what they were wearing, but more about how they carried themselves. They were growing into beautiful young women, both inside and out. *Where did the time go?* I thought. *It must be something in the water,* I mused. *All these kids are growing up so fast!*

We exchanged hugs and kisses and put their side dishes in the kitchen with the rest of the food.

"Wow, is that peach cobbler I smell?" Peyton asked, walking into the kitchen.

"Yes, it is!" I answered, laughing.

She looked like she wanted to skip the rest of the meal and go straight to the desserts. My suspicions were confirmed when I informed her we also had cheesecake topped with whipped cream and strawberries, and her eyes lit up like a Christmas tree.

We were still standing in the kitchen catching up when the doorbell rang again. It was my cousin Pam and her husband, Eric, along with Michelle and her fiancé, Jay.

Ever since my cousins relocated from Chicago to Atlanta, our interactions had been few and far between. Off the top of my head I couldn't even recall the last time I'd seen them. Given all that I'd been through in the last five months, the sight of them now produced some very powerful emotions. We'd been very close as children, and in that instant I realized how much I'd missed them.

Before we even got started on our greetings the doorbell rang again, and this time it was Anita and Gerri. Everyone had arrived, and I was so excited to see them all I didn't know who to give my attention to first. Gerri and Anita had traveled back to Chicago for the funeral, and that meant more to me than they knew. We started out being coworkers, and over a period of fifteen years or more we'd spent forty hours or more a week together. We were friends and we became family. Seeing them again made me acutely aware of how much I missed them too.

Once all the greetings and introductions were out of the way, we got down to the business of enjoying the meal we'd all had a hand in preparing. While we ate Kenny's ribs, chicken, sausage, and all the sides everyone else contributed, we got caught up on what had been happening in everyone's lives.

"Are you enjoying your time with your grandbabies?" Gerri asked.

"I am. Every time I see them, I'm more aware of how much of their lives I've missed. They are growing up so fast. It had been our plan to spend more time with them when we retired; I guess it's up to me now. I didn't think I'd have to do it alone, but I've made a commitment to myself that no matter where I end up, I'm going to make a concerted effort to be more present in their lives."

"I know you planned to move to Houston, but have you ever considered moving here to Atlanta?"

I was still so committed to my plan to move to Houston, I had to admit I had not, up until then, ever considered moving here. Anita's question gave me something to think about; in fact, it planted a seed that would continue to grow moving forward.

"Well, I have to say, you sure don't look like what you've been through," Anita said.

"Yeah," Gerri chimed in, "You look great! You've lost a lot of weight."

"Thanks," I said. "Thank God I don't look like what I've been through, because I would look a hot mess! I have lost weight, but not intentionally. I mean, I haven't been dieting. I only sleep about two to three hours a night, and I don't have much of an appetite. I think I've eaten more in the last few days than I have in the last five months.

"My pressure was up the last time I went to the doctor. After running some blood tests to check my vitals and rule out any serious problems, she said my elevated pressure and the weight loss were symptoms of the stress I've been under. Aside from wanting to see Kenny and the kids, that was the other reason I wanted to make this trip. I needed an escape from my current reality."

"So what's next?" they asked.

"I bought myself a little time to get things organized and figure out what I need to do. I have some decisions to make, but in the meantime I'm just trying to get adjusted to being alone."

"How long are you going to be here?" Gerri asked.

"I'm here for three more days, and then I have to get back. I have paperwork to complete and return to the bank, and fortunately I have some customer orders coming up. This is a great time for my business—weddings, showers, birthday parties, anniversaries, and family reunions."

"That's great! So business is good?"

"It's growing. I'm hoping to continue to build it and transition at least some of it to Houston. I'm so glad Garry encouraged me to get started before we moved. It's the only thing that has kept me from totally losing my mind."

"Excuse me, Miss Arlita, but is it okay if I have some of your peach cobbler now?"

Peyton had waited for as long as she could, and apparently she wasn't the only one, I thought, laughing. At the mention of the cobbler all conversation ceased, and everyone headed to the kitchen. I took the cheesecake from the fridge too, but as I expected, the cobbler was the first to go.

"Kenny, if you want some of this peach cobbler, you better get in here because it's going fast!" Anita warned.

Kenny just laughed. "I'm not worried," he said. "I've got the baker here. I can always get another one."

Everyone laughed.

"He doesn't need me," I said. "He makes a cobbler just as good, if not better than mine."

"That's because I had you to teach me," he said, smiling and hugging me.

After everyone had dessert, we talked for a little while longer, and then things started to wind down. We said our goodbyes and promised to keep in touch. When all of the guest were gone, I finally sat down and reflected on the day and began to mentally prepare myself to leave the temporary peace I'd found.

"You okay, Mommy?" Kenny asked, sitting down beside me.

"Yeah, baby, I'm okay. Just thinking about going home. I need to get back . . . but I don't want to go back. I've enjoyed you and the kids so much."

"We've enjoyed you too, and I wish you didn't have to go back either. I really want the kids to get to know you better, to know you the way I know you. They need that, they need you in their lives, especially now."

I didn't recognize it right then, but the seed was growing.

Three days later I was heading to the airport to catch a plane back to Chicago. Before we left, I said my goodbyes to the children. I tried not to notice the tears pooling in McKenzie's eyes as she hugged me goodbye, fearing I would lose control of my own.

"It's okay, baby girl," I said. "I have to go back now for reasons I know you don't understand, but I promise you . . . we'll see each other again real soon."

Chapter Twenty-Six

WHEN I RETURNED TO Chicago, I kept my mind and my hands occupied. From sunup to sundown, I busied myself baking, decorating, and packaging orders. When I wasn't baking, I searched the internet and watched the Food Network for inspiration. I spent my days experimenting with new recipes, trying to create new desserts to offer my growing customer base. I challenged myself to act as though my life was normal, but late in the midnight hour, I couldn't run from the truth.

After I turned off the oven, put away my mixer and all my other baking tools, turned off the light, and retreated to my bedroom, I couldn't hide from myself. Alone in my room lying in a bed that no longer offered comfort or sleep, I had to face the truth: that nothing about the life I was living was normal, and probably never would be again.

No matter how busy I was, or how thankful I was for that blessing, the fear and the uncertainty about my future were always there lurking just below the surface of my consciousness. I went about my days filling up the hours with my baking, church, and the occasional lunch or dinner with family and friends, but I felt stuck. I couldn't go back, and until I knew where I was going, how I was going to get there, and what I was going to do when I got there . . . I couldn't go forward. There were simply too many unknowns. Intellectually, I think deep down I knew I was probably going to wind up having to sell my house as we had planned, but emotionally I wasn't ready to go there yet. So day after day, I continued to live this temporary life, in between here and there. I focused on trying to make as much money as possible and hold on to it for as long as I could. While I tried to convince my family and friends I was okay, I worked just as hard to convince myself.

I had several birthday parties and showers on my calendar, but the event I was most excited about was my niece's baby shower. Summer had relocated to Alabama the year before and was returning for the second time that year for her baby shower. Donna was excited about being a grandmother again, and especially happy for her firstborn, who would soon be giving birth to her firstborn.

The whole family was looking forward to this baby, and with a tinge of sadness I thought about how excited Garry would have been to welcome this new addition to our family. He had been there when Donna's youngest, Staci's, children were born. He had held and cared for Indya and Isaiah from day one, and he would have been both proud and thrilled to do the same for Summer's child.

Summer, like her mother, had been a big encourager and supporter of my business. When they decided to have the shower in Chicago, she called me and ordered cupcakes. I was looking forward to impressing her with my skill. More than that, I was looking forward to seeing her again, and seeing with my own eyes how she was handling her first pregnancy.

"Hello."

"Hey, little mommy."

"Hey Auntie, how are you doing?"

"I'm okay, trying to heed everyone's advice. Just taking it one day at a time. How are you doing? How's little Jason, is he behaving himself?"

"He's okay, he's very active."

"And let me guess, he's always most active when you're trying to sleep?"

"Right!"

"I know the feeling," I said, laughing. "Your cousins, especially Kevin, would be quiet all day, and time I lay down, they would decide to play kickball inside my stomach."

"Exactly!" Summer said, laughing.

"Did you get the pictures I sent you?"

"Yes, I did. The cupcakes look delicious, and I like all the colors. I still have to talk to Mama and Staci about the color scheme, though, and I'll get back to you about what color I want for the shower. Looking at the guest list, I'm sure I'm going to need about three or four dozen."

"Okay, no problem. You let me know as soon as you can. I've missed you, baby girl. I'm really looking forward to seeing you."

"I'm looking forward to seeing you too, Auntie. I still can't get used to the idea that Uncle Garry won't be there."

"I know the feeling, baby. I don't know if I'll ever get used to that!"

Summer's baby shower wasn't the only personal event coming up soon. My mother's eightieth birthday was coming up in September. Losing Garry had made me acutely sensitive to seizing the day and not putting things off. I gave her a surprise birthday party for her seventy-second birthday, eight years earlier. I knew then more than ever before that tomorrow wasn't promised to any of us. Eighty was a major milestone, and it warranted a major celebration.

While I was trying to decide just exactly how I was going to mark the occasion, Juanda called.

"Hey, sis, how are you doing?" she asked.

"I'm okay, girl, trying to stay busy."

"Yeah, how's that going?"

"Pretty good, actually. Thank God this has been a busy time for me, and I'm really hoping it lasts through the end of the year. I applied for the unemployment forbearance program through the bank. That will give me nine months to get my act together and decide what I'm going to do about this house, about my life. But enough about me, what's up with you?"

"I'm okay, working hard. I was calling because I need a favor, sis."

"Okay, what do you need?"

"Well, Mom's birthday is coming up in November. She'll be eighty, and I want to do something very special. I coming to Chicago on business in October, and I want you to go with me to find a venue for her party. I'm also thinking about providing gift bags with favors for the guests, and I was wondering if I could have everything shipped to you. I was also hoping you wouldn't mind assembling the bags?"

"Wow, I didn't realize our moms were the same age. I was just sitting here trying to decide what I'm going to do for my mom. Her eightieth birthday is in September. Unfortunately, with all that's going on right now, I'm not going to be able to do anything on that grand a scale. I do want all her grands and great-grands involved, though. I'm thinking of a big family dinner at my house. I want Kenny, April, and the kids to come, and I'll invite some of her close friends. In answer to your questions, though, yes, I'd be happy to help with your mom's celebration. Whatever you need me to do."

CHAPTER TWENTY-SEVEN

AFTER TALKING TO JUANDA, I looked at the calendar and realized Summer's shower was less than two weeks away. Mom's birthday was on the twenty-second of September, and if I was going to do anything, I needed to start planning. I decided the celebration would definitely be at my house, and the first thing I needed to do was touch base with Kenny.

Since Kenny lived the farthest away, I needed to call him and make sure he and April and the kids would be able to come. Mom's birthday fell on a Sunday, but I decided to have the dinner that Saturday. If Kenny could come, that would give him a day to rest before he had to make that long drive back to Atlanta.

"Hi, Mommy," he said, answering the phone when I called. "You okay?" he asked.

"Yeah, baby, I'm okay. How is April and my grandbabies?"

"April's good, and the kids are okay for the most part. McKenzie is still taking Dad's death hard, and she keeps reminding us that she doesn't like you being up there alone."

"I know, bless her heart. I don't really want her worrying about me, but at the same time, I have to admit, it does make me feel good to know she's concerned. You guys are so far away, and I often feel like I'm out of sight, out of mind. It's good to know she thinks about me when I'm not with her, as much as I think about her . . . about all of you."

"Yeah, she definitely thinks about you, especially now. Are you sure you're okay, Mommy?"

"Yes, I'm sure. I called to talk to you about your grandmother."

"Why, is there something wrong with Grandma?"

"Naw, she's fine, but her birthday is coming up next month. She's turning eighty. I want to do something for her birthday. I'm thinking a big family dinner with the whole family and a few of her close friends.

"I was calling to see if you all would be able to come up for the celebration. If so, I was wondering if you would help me out by doing the grilling. Her birthday is on the twenty-second, which is a Sunday, but I was thinking about having the dinner on that Saturday."

"Let me take a look at my schedule. If I don't already have that weekend off, I'll see if I can switch with somebody."

"And if you can come, you don't mind doing the grilling? I'll take care of everything else."

"Of course not, Mommy, you know I don't mind. Whatever you need me to do."

"Okay, baby," I said, breathing a sigh of relief. "I'll start working on a tentative menu. You let me know as soon as you can about the date, and I'll proceed from there."

After hanging up the phone, I jotted down some side dishes to go along with the meat. I decided not to proceed any further until I knew for sure Kenny would be able to come. I had the family covered, but I wasn't sure about Mom's friends, so I decided I'd better check in with the guest of honor.

"Hey, lady, what are you up to?" I asked when she answered the phone.

"Nothing much, I was just sitting here watching TV."

"Have you been feeling okay?" I asked.

"About the same. The pain never goes away; it's just better or worse from one day to the next. I have my good days and my bad days."

"And today?" I asked.

"So far today is an okay day. What's up, are you okay?"

I know they mean well, but I'll be so glad when people stop asking me that, I thought to myself. "Yes, Mom, I'm okay," I answered. "I was calling about you."

"What about me?" she asked.

"Well, I'm sure I don't have to tell you this, but you have a pretty big birthday coming up soon, lady."

"Yeah, I'm going to be eighty years old," she said, sounding very unenthusiastic.

"Right, that's a big deal, and I was thinking we need to celebrate this momentous occasion. I'd like to throw you a party, and in addition to all your family, I wanted to know who else you'd like me to invite. And don't bother telling me I don't have to do anything special," I said, anticipating her response.

"Okay, I won't tell you that, smarty-pants, but I will tell you not to go spending a whole lot of money. I appreciate the thought, but all I need is my family. I'll be grateful just to make it to my birthday. You're by yourself now, baby, and you don't need to be spending a lot of money on me."

I knew she meant well, but I really didn't need to be reminded that I was alone.

"Don't you worry about the money. You're turning eighty, and that's a real big deal, and no amount of money is too much to celebrate that, even for me. So, who do you want me to invite to your party?"

Thirty minutes later, I finally got off the phone, but not before she reminded me at least three more times I needed to save my money and not spend it on some elaborate celebration for her. I laughed to myself when I hung up the phone. *Yeah right,* I thought to myself. *If I didn't do something to mark the occasion, I would surely never hear the end of it!*

A couple days later while in the store shopping for the supplies I needed for Summer's cupcakes, my phone rang. I managed to fish it out of my purse just in time to catch Kenny's call.

"Hey, little lady, what are you doing?"

"Hey, sweetie, I'm in Walmart right now. What's up?"

"Nothing much. I was calling to tell you I checked my schedule for Grandma's birthday weekend. I don't have that weekend off, but I was able to switch with a coworker. We'll leave early Friday morning, so we should get there around six or seven that evening."

"That's great!" I said with a sigh of relief, pleased they would be able to make it. "I had to tell Mom about the dinner so she could tell me which of her friends she wanted me to invite, but she doesn't know you guys are coming. She will be so surprised! So, if you happen to talk to her, don't mention it. I'll make sure I have all the meat at the house. Do you want me to season it, or do you want to do it? If you send me the ingredients for your rub, I'll make sure I have everything you need on hand."

"Okay," he said. "I'll text them to you, and I'll season the meat when I get there and let it marinate overnight."

"Sounds good, baby. I'm so glad you all are coming. She will be so surprised and happy to see you."

"I'm glad too. It will be good to see her . . . to see all of you for a happy occasion."

Long after I got home from the store, Kenny's words echoed in my head. I remembered having those exact same thoughts when my house was full to the gills with family and friends five months ago. I remembered wishing we'd all been together for a happy occasion and not a funeral. Garry loved to entertain as much as I did, and he would have been charged to have everyone over to celebrate Mom's birthday. Aside from having the opportunity to see all his children and grandbabies at one time, he would have been thrilled to show off his grilling skills. He would be greatly missed at this family gathering, but I was determined to do everything in my power to make it a happy occasion despite his absence.

CHAPTER TWENTY-EIGHT

THE COLOR SCHEME FOR the shower had been decided upon, the cupcakes were made, and the shower was tomorrow. I was so excited to see Summer. Though we'd talked on the phone several times since Garry's funeral when she announced her pregnancy, I hadn't seen her since then. When we talked, I tried to gauge from her voice how she was feeling, how she was handling the pregnancy. I was glad I'd finally get to see with my own eyes how she was really doing.

When I finally saw her the next day, I breathed a sigh of relief. She was absolutely glowing. She looked healthy, she looked happy, and there was no doubt she was truly looking forward to the birth of her first child.

"Whoa, Auntie, look at you!" she said when she saw me. "You look great, you've lost a lot of weight."

"And it looks like you found it," I said, laughing and patting her stomach affectionately. "It looks good on you too."

We hugged each other for a long time and then looked each other up and down, both inwardly seeking answers to the same questions. *How is she really doing? How is she really feeling?*

"How are you really doing?" we both asked at the same time, and then we both laughed again.

"You first, Auntie," she said, suddenly looking at me with serious eyes. "All the way here, I've been trying to prepare myself to face the fact that I won't see my Uncle Garry. I'm still trying to wrap my head around the fact that he's gone, that he won't get to see and bond with this baby."

Her eyes clouded up as she rubbed her stomach. I could feel those familiar tears that never seemed to dry up as I thought the same thing myself.

"I can't imagine what you're going through, Auntie. You have to live with his absence every day. You look great, but how are you really doing?"

"You're right, baby girl. No matter how hard I try, I cannot escape his absence. My house is empty, my bed is empty . . . my heart is empty! There are days when I literally cannot stand to be there without him, and yet there are days when I cannot bear to leave it because he is there in every room. People keep telling me 'in time' the pain will pass and my joy will return. The problem is, no one can tell me how much time.

"It's been six months, and the pain hasn't faded, not even a little bit. I get through each day telling myself the next day will be better, the next twenty-four hours will be less painful, but I wake up every morning to more of the same. I don't want to upset you, especially now, but I can't pretend to be something I'm not, not to you of all people, sweetie. You have that special anointing. I knew it a long time ago; you see deeper than others, and I suspect I couldn't fool you even if I tried."

"True," she said, nodding her head. "I felt your pain in my spirit when we talked on the phone, but now my eyes have confirmed it. No one can tell you how much time, Auntie, because no one knows. Time doesn't belong to us; it's both a blessing and an instrument from God. Do you remember the conversation we had about Uncle Garry and the church?"

"Yes," I said, smiling and fondly remembering that conversation. "I was a little taken aback by the boldness and the advice of one so young. But everything you said came to pass. What pearls of wisdom do you have for me this time?" I said, laughing.

"Well, I suspect you've spent the better part of every day for the last six months praying and asking God to deliver you from your pain."

I nodded my head again.

"You've been praying for deliverance, instead of asking him to give you the strength to live through it and the discernment to discover the blessing that lies within."

Before I could react to her last statement, she raised her hand. "I know what you're thinking . . . how could I dare to suggest that losing Uncle Garry was a blessing? No matter how hard it is to lose a loved one, there comes a time when we have to acknowledge they never leave us empty handed. You and Uncle Garry were together for a long time, and though you probably did not realize it at the time, he gave you—*left* you something far greater than the life you led: the family you made together and the love you shared. What I believe is the grief and the pain you are experiencing is God's instrument, his time . . . the time you need to discover what that is. I believe during this time, you will discover things about yourself that might not otherwise have been revealed to you, were it not for this time you want so desperately to escape from. I believe, Auntie, a day will come when you will discover your life has not ended. It did not end when you lost Uncle Garry, but in fact, a new life is only just beginning."

Taking my hand in hers and looking deep into my eyes, she said, "In his own way, Uncle Garry left you many things you will discover have prepared you for this new life. How long will it take, you ask? As long as it takes."

Throughout the rest of the shower, I watched my lovely anointed niece. I observed the glow on her face and the aura that surrounded her. I laughed and played along with the shower games, but in the back of my mind I replayed her words, trying to make sense of them and accept them. She had been right before, and I knew then what I know now: she was a messenger. I left the shower in peace knowing that she was doing much better than I. I trusted in what I saw and in God, and believed that she would in the next two months bear a healthy and happy baby who would be loved and cared for by our entire family.

I meditated on her words when I returned home that night, and I did pray a different prayer. I prayed not for deliverance, but strength and patience.

"Okay, God, so I guess there are some things I need to know about myself. Apparently there are things I need to know that will help me going forward, so I'm asking you to bless me not only with patience, but the ability to see and hear what I need to know."

I had no idea when I went to sleep that night that I would soon remember vividly her words and my prayer. Despite my prayer, I was still hoping the storm was almost over . . . little did I know it had only just begun.

Chapter Twenty-Nine

T HE WEEKS AFTER SUMMER'S baby shower passed quickly. All Mom's invited guests had confirmed their attendance, the food and decorations had been purchased, the side dishes were made, and the big celebration was just a couple of days away. Since I started the business, Mom had become partial to my cupcakes, especially my red-velvet cupcakes. In lieu of a birthday cake, she decided she wanted cupcakes. Indulging her wish, I decided to bake a dozen of her favorites, as well as a half dozen each of my three other top sellers.

On a daily basis in the midst of all the party preparations and all my other activities, I recalled Summer's words to me. Every day I woke expecting some miraculous revelation, some sign of the gift of knowledge Garry was supposed to have left to me. With great anticipation, I looked for some little nugget about me that would help navigate whatever future God had in store for me.

When I wasn't busy filling customer orders, cleaning the house, or preparing food for the party, I sat for hours in front of my fireplace staring at Garry's urn on the mantel talking to him. I no longer cried and berated him for leaving me; instead I sat quietly, hoping desperately to feel something . . . anything. Sometimes I talked quietly, asking him to show me a sign, to share his wisdom. "Tell me,"

I pleaded, "besides the insurance money . . . what did you leave me? What am I not seeing? What am I supposed to see?"

Every night as I lay in my empty bed unable to sleep, I prayed for patience. I prayed for strength to get through the next day. I prayed for shoulders broad enough to bear the responsibility left to me. I tried with all my heart not to give in to frustration, but with each passing day, like some alien invader, it crept further and further into my spirit.

Next to his urn was a plaque we'd received from the funeral home. On it was a picture, the same picture that was on the cover of his obituary. The picture had been taken on our thirtieth wedding anniversary and vow renewal. He was smiling a big, brilliant, beautiful smile. He looked happy and at peace. It was a look I'd rarely seen over the last twelve months of his life. The look he'd worn most often was one of extreme fatigue and pain that radiated from the top of his head to the soles of his feet. I thought at the time the pain was physical, a result of working so hard and for so many years on those bad knees of his, but I realized in those last days of his life, the pain he bore on his face went much deeper than the physical, and it extended far beyond his face.

I closed my eyes and remembered with a sharp pain in my heart those last days.

I remembered in vivid detail the way he would just suddenly drift off. The look of pain intensified, but there was something more, something I couldn't quite identify. He looked like something was weighing on him. Remembering now, I wondered what he'd been thinking. What had he been struggling with? Was he contemplating even then the future he knew I'd be forced to face without him? I thought about the many cryptic conversations we had throughout that last week. I recalled the words he said, words I'd tried so hard to ignore at the time, not wanting to acknowledge what they might have meant. "You're stronger than you think you are, sweetheart.

You'll be just fine, baby." He said those words over and over again, and I tried to ignore the pain in my heart and my gut—that internal warning that something was very wrong.

I was so engulfed in my memories it took several minutes for the sound of my phone ringing to penetrate my brain. Looking around frantically for it, I realized I'd left it in the kitchen on the counter and made a mad dash to catch it before it stopped ringing.

"Hello!" I practically shouted when I finally reached it.

"Hey, sis," Juanda responded to my frantic hello. "Are you okay? You sound out of breath."

"Hey, girl. Yeah, I'm fine, I just had to run to catch the phone. I was in the family room and it was in the kitchen."

"Are you sure you're okay?" she asked, sounding like she didn't believe me.

"Yeah, I'm fine, I was just having a moment. What's up with you?" I asked, trying to change the subject.

"You know you're not fooling me for one second. You're trying to change the subject, and I'm gonna let you slide—just this once. I called because I wanted to remind you I'm going to be in town the first weekend in October for a seminar. I wanted to know if I could stay with you over the weekend. The company is putting us up in a hotel for the week during the seminar. I also wanted to go look at some venues over the weekend, and I wanted to know if you think you're still up to going with me?"

"Yes, and yes, and I can't believe you even asked me either question. I already promised you I'd help you in any way I can with your mother's party, and of course you're staying with me!"

"Well, I didn't want to just take it for granted, but thanks! Now that we've gotten that out of the way, you wanna tell me what's wrong?"

"Nothing's wrong," I said, laughing. "I was having a one-way conversation with your brother," I said, more seriously. "It got a little emotional."

She didn't say anything for a few minutes, and I could feel she was struggling with her own emotions. "I understand, sis," she said finally. "I can't wait to see you next month. It sounds like you're long overdue for one of our talks."

"And a hug," I said.

"Several, in fact. I can't wait to see you either."

"How are the plans for Mama Evelyn's birthday celebration coming?"

"Everything is right on schedule. Kenny and his crew will be here tomorrow. She's going to be so surprised. She doesn't know they're coming. I think she's going to be very pleased."

"I'm sure she will. Take lots of pictures. I'm afraid I've got to run now, I've got a meeting to get to. We'll talk more soon."

"Okay, sweetie, talk to you later. Love you, girl!"

When I hung up the phone, I looked at the time and was shocked. *Wow, where has the day gone?* I thought. All my emotional musings had left me weary of both mind and body. I wanted nothing more than to turn off the lights, lie down in my bed, and slip into mind-numbing sleep, but if I was going to stay on schedule, I had more work to do before I could even think about sleeping.

I went into the kitchen and began organizing dry ingredients for my cupcakes. Afterward I made my signature cream-cheese frosting, then set out my eggs and butter so I could get an early start in the morning. The rest would have to wait until then. By the time I finished the frosting, I was so exhausted I could barely see straight. I had been running on fumes for days, and my body was finally telling me enough is enough. I put the frosting in the fridge to set, and just before I turned off the lights, I took one more look at Garry's picture on the mantel.

"I'm not done with you yet," I said. "To be continued."

After setting the alarm, I turned off the lights and headed upstairs. *Please, God,* I prayed as I got ready for bed. *Please let me sleep!*

CHAPTER THIRTY

COMING UP THE STAIRS, my legs and arms felt like lead weights, and I could barely keep my eyes open. By the time I shed my clothes and crawled into bed, I fully anticipated I would pass out as soon as my head hit the pillow. Unfortunately, as soon as I turned off the lights, my eyes refused to close. My brain refused to respond to the pleas of my weary body and shut down. Every thought I had managed to keep at bay throughout the day suddenly returned with a vengeance and would not be further denied.

Accepting the inevitable, I lay there and allowed my thoughts to roam free. As excited as I was about celebrating my mom's birthday, I thought of my own coming up shortly with a mixture of sadness and excitement. Sadness because this would be the first birthday in forty years I would spend without Garry. He always acknowledged my birthday in small, little ways that meant so much. There had not always been expensive gifts or dinners or lavish vacations, but there had always been a card on my pillow. Sometimes there was a cluster of balloons in the middle of the bed, or a small bottle of my favorite perfume. Sometimes he would cook me a special dinner or plan a spontaneous long weekend. No matter what else he did, he always made sure I was never alone on my birthday. In a way he had assured that again this year, though he probably had no idea he wouldn't be here himself.

After we acquired our time-shares, he was always encouraging me to take a "girls' weekend."

"You have more vacation time than I do, Kitten," he'd say. "Why don't you get a group of your girlfriends together and go somewhere? You can do a long weekend, or hell, if they can get the time off, take a week. We will never be able to use all of the time we have together, so at least you might as well enjoy it."

After I booked my trip to Atlanta to see my grandbabies, I felt adventurous enough to take Garry up on his suggestion. I decided I didn't want to spend my birthday at home alone, so I called Joyce and invited her to join me for a long weekend at the Dells. Joyce was delighted at the offer, so we decided to extend the invitation to one other person. I invited Donna first as a way of thanking her for all her help in organizing the repast after Garry's funeral.

"Oh, sis, I would love to join you," she replied when I asked. "But I'm saving my vacation days to go see Summer and the baby later that month."

"Oh, of course," I said. "The new mommy and grandbaby come first. I totally understand. It's okay, I'm gonna need all of you to help me utilize these time-shares, so no problem. Maybe next time."

I called Joyce back and told her Donna couldn't go. "Your turn," I said. "You pick somebody you want to join us and invite them."

She asked our mutual friend and choir member Linda, and she gladly accepted our invitation. I chose the Dells because it was within driving distance, so nobody would have to come up with airfare. Since they were my guests and I was driving, the only thing I asked was that we share the cost of the gas.

My last thoughts before I finally passed out were how proud I was of myself. I was learning to do things for myself by myself, things that I'd always relied on Garry to do. I chose the resort, I called the time-share, gave them the information, and paid the exchange fee. My birthday, October 10, fell on a Thursday, so I would actually be home on my birthday, but we booked the resort from the eleventh through the fourteenth. I planned to celebrate that weekend with my girls!

Our itinerary consisted of shopping, eating, movies, and plenty of late-night girl talk accompanied by lots of wine and snacks at the resort. When I planned the trip, it was to be a wonderful celebration, a symbol of my new independence and my new reality spent with good friends. I had no idea it would end in life-shattering heartbreak for me and my family, another terrible blow to my already fragile existence. I had no idea that from that year forward, the date October 14 would be indelibly burned in my brain and forever marked in my heart with sad remembrance.

♦

I HADN'T GOTTEN THE best night's sleep, but I had managed to get in about three or four hours. That would have to do. I got dressed and went down to the kitchen, plugged in my mixer, and got busy making the first batch of cupcakes. Every now and then I glanced up at the clock and smiled. *Kenny will be here soon*, I thought, getting more excited by the minute. I turned to the music station on the TV, cranked up the volume, and tried to work myself up into a party mood. *This isn't about you*, I said to myself. *Tomorrow is Mom's day, so nothing but happy thoughts!* I was determined to pull myself together and give her a birthday celebration she would remember for the rest of her life.

"Hey, lady," I said when my phone rang. "Hold on, let me turn down this music."

"Are you having a party over there?" she asked when I came back to the phone.

"Nope," I said, laughing, "just trying to get into the mood for tomorrow. How are you feeling today?"

"I feel pretty good," she said. "I was just calling to see if you need me to do anything for tomorrow."

"Absolutely not!" I said. "Have you forgotten this is your birthday party? You don't really think I'd put you to work for your own party, do you?"

"Well, I don't mind helping out. I hate the thought of you doing all that work by yourself."

"Who said I was doing it all by myself, missy? Don't you worry, I've got everything under control. You just concentrate on making yourself gorgeous for your guests tomorrow. Kevin will stop by and scoop you up when we're about ready. I'll call you and give you a heads-up when he's on his way, and yes, before you ask again, I'm sure I don't need you to do anything but enjoy your birthday celebration."

"Okay," she said, laughing. "I'm not gonna offer again."

"Good!" I said, laughing too. "Now, is there anything else? 'Cause I got to get back to work."

"I guess not. I'll see you tomorrow."

Shaking my head when I hung up the phone, I laughed out loud again. *You ain't fooling me, woman,* I thought. *That was a fishing expedition, but you're just going to have to wait until tomorrow.*

Between the music and baking the cupcakes, I was able to keep my mind focused on the task at hand. I deliberately avoided even looking in the family room so I wouldn't get distracted. When I took the last batch of cupcakes out of the oven, I glanced up at the clock and thought to myself, *Kenny should be here any minute now.*

I sat the cupcakes on a cooling rack on the counter with the earlier batches, and then ran upstairs for a few minutes. No sooner than my feet hit the kitchen floor as I came back downstairs, I heard a car door slam. Smiling, I ran to the living-room window and looked outside.

Much to my delight I saw Kenny's truck in the driveway. He was unloading the luggage and the kids were headed for the front door.

I ran to the door and snatched it open, then opened my arms wide to receive my grandbabies. The next twenty minutes were spent exchanging hugs and kisses. I couldn't take my eyes off the children, nor could I believe what I was seeing. All three looked as if they'd grown at least two to three inches since the last time I saw them. *Impossible*, I thought. *That was only about two months ago.*

"Are those cupcakes?" the girls asked in unison, licking their lips.

"Yes, they are," I said, laughing. "They are for Nana's party tomorrow. Sorry," I said as their little faces fell. "You're going to have to wait until tomorrow. Besides, I still have to frost them."

"Where should we put our stuff, Mom?" Kenny asked.

"You and April and Mason will be in Kevin's room, and the rest of the kids are bunking in the basement."

When they'd put all their stuff away, I asked if they were hungry.

"Not right now," Kenny responded. "We stopped and ate just a little bit before we got here. Maybe a little later."

"Okay," I said, "just let me know when you're ready."

We sat down and got caught up while the kids went down to the basement to watch TV.

"So how's it going, Mom?" Kenny asked.

"I've had a couple of realtors come out and assess the house for me. I'm not having any luck getting the mortgage adjusted, so as much as I hate to do it, I'm going to seriously think about putting it on the market and hope I can do a short sale. I've still got a little time, but I'm definitely going to have to make a decision by the first of the year."

"I understand, Mom. I know you wanted to keep the house in the family, but you have to do what's best for you. What are Kevin and Jillian going to do?"

"Well, they will probably stay with me until I sell the house, unless they decide to move back into the city sooner. This is a very long and expensive commute for them."

"Where is Kevin?" he asked.

"They're both at work," I answered. "They'll be here later. They're going to bring Noah and David with them. They have a big-screen TV down there; they can have a big pajama party and make all the noise they want to. The only thing I haven't thought about is Mason trying to keep up with them, but he seems to be navigating those stairs pretty well."

"Yeah," Kenny said, laughing. "He'll be just fine. Where's the meat you want me to grill for tomorrow? I guess I should start getting that ready."

"Okay," I said, getting up to retrieve it from the outside fridge. "Here are the ribs and the chicken. I guess there's nothing to do to the sausage but cut it up. I bought legs, wings, and boneless breasts so you don't have to cut up the chicken."

"Cool," he said. "The most work is the ribs, but these look pretty good. Very meaty."

"They better be," I said, laughing. "They cost an arm and a leg!"

I started working on something to feed the kids later while he worked on the ribs. I decided to keep it simple: hamburger sliders and french fries. There would be plenty of food tomorrow.

"By the way, little lady," Kenny said while I was busy cutting up potatoes for the fries. "You've got a birthday of your own coming up soon, right?"

"Yep, I do. On the tenth," I answered.

"So, you got any plans?" he asked.

With a smile that masked the sadness in my heart, I said, "Yes. I booked a weekend getaway with my girlfriends at the Dells. Your father was always encouraging me to use the time-share without him because I had more vacation time than he did. This will be the first time in forty years that we haven't been together on my birthday. I decided to take him up on his suggestion."

I looked in the direction of his picture for the briefest of seconds. "I did it for myself . . . by myself. I think he would be proud of me. I guess I'm going to have to get used to doing that going forward."

"I know he's proud of you, Mom," he said. "I'm proud of you too. You can do it. I know you think Dad did everything for you, but I think you don't give yourself enough credit. I know you're going to be just fine," he said and hugged me.

Chapter Thirty-One

THE SLIDERS WERE DONE and I was just finishing up the last batch of fries when Kevin and Jillian walked in with Noah and David. After exchanging hugs, the brothers began trading their usual barbs back and forth. Noah and David joined their cousins in the basement, and instantly the noise level in the house escalated several octaves. McKenzie and Londyn adored Noah and David, and it was easy to tell from all the laughing and squealing coming from the basement, they were delighted to see them.

There were only five adults and five children in the house, but it sounded like at least fifty more.

I smiled warmly and felt a sharp tug on my heart as I listened and observed the camaraderie between my sons and their children. Garry had planned to retire next year, and we were going to move to Houston. It would have been hard to leave the house after all the wonderful years we spent there, but now it would be doubly hard to walk away. It pained me to think my grandchildren wouldn't get to know and love this house the way we did. It made me very sad to think this might very well be the last time they got to enjoy it.

I sat all the food out on the counter and called the children to come and eat. I laughed and marveled at how fast it disappeared, seemingly in the blink of an eye. *No wonder they are growing so fast,* I thought. I laughed again, thinking I was glad I didn't have to feed them all the time. Kenny had finished seasoning the meat and put it away. I'd cleaned up from the buffet-style dinner we ate, and now the adults sat around the kitchen table talking. The children had retreated back down to the basement and their video games. It was quieter as everyone was starting to feel the fatigue of the day.

April and Jillian helped me move some things around in the dining room while we talked. As usual, the conversation led to memories of Garry and how much he would have enjoyed playing grill master for the party tomorrow. Kenny had learned from his father and grandfather, and then developed and honed his own set of skills. Smiling with anticipation, I knew without a shadow of doubt how happy my mom would be to see her youngest grandson and his family. Even more, I knew she would be thrilled to be eating his delicious ribs.

I went down to the basement and checked on the kids, making sure they had enough linens, and warned them not to stay up too late, knowing even as I spoke the words I was wasting my breath. Returning upstairs, I hugged and kissed everyone else and told them I was turning in, even though I knew sleep was a long way off for me.

Maybe it was having my children and my grandchildren all together under the same roof, or maybe all those sleepless nights had finally pushed my body beyond its limits, but contrary to what I believed when I headed up the stairs . . . I did sleep. Unlike every other night for the past seven months, when I shed my clothes, slid between the sheets, turned off the lights, and laid my head on the pillow, I was out like a light.

No horrible nightmares remembering all the blood on the kitchen floor after the paramedics carried Garry out to the ambulance, having exhausted all efforts to revive him there. No lying there staring up at the ceiling wondering what I was going to do with the rest of my life, how I was going to live without him. No worrying what I was going to do about the house, or how I was going to move myself and my mother to Houston—alone. Nothing. Nothing but blissful, blank, uninterrupted sleep!

I woke the next morning feeling rested, renewed, and restored. That heavy blanket of sadness that usually covered me was temporarily absent. While Kenny and April prepared breakfast, I frosted the cupcakes and finished setting up for the party. Kenny had fired up the grill at the crack of dawn, and if the smells wafting in from the patio were any indication, we were in for a treat: some great Carter barbeque.

Chapter Thirty-Two

"WHAT TIME IS THIS party kicking off?" Kevin asked, coming down into the kitchen.

"I told everyone between three thirty and four. I'm going to call her and tell her you'll pick her up at three thirty."

"Okay, sounds good. I'm going to take the boys to get a haircut. Is there anything you need me to do before we leave?"

"Yes, please. Would you bring two of those long tables in from the garage?"

"Sure."

The smell of breakfast brought the kids up from the basement, all talking at once as usual. After giving me hugs and kisses, they sat down and devoured pancakes, sausage, bacon, and eggs in record time. I managed to snag one pancake and a piece of bacon before everything disappeared.

"Do you want me to fix you some more pancakes and bacon, Mommy?" Kenny asked, laughing.

"No, I'm fine, baby. This will hold me till later."

After breakfast, Kevin and David brought the tables in from the garage and set them up in the dining room.

"Do you need me to do anything else, Grandma?" David asked.

"Yes, sweetie. I need you and Noah to bring in the cooler, fill it with ice, and start putting water and soda in it for me."

"Okay," he said and yelled for Noah to come help him. Soon afterward they left to go to the barber shop. Kenny continued to man the grill, April made a special punch from a recipe she'd found on the internet, and I made my special sauce for the ribs and chicken. When everything was set, we all went to shower and change for the party.

Kevin left to go pick Mom up, and right around four o'clock her guests started to arrive. She made her grand entrance around four fifteen, and soon the party was underway. The look on her face when she walked through the door and saw Kenny and his family was priceless. It brought tears not of sadness but pure joy to my eyes as I beheld the beaming smile and complete surprise that spread across her face.

Pretty soon the house was full. She was holding court at the kitchen table, bragging to everyone that her baby had put this party together for her all by herself. Everybody was eating, talking, laughing, and having a great time. I would have loved to have given her a big fancy party at a banquet hall with all the bells and whistles, but I had a feeling she was enjoying this much better.

I went around and took pictures of her with all her guests and with her grands and great-grands. As I looked through the lens of the camera, I observed the smile that never left her face. While everyone else was laughing and talking, I was watching. *Eighty years old*, I thought to myself. *My mom is eighty years old!* She didn't drive anymore, and she was deathly afraid of flying. I'd already checked and found travel by train from Houston to Atlanta was expensive— more expensive than flying, not to mention it would take a day and a half. It would take approximately twelve hours to drive from Houston to Atlanta, and I knew I couldn't do that drive by myself.

The only way she'd get to see Kenny and her great-grandchildren would be for Kenny to make the trip to Houston.

With three children and the rising cost of airfare, that would mean he'd have to drive, and that wouldn't be fair to him. I sat there watching everyone, especially my mom, having a good time, and a light went on in my brain. I was right yesterday when I said it wasn't about me. I didn't have the luxury of doing just what I wanted to do. I had to consider what was best for everyone I loved, just the way Garry would have. For the last fifteen years I'd been dreaming and waiting to go to Houston, but today was today. It was no longer about what I wanted, and I was no longer convinced that Houston was where I needed to be.

Mom was thrilled with her birthday cupcakes, and the rest of her guests enjoyed them too, especially her great-grandbabies. I'd made more than enough of everything, and I sent everyone home with to-go boxes.

Before she walked out the door to go home, she hugged me really tight and said in a voice thick with emotion, "Thank you, baby, I had a wonderful time."

"I know," I said, hugging her back. "It's written all over your face. Plus, I have proof," I said, holding up my phone. "I have pictures! I'm glad you had a good time, Mom. I love you, happy birthday!"

"Thank you again," she said, her eyes filling up with tears.

I brushed away a tear, holding back tears of my own, and said, "You're welcome," as she turned and walked out the door.

Sleep didn't come as fast that night. I lay awake for quite a while, weighing what I wanted to do against what I was beginning to feel in my heart needed to be done. I prayed and asked God to give me guidance. My mother had fewer years ahead of her than I did. Knowing her limitations, could I really deny her the opportunity to spend as much time as possible with her great-grandchildren, or them her love and guidance? Could I really be that selfish? My last thought before I drifted off was that God would help me make the right decision for all of us, because whatever decision I made would affect all of us for the rest of our lives.

CHAPTER THIRTY-THREE

I WOKE THE NEXT morning to the muted sounds coming from the basement. My grandchildren possessed an endless supply of energy, like the flow of water from a faucet you just can't seem to turn off. After all the activity of the day before and the late night, they still managed to be up at the crack of dawn. Judging from the sounds I could just barely make out, they were speaking in their own private "cousin language" while alternately playing video games or watching the Disney Channel.

I could just barely hear the low rumble of Kevin snoring across the hall, and smiled as I wondered if his snoring had kept Kenny and April awake. After years of sleeping with his dad, it didn't bother me at all; on the contrary, I found the sound oddly comforting. There was a peace in my house that morning; there was a peace inside of me. I was pleased that I'd been successful in giving my mom a memorable birthday. Her birthday celebration had given us all an opportunity to bond under happier circumstances. It had also provided some clarity for me as to what my next steps should be.

My pastor always said God sends a word, followed by confirmation. That morning I believed he'd sent me a word, and I vowed to pay close attention as I waited for the confirmation. It didn't take long. It was still very early. The children seemed content downstairs, and the other adults seemed in no hurry to stir. I snuggled down in the covers and closed my eyes for an intended second and woke up almost an hour later to the smell of bacon cooking. It was obvious from all the noise coming from the kitchen everyone was now up except me.

"Morning, sleepy head," Kenny said as I came down the stairs into the kitchen. "You must have been tired. That was one heck of a party you threw yesterday."

"Thanks to you, baby. Thanks to all of you," I said.

"Are you hungry?" he asked.

Stealing a line from my grandson, I said, "I can eat."

Everybody laughed, especially my grandson David because that was his line.

We lingered over breakfast talking about any and everything, everyone seemingly reluctant to leave one another, as if we all sensed it would be a long time before we would be together like this again. The day passed too quickly, and soon it was time for Kenny, April, and the kids to get a few hours of sleep so they could head out very early in the morning for the long drive back to Atlanta.

I stayed up to put away the food from dinner and pack them some food for the road. There were some cupcakes left over, and I made sure to include those. I wanted to be up to say goodbye, so I didn't get in bed, I just curled up in my recliner. Kenny was right. I was tired; the events of the last two days were catching up with me. Even though I'd mercifully enjoyed two good nights of sleep, they didn't quite make up for the many sleepless nights that preceded them.

I closed my eyes for what seemed like minutes but turned out to be a couple of hours. The sound of Mason's voice, not happy about being roused from a sound sleep, alerted me to their imminent departure. I opened my bedroom door and stepped in the hall just in time to see Kenny descending the stairs with their luggage. April was busy rounding up the girls.

"I packed some food for you guys to take back with you, including some cupcakes," I said to April, looking at Londyn, who favored me with a sleepy smile.

"Thanks. Were there any of the red velvet left?" she asked.

"Yes, and some of the lemon Mason liked."

The scene at the front door was pure déjà vu. Kenny was still loading up the truck; April, Londyn, and Mason were already inside, but McKenzie lingered. As before when they left after the funeral, she seemed reluctant to leave me. She looked up at me with watery, sleepy eyes and hugged me tight.

"Why can't you come with us?" she asked.

I sat on the bench in the foyer and took her into my arms, rocking her gently. "Oh, Kenzie bear . . . I love you so much, baby. I wish I could come home with you, but I just can't right now. I promise you, though, it won't be a long time before I see you again."

Glancing up over the top of her head, I saw Kenny standing silently in the door allowing us to have our moment. I looked into his eyes, and what I saw there let me know something had shifted. Every fiber in my being was telling me that a decision was being formed, and not the one I thought I was going to make. I could hear my pastor's words: "First comes the word, and then confirmation."

"Come on, Kenzie," he said finally. "We've gotta go, baby girl. I've gotta get you guys back to Atlanta."

She slowly left my arms and hugged me again before she walked through the door out to the car. I walked out onto the porch with Kenny, not trusting myself to speak, but finally managing to say "Call me" after he hugged me.

"I will," he said, "as soon as we get home. I love you, Mommy."

For the second time in seven months, I stood on the porch and watched as his taillights disappeared from my sight. I locked the door, set the alarm, and turned off the lights. Walking into the family room in the dark, I stood in front of Garry's urn. I stood there for a long time, listening, waiting . . . feeling.

Finally I said aloud, "Tell me what to do. Tell me what you would have me do." I don't know if the question was addressed to Garry or to God; I don't know which one heard it. Maybe they collaborated— but I didn't have to wait long for my answer.

After Kenny left, I knew I wouldn't be able to sleep, so I curled up in my recliner to wait for their call. Not expecting a call till much later in the morning, I was startled first by the fact that I'd fallen asleep, and second by the sound of my phone ringing. Glancing at it, I saw that it was Kenny. I noted the time as well and realized they had not been gone long. My heart began to beat rapidly as I punched the button to answer it, immediately expecting to hear the worst.

"Hey," I said. "I know you guys are nowhere near home. Are you okay?"

"Yeah, don't worry, Mommy, we're fine . . . Well, we're not hurt, at least. I wouldn't say we're fine, especially your granddaughter."

"Mac?" I asked.

"Yes, she's been crying ever since we left. Look, we're going to call you when we get home. We need to talk, okay? I mean seriously! I know what you planned, but April and I want you to seriously consider another plan."

"Okay, son" was all I said.

I didn't need to wait until they got home. When I hung up the phone, I was up the rest of the night, having already figured out what plan they wanted me to consider. Even though a little voice inside of me screamed, *But what about the dream?* I was reminded of the message I'd been receiving over and over throughout the last few days. It was no longer about my dream; it was about my reality. It was no longer about what I wanted; it was about what was best for my family. Garry was gone, but I couldn't pretend that I was in this alone. Every choice, every decision I made, would impact my children, my grandchildren, and my mother. I was slowly, albeit reluctantly, coming to terms with the knowledge that it was time to put the dream to rest.

Obviously God had a plan. He hadn't completely revealed it to me, but I had to trust that he had one and then pray for the wisdom and the courage to follow it. The sun was up, the world outside my bedroom was getting on with the day, but I had not stirred from my chair. I was exhausted from not having slept and from the battle raging between my head and my heart all night long.

I knew before I answered the phone Kenny and April were going to ask me to consider moving to Atlanta instead of Houston. All night I'd been back and forth weighing the pluses and minuses of that decision.

In Houston I had my sister. I also had friends I'd made over the years during my many visits. I knew my sister, one of my biggest supporters, would make sure I had an active social life. I also knew she would without hesitation use her connections to help me establish my business there. On the other hand, I had no blood relatives in Houston, and visits to my grandchildren would be limited, at least for Mom, to the number of times Kenny could drive there.

In Atlanta, besides Kenny, I had other family members I could rely on if I needed help. Living in the same state would afford both me and Mom the opportunity to bond with Kenny and his children. I would have a chance to make up for all the time I'd missed out on in their early years, and Mom would have a chance to enjoy them in her later years. I would miss all my friends from Chicago, but as hard as I tried, I really couldn't find a downside to moving to Atlanta, except for one. I would have to give up my dream of moving to Houston and reuniting with Juanda.

So we had our conversation. I listened to everything they had to say, and just as I suspected, they lodged a full-on campaign to get me to move to Atlanta. They presented all the arguments I'd already considered and one compelling argument that all but sealed the deal. Kenny reminded me that moving to Atlanta would not only give his children the opportunity to know and bond with the mother he knew and loved, but it would finally put to rest his oldest daughter's concerns about me being alone. Remembering McKenzie's tearful departure tugged at my heart, and I knew that my fate had already been decided. The only thing left to do was accept it, and break the news to Juanda.

CHAPTER THIRTY-FOUR

AFTER OUR FIRST VISIT to Houston to see Juanda, a seed was planted, a dream was born, and a plan was formulated. I fell in love with her city and decided when we retired that's where I wanted to go to reunite with the sister God had blessed me with.

She had appeared in my life like a well-timed angel, the answer to a lifelong prayer, not from my mother's womb but straight from my heavenly Father's heart. Born out of his love for me and his infinite wisdom and knowledge of exactly what I needed and when.

Fortunately Garry liked Houston too. He knew how much I missed Juanda after she relocated, and he really didn't care where we went, as long as it was far away from the bone-chilling cold of Chicago. Every time we visited, the dream got bigger and my resolve stronger to follow through with the plan. Now, fifteen years later, I couldn't believe I was seriously considering backing out of the plan. Even more disturbing was the thought of trying to explain to Juanda that we wouldn't get to realize the dream we'd nurtured all these years.

One of Juanda's favorite cakes was German chocolate, and I promised to make her one on her next visit to Chicago. So on the morning of the day she was to arrive, I was standing in my kitchen frosting the cake I promised her. I'd been stressing about the conversation I knew I had to have with her for the past several days, and on that morning, I had a raging headache and upset stomach.

Over and over again, I practiced in my head what I would say— how I would break the news that I wouldn't be coming to Houston after all. I thought about all of the houses we'd looked at together and how excited we'd both been about finally being together again, and I dreaded the look of disappointment on her face when she heard the news. I assumed that like me, she would be crushed to find that the dream we'd nurtured for the past fifteen years would not come to fruition.

When she arrived later that evening, we went straight to her favorite place and picked up Italian beef sandwiches and fries for dinner. I tried to act like nothing was wrong, but when we returned to the house I barely touched my food, and it didn't take her long to see past my façade. She'd been talking a mile a minute ever since we sat down, and I hadn't heard a word she said. She picked up her sandwich to take a bite, then looked at me and sat it back down.

"Okay, sis, you've been acting strange ever since I walked through the door. At first I thought you were just tired, but now I know something's wrong, so spill!"

"Finish your sandwich," I said. "We need to talk."

"The sandwich can wait. What's wrong?"

"Okay, well let's go upstairs."

When we went upstairs, we sat on the bench at the foot of my bed. I sat there for a long time trying to find the right words and willing myself not to cry.

"Okay, you're making me really nervous, sis. Whatever it is, I can handle it. We can handle it. Just tell me."

"Sis, you know how much I've missed you, and how much Garry and I were looking forward to moving to Houston so we could be together again. After he died, I had every intention of following through with our plan, but . . ." I hesitated, feeling the tears begin to sting behind my eyes. "Things have happened. I've had to reevaluate my priorities, and—"

She stopped me before I could finish. "Sis," she said, taking my hand, "are you trying to tell me that you're not moving to Houston?"

"Please don't be mad," I said. "I know you've looked forward to this as much as we have."

"Mad? Are you kidding? Oh, sis, I'm not mad. I wondered how long it was gonna take before you told me. Or, I guess, maybe I should say how long it would take you to realize that where you need to be is Atlanta."

I couldn't believe what I was hearing. I didn't know what surprised me more: the fact that she wasn't upset with me, or the fact that she already knew I was going to move to Atlanta. I'd only realized that myself a couple of days ago.

"Wait! How did you know I was considering moving to Atlanta?"

"I didn't know until Sean told me," she said, laughing.

Now I was really confused. "How did Sean know? I only just began to seriously consider it a couple of days ago, and I haven't even told Kenny and April yet!"

"You do know our boys talk, right? Apparently Kevin, Kenny, and Sean have been talking, and they decided you need to go to Atlanta, and Sean said I shouldn't be selfish and stand in your way. I put myself in your shoes, and I thought about how blessed I am that my grandsons are only two hours away. Don't get me wrong—I want you to come to Houston, as selfish as that is, but I completely understand and agree with the boys that right now, at least at this point in your life, Atlanta is the place you need to be for you, and for Kenny and your grandchildren as well. So now that we've established that I'm not upset with you . . . can I please have a piece of my cake?"

I was so relieved that she wasn't upset, and more confident than ever that God was steering me in this new and different direction. My stomach was no longer tied up in knots, and my headache had disappeared. I was laughing and crying all at the same time.

"Yes," I said, laughing. "I'm suddenly starving, so I'm going to finish my sandwich, and then I'm also going to have a piece of *your* cake!"

Chapter Thirty-Five

AFTER FINISHING OUR DINNER and our cake, we stayed up half the night talking about everything from love lost to our children and grandchildren. We talked about the dream we almost had, and as much as it wasn't necessarily the decision I wanted to make, we both agreed it was the right decision to move to Atlanta.

The next morning we got up and went to look at the potential venues she had chosen for her mother's birthday party. All too soon, our time together came to an end.

"Thanks for going with me today, sis, and thanks in advance for all your help with the party."

"You know I love your mother. It's my pleasure to help out."

We both held on a little longer and a little tighter as we hugged goodbye.

"I love you girl, and I'm absolutely not upset with you about moving to Atlanta. I know without a shadow of doubt, if I were in your shoes, I would be making the same decision."

"Thanks, sis, I really needed to hear that. I love you. I'll see you next month."

Having made up my mind, I called Kenny to give him the good news.

"Hey, Mommy," he said when he answered the phone. "How are you doing?"

"I'm okay. Is April home?"

"Yeah, she's here. What's up?"

"Okay, can you both get on the phone or put me on speaker? I have something to tell you."

After a few minutes, I heard April say, "I'm here."

"Well, I've given it a lot of thought and a lot of prayer, and I talked to Juanda."

"And?" Kenny said, interrupting me. "What did you decide?"

"I've decided that moving to Atlanta is probably the better choice to make under the circumstances, but I'm going to need your promise that you're going to help me make this move, and that I can count on you to help me out with your grandma as well as getting my business established down there."

"You can absolutely count on us to do all three," they both said.

"Well, there's a lot I have to work out, not the least of which is finding a place to live. We'll talk more about that later, but we can start with that. Can you guys find me a realtor?"

"No problem," Kenny said. "And Mom . . . I know how much you wanted to go to Houston, but I promise we'll make sure you won't regret moving here."

"I'm sure I won't regret it, baby. It's just going to take a little getting used to."

I sat in my recliner for a long time after they hung up the phone. Making peace with that decision was just the beginning. I had a million other decisions to make related to the move, but they would have to wait for another day. I only had a few days to get ready for my birthday getaway with my girls. Everything else would have to wait until I got back.

I needed to get the car checked out and start packing. We all decided we would bring snacks for the resort so we wouldn't have to eat all our meals in restaurants. The unit came with a full kitchen, so we could make breakfast and or lunch—even dinner if we didn't feel like going out. Both Joyce and Linda loved German chocolate cake, so I decided to thank them for sharing their weekend with me by baking one to take with us. Among other things, that would be my contribution to the snacks. I also wanted to get them some small gifts to commemorate our trip as a token of my appreciation. When I dragged my suitcase upstairs from the basement and sat it on the bench at the foot of my bed, my spirits suddenly lifted. The anticipation of our trip began to set in, and I decided to put all thoughts of moving on the back burner.

Two days later I stood in my kitchen for the second time in a week putting frosting on a German chocolate cake. The gifts had been purchased along with a couple of bottles of wine, and I was almost finished packing. We decided to leave from my house, and I would drive my car. The night before we left, I couldn't sleep because I was so excited. It was not only my first "girls' getaway," but it was the first road trip in which I would be doing the driving. Whenever we went on a road trip, Garry had always done all the driving.

Joyce's husband dropped them off the next morning, and after we loaded up the car, we were on our way. The time passed quickly as we all talked about men, our children, church . . . how good it was to be leaving all our stresses behind, and how much fun we planned to have. Traffic was good, and except for the conversation inside the car, the trip was thankfully uneventful. The directions I printed out took us right to the door of the main building. After we checked in, we found the cottage we had been assigned to and took our luggage inside. The unit had one bedroom on the first floor with two twin beds and a bathroom. There was also a kitchen, dining area, and family room, as well as an enclosed patio on the first floor. The master bedroom and bath were upstairs. The girls decided I should take that.

We deposited our luggage in our respective rooms and then set out to find a Walmart so we could purchase some more food and wine for our stay. When we returned, we opened up a bottle of wine, munched on snacks, and talked till the wee hours of the morning. It was so good to have someone to talk to about everything I was going through, someone who wouldn't judge or try and tell me what I should be feeling instead of just listening and helping me deal with what I *was* feeling.

The next morning we slept late, had a light breakfast, and set out to explore the area. We'd already looked up the location of some of the restaurants and the nearest mall, and decided to do some shopping. I hadn't bought or even thought about buying any clothes since my trip to Houston in March, so I was pleasantly surprised to discover I had lost some weight. I was looking for a dress to wear to Juanda's mother's birthday party and was pleased to find I needed a size smaller than I normally wore.

We found the perfect dress and a couple of other items, and after shopping we had an early dinner at Cracker Barrel. We spent another evening at the resort drinking wine, talking, laughing, and sometimes crying. It was not only a fun weekend, but it turned out to be very therapeutic. I'd kept my feelings bottled up inside for months, afraid to let anyone know how I really felt. Wanting people to think I was fine because I believed it made them feel better to think so. Finally, I could tell it like it was. Finally, I felt free to embrace my truth and feel comforted and not judged.

The next day was Sunday. It would be my official birthday celebration with the girls, and our last full day at the resort. Even though I'd rented the unit for the whole week, Joyce and Linda had to get back to work, so we were only staying until Monday afternoon. We were going to see a movie, and then go out for a steak dinner with all the trimmings. As much as I was looking forward to that steak dinner, it made me sad to remember the last time I had one was with Garry on our trip to San Diego, our last vacation together.

We stayed up late Saturday night and slept late Sunday morning. After a light breakfast, we lay around chillin' until it was time to get dressed to go out. We left that night looking forward to the movie and to the dinner, grateful that we wouldn't have to get up early the next morning to pack and leave. Even though I didn't have a job to return to, I was in no hurry to return to all the decisions I had to make about moving. Just the thought of packing up thirty years of memories made me overwhelmingly sad and mentally exhausted.

As we drove to the theatre, I don't know what Joyce and Linda were thinking about, but I knew none of us could ever have anticipated the devastation the morning would bring.

CHAPTER THIRTY-SIX

THE MOVIE WAS GREAT and the dinner was excellent. We had a wonderful time that continued on well after we returned to the resort. We stayed up late talking and finishing up the last bottle of wine. Since I'd rented the resort for the whole week, we didn't have to leave by eleven the next morning. We could sleep late if we wanted to and take our time packing up to leave.

The weekend had been everything I'd hoped for and more, and yet when I finally went upstairs to go to bed, I felt an unease that was all too familiar. I lay awake for hours feeling an overwhelming sense of doom, but I couldn't figure out what could possibly be wrong. I tossed and turned, unable to shake that uneasy feeling, the same feeling I had just before Garry passed.

I finally drifted off, but woke feeling exhausted. Since we didn't have to get up early, I intended to linger in the bed a little longer. My plan was interrupted by the sound of my phone alerting me to a text message. I fully expected it to be from either Kevin or Kenny, checking to see if I was having a good time. I was totally not prepared for who the text was from, or what it was about.

Looking at the phone, I saw that it was from Donna, asking me to pray for my niece Summer, saying that she was being rushed to the hospital. Summer had given birth to a beautiful baby boy just nine days earlier. I was shocked and confused by the text because up until that moment, I believed that both mother and son were doing fine.

I didn't hesitate to text back and tell Donna that of course I would be praying and to keep me informed of her status. I could hear that Joyce and Linda were already up, and I started down the stairs to tell them about the text and ask them to pray with me. My foot barely touched the last step leading into the family room when I received another text.

The second I read it, the room started to spin and I thought I would faint. My eyes registered the words, but my heart immediately rejected them. "NO, NO, NO," I said over and over again as the tears began to fall. Joyce and Linda came out of their room to see what was wrong, and I tried to tell them, unable to put together a coherent sentence.

"Niece, gone . . ." was all I could say. *Not possible,* I thought to myself. *I must have misunderstood her text.* "Summer is gone," it said. In retrospect I know it sounds stupid, but my very first thought was *Gone where?* She couldn't possibly mean what it sounded like. Summer couldn't be . . . dead! She just had a baby . . . she had a son . . . she was getting married! None of it made any sense.

My heart was beating so fast. I was walking around in circles thinking to myself, *This can't be happening again!* I had to call somebody; I had to find out what was really happening. The entire time we'd been at the resort, I'd been having trouble with my internet service. Sometimes I couldn't get any service at all unless I stepped outside onto the porch.

I stepped outside and dialed Donna's number, but didn't get an answer. I called Kevin, and as soon as he answered the phone, my heart sank. The sound of his voice told me everything I didn't want to know.

"Yes, it's true, Ma," he said, his voice thick with emotion. "She's gone; she died before she made it to the hospital. When are you coming home?" he asked.

"We were going to leave later this afternoon, but I'll be on my way as soon as we can get packed up."

"Are you okay?" he asked.

"No." It was all I could say, feeling like I was on the verge of hysteria.

I had a million questions, the least of which was "Why? How could this be happening again?"

"I don't want you to try and drive, Ma. Can Joyce drive back?" he asked.

"I'll ask her. I'm sure she won't mind under the circumstances. Depending upon the traffic, it should take us about three hours. Can you meet me at the house? I want to go straight to Donna's."

"Yes, of course, I'll take you there. Everyone is at the house."

"Okay, I'll call you when we get close. I couldn't get Donna on the phone. Would you please tell her I'm on my way back? Tell her I love her and I'll be there as soon as I can."

"She knows, Ma, but I will tell her. You all be careful."

I went back inside and tried once again to explain what was wrong. "I don't really know any of the details, but apparently my niece died just a little while ago. One minute my sister was asking me to pray because she was being rushed to the hospital. That's what I was coming downstairs to tell you and ask you to pray with me. Two seconds later, I got another text saying she was gone."

Tears running down my face, I couldn't go on. I just sat there shaking my head.

"We'll start packing up so we can get you back," Joyce said.

"Yeah," Linda said. "We'll drive. You shouldn't try and drive as upset as you are."

"Thanks. I didn't want to ask, but you're right. I'm in no shape to drive."

About an hour later, we were packed, dressed, and ready to head back to Chicago. I sat in the back seat, alternately crying and wishing this was some horrible nightmare I could wake up from. I'd lost a husband, but my sister had just lost her child—her firstborn. Lord, what could I say to her? How could I comfort her? I had very personal knowledge of the depth of her despair. My pain, though different in its origin, was still so fresh, I didn't know if I had it in me to be the strength and comfort she had been for me. The trip to the Dells had seemed relatively short. The three hours had passed quickly, and I remembered being so proud of myself for having driven it the whole way. Now, sitting in the back seat, the trip back to Chicago seemed to take forever.

I was anxious to get back so I could see Donna and try to find out exactly what had happened. I also wanted to see what I could do to help her and the rest of the family. Staci had lost her sister; her kids had lost their beloved auntie. I knew they had to be hurting just as much as Donna.

After what seemed like an eternity, we finally pulled up in my driveway. Joyce's husband was waiting. He was talking to Kevin, who had arrived to drive me over to Donna's. Just seeing Kevin's face produced a fresh batch of tears and reminded me of another very painful day. When I climbed out of the back seat, my legs felt weak and my hands were shaking. Thinking about the days ahead, I asked God how and why this was happening to our family again, and so soon.

Joyce, Reggie, and Linda all hugged us. "We are so very sorry for your loss," Joyce said with tears in her eyes. "Please tell Donna she and her family are in our prayers, and please let us know if there is anything we can do."

"I will," I said. "I had a wonderful time despite the way the trip ended. Thank you so much for sharing *your* weekend with me, and thanks for driving back."

"We had a wonderful time too, and you don't have to thank us for driving back. There was no way we would have let you drive under the circumstances. You go now and be with your family, and I meant what I said—if there is anything I can do, don't hesitate to call."

Kevin took my luggage inside, and then we left to go to Donna's. All the way there I prayed and asked God to give me strength, to give me the right words to comfort my sister and the rest of the family. Even as I thought about comforting them, I remembered my last conversation with Summer and my heart broke. I realized I hadn't seen her since the baby shower, and I'd only talked to her once since she had the baby. She sounded tired, and considering she'd just had the baby, I didn't think her fatigue was out of the ordinary. I had no idea she was ill. I had no idea it was the last time I would ever hear her voice.

My heart ached, and I tried desperately to stem the flow of tears that leaked from my eyes. I tried to stop the sobs that escaped my throat, thinking, *I have to pull myself together. I can't fall apart. I have to be strong for my sister.*

CHAPTER THIRTY-SEVEN

W HEN I STEPPED ACROSS the threshold into Donna's house, I was instantly assailed by the memory of coming into this house eight months ago. For different reasons, I felt the same sense of shock and disbelief. The pain I felt was strong and pervasive, at once overwhelming me and rendering me helpless. I could see Donna sitting at the kitchen table staring blankly at the computer screen in front of her.

The kitchen was just a few steps from the living room, and yet it seemed to take me an eternity to cross the distance, all the while praying for God to open my mouth and allow the right comforting words to spew forth. When I finally found myself standing by her side and she turned to acknowledge my presence, I saw immediately it was not words she needed, but the comfort of my outstretched arms.

The floodgates opened up as she leaned into me, and I held her until she temporarily emptied out the pain stored in her heart. I knew from personal experience the release was only temporary, for there would be many more tears to shed in the coming days. I decided to postpone my questions about what had happened, for I knew the why was not important now. Facing the reality that her beautiful daughter was gone, acknowledging and accepting that she would never hear her voice again or share that bonding experience she had been so looking forward to with Summer and her days-old grandson, finding some semblance of peace . . . that was all that mattered now.

I asked the only question I felt was really relevant at the time. Rubbing her back, I looked at her through my own tears and asked, "Sis, what can I do? How can I help?" I knew from my own recent experience there were arrangements to be made, and people to notify. It suddenly occurred to me that I had not contacted my mother to let her know I had returned home. She knew I was due back today, and she was probably wondering and worrying about why I hadn't checked in with her.

Donna's phone rang, and when she took the call, it gave me an opportunity to step outside and make a call of my own.

"Hey, Ma," I said when she answered.

"Hey," she said. "Are you home?" she asked.

"Yes, I came back a little earlier than I planned."

I held the phone for a long time trying to keep it together, but the thought of saying the words was too much. I began to cry again, and I couldn't stop. All the pain I'd tried to hold at bay in front of Donna came bubbling to the surface, and I couldn't push it back down. Kevin was sitting in the open garage talking to Karl, and when he saw my distress, he came and took the phone from me. The reality of it all hit me with such force I felt like I'd been kicked in the gut. I doubled over in pain so fierce it nearly took my breath away. As he explained to my mother what happened, I sobbed. I remember shaking my head and walking back and forth in the driveway saying, "God, I can't do this again, it's too much . . . it's too soon."

I cried until my head hurt and my throat felt raw, and then as suddenly as the pain had assaulted me, another feeling took over. I wouldn't describe it as peace, more like a revelation. As if God himself had responded to my cries. I realized as painful as this was for me, it was not about me. As much as I shared this loss, it was time for me to put my feelings aside and concentrate on my sister. She needed me to summon my faith so I could shore up hers. She needed me to summon my strength so I could be hers. What she didn't need was for me to fall apart. It was time for me to get it together so I could offer her the same level of comfort she had given to me.

For reasons perhaps neither of us would ever fully understand, a new bonding was taking place, born out of our shared experience. God had flipped the script, and now it was my turn to be the strong one—it was time for me to take control. Among other things, as she had eight months ago, I took on the responsibility of organizing and overseeing the repast.

I look back on those days now and understand more about the message my beautiful niece had given me the last time we talked. "When the people we love leave us, they never leave us empty handed." In the coming days, I would come to acknowledge all the things Summer left us.

As I sat behind my sister in the sanctuary at Summer's homegoing service, I listened to the minister as he delivered her eulogy. I tried to stay focused; I tried not to let my mind wander to a time not too long ago when I sat in that same spot. I was determined to remember my revelation that none of this was about me. I couldn't allow my memories to overtake me.

I listened as the minister gently admonished us about saying and even thinking that Summer was "gone too soon." He reminded us that Summer had not belonged to us, she belonged to God. She had been here on loan. She had an assignment that, whether we knew it or not, she had completed, and God had called her back home. It was his call, not ours. It was his prerogative, his will, and it mattered not that we were not ready to let her go. *She* was ready, she had done what God sent her here to do, and he had called her home.

I sat there thinking, *She was only thirty-six. How could she be ready? She just had her first child. How could she be ready? She was about to get married—how on earth could she be ready?* As if the minister or God himself had heard my questions, he went on to say it did not matter when we began or when we ended; it was not about the sunrise or the sunset . . . but what happened in between.

He told us, reminded us, that Summer had accomplished more in her thirty-six years than most people who lived to be three times her age. He reminded us of her anointing and all the people's lives she had touched and how blessed they were for having been touched by her. He reminded us of the gift she had left us: her precious son. I sat up, suddenly remembering Summer saying, "They never leave us empty handed."

He said more, but it all amounted to the same thing. He told us not to be angry with God, for he had not unceremoniously taken our beloved Summer away from us, he had simply brought her back home. They were playing her favorite song, "Take Me to the King." My eyes were closed. My heart was being ministered to by the song, which was also one of my favorites. My mind was thinking about all the minister had said. I knew he was talking to Donna and the rest of the family about Summer, but he could just as easily have been speaking to me about Garry. I'd been guilty of accusing God of taking him too soon; I'd railed over and over again that I was not ready. I was convicted by my audacity, knowing now that it had not been about me or my readiness.

As the song reached a rousing crescendo, I could hear weeping in the background. I opened my eyes and saw that it was not Donna. Her head rested gently on Karl's shoulder, as she was locked in silent grief. The weeping grew louder and turned into gut-wrenching sobs. I looked down the row at Staci and the children. Their faces were awash with tears, but the sobs were not coming from them.

I looked around, seeking the source of the sobs that had increased in volume and intensity, and suddenly noticed my son. Kevin was standing in the corner, doubled over in visible pain that I recognized was more emotional than physical. He was emptying out everything he'd been holding in for months. I knew that he was devastated by the loss of his cousin and friend, but I also knew his sobs were just as much for the father he'd lost, a loss and subsequent grief that up until now he'd not given into.

I wanted to comfort him, but I knew all too well he needed that release. I was having difficulty holding on to my own composure, so I stayed where I was and prayed. I prayed that the hand of God would comfort him as only he could.

When the service was over, I left and preceded the family to the banquet hall where the repast was to be held. I immersed myself in doing what I needed to do for the family. *I'll have plenty of time later to give into my feelings … my grief,* I thought to myself. *For now, I need to stay strong for my sister. For the family.*

Chapter Thirty-Eight

WHEN I FINALLY RETURNED home from the repast, I was physically and emotionally exhausted. My feet ached and my head hurt, probably from concentrating so hard on trying to keep my emotions in check. I barely ate at the repast, but I had no appetite. My only desire was to get off my feet. I began to take off my clothes on the way up the stairs to my bedroom. When I walked into the room, I fell across my bed and cried. I finally gave in to everything I'd been holding in all day.

I cried for my sister. I couldn't even imagine burying one of my children. I cried for that sweet baby boy who would never know his mother. I cried because I would never again get to see her radiant smile, hear her infectious laughter, or be blessed by the amazingly intuitive words of wisdom from one so young. I cried long and loudly until my throat hurt, my eyes were swollen, and I was sure there wasn't another drop of water left in my body.

After washing my face and putting on a gown, I went down to the family room. I sat on the couch in the dark and looked up at Garry's urn on the mantle.

"Donna and I are counting on you to look after Summer," I said.

I smiled as I thought to myself, *Knowing Summer it will probably be the other way around—she will be looking after her Uncle Garry.*

"You tell her not to worry. We will love Jason like he's our own. We will take good care of him, and when he's old enough, we'll make sure he knows all about his amazing mother."

I sat there for a long time in the dark, waiting for some kind of response. As usual, there was none—or so I thought.

Weary beyond words, I finally climbed the stairs back up to my room. I lay down on the bed again and suddenly felt the most amazing calm and sense of peace. Lying very still, I allowed it to wash over me like a comfortable old blanket. My eyes started to flutter, and just before I succumbed to the fatigue of the day, I smiled, feeling his presence, and said, "Thank you!"

I gave myself a couple of weeks to try and regroup after Summer's death, and then I got down to business. Her death had hit me hard and reinforced my awareness of just how unpredictable life was. There was no more time for procrastination; it was time to put my priorities in order. If I had to start over, begin a new life without Garry, there was no more time to waste.

I came to the conclusion that the bank had left me no choice. I was going to have to sell the house. I called Juanda and asked her for a recommendation. I needed a realtor to come out and look at the house and tell me what I needed to do to get it ready to go on the market. She gave me the number of a realtor and friend who had facilitated the sale of her last two homes before she moved to Houston. He came, walked through, and gave me his suggestions. He also checked for houses that had sold in my area recently to give me an idea what my house could possible sell for. He then gave me the name of a realtor he had worked with often who specialized in short sales.

I went over all the notes I took and let all the information marinate for a couple of days, then I went to work. I had to buy light fixtures for some of the closets, and more smoke detectors. I also decided to remove the wallpaper in the downstairs bathroom and retile the floor. In addition to all the cosmetic changes, there was a long list of certifications I had to have for the city. I needed to get certifications for the furnace, air conditioner, hot-water heater, and the fireplace. I also discovered some of my outlets were not up to code and needed to be replaced. It seemed like the more I crossed off the list, the more it grew. It was a frustrating and daunting experience.

Every night I went to bed telling myself, *You can do this!* Every morning I woke up to something new and thought, *I can't do this alone!*

In the midst of all the things on my list, I spent every free hour on the computer browsing realtor websites looking for a house to rent. Because of Mom's back condition, it had to be a ranch. I also wanted a split-floor plan with the master bedroom on one side of the house and all the other bedrooms on the other. That way we could coexist in the house and both have our privacy.

I really wanted what was called a "bonus room." Most of the houses I'd looked at and really liked had them. The houses were listed as one-and-a-half-story because the bonus room was usually upstairs over the garage. It would give me an extra guest room and a place where my grandchildren could sleep and play when they visited. I began to make a list of all the houses that appealed to me and fit into our budget. Kenny and April found a realtor, and we'd been talking on the phone once or twice a week about what I was looking for. Every couple of days he sent me a list of his inventory, and I added the ones I was interested in to my growing list. It took me to the middle of November to get all the cosmetic changes taken care of. The certifications would have to wait until I was closer to actually putting the house on the market, so hopefully I would only have to have them done once. The next thing on my list was to find an attorney to represent me and handle the short sale. Fortunately, the realtor had someone in mind. She gave me the name of an attorney she had worked with before and I called him.

I told him about my husband's death and everything I'd been through since. I told him about all the bank had put me through and their lack of cooperation.

"I've come to the conclusion if I'm ever going to get past my grief, find some peace of mind, and repair the broken pieces of my life, I'm going to have to sell this house. Even if I could afford to stay here, it's too painful being here without my husband. I need a fresh start somewhere else. My unemployment has run out, and if I start using the insurance money, I'm afraid I'll ultimately lose the house anyway and then have nothing left to start over with."

"Mrs. Carter, it's been my experience that is exactly what will happen. I've seen too many clients lose their savings, their retirement, and everything else trying to hold on to a house. The bank doesn't care about your grief or your circumstances; they only care about their bottom line. They have whole departments dedicated to stringing you along. I've seen it happen too many times, and I don't want it to happen to you.

"My suggestion is if you have someplace else to go, you need to move as soon as you can, while you still have the money to do so. We will put the house on the market. I'll work with the realtor to get it sold, but I have to warn you, short sales can be a long, drawn-out process—the bank isn't going to make it easy. If peace is what you need, your best chance is to get out of the house as soon as possible. Tell the bank you intend to sell the house, tell them you are being represented by an attorney. Give them all my info, and tell them from now on, any communication should come directly to and through me."

I felt a sense of relief immediately after our conversation. Just knowing that I now had an advocate, someone to act on my behalf with the bank, made me feel like a huge weight had been lifted from my shoulders. Once my mind was made up and the attorney confirmed moving was the right thing to do, the next step was tackling the very emotional task of packing up thirty years of my life.

It had taken me months to summon the emotional strength to pack up Garry's clothes and things. I let the boys take what they wanted, gave some to close friends, and donated the rest to Purple Hearts. I'd had a couple of garage sales over the summer, but I still had a ton of things I knew I was going to have trouble parting with.

I had put it off long enough, and time was running out. I decided whether the house sold or not, I wanted to be out by the end of April 2014. I picked up the calendar a week before Thanksgiving and circled April 28 in red. I had to find a place to live in Atlanta, get me and Mom packed, and move into our new home by April 28. That was the target date.

I sat at my desk staring at that calendar and wondered how the hell I was going to pull that off. I went to church that following Sunday and received my answer: "Do you believe God has the power to answer your prayers?" That was the question my pastor asked the congregation that Sunday morning.

"It's not enough for you to *say* you believe it," he said. "If you really want God to move on your behalf, you have to demonstrate your belief. You have to show God you believe; you have to operate and function like he's already answered your prayer." He went on to say, "So you want to move? Start packing! You go home today and pack just one box. Start with one box. You show God you believe he will open up a window and pour out a blessing, and I guarantee He will make it happen!"

I sat up a little straighter in my seat and looked around, startled. *Does this man have my home bugged?* I thought. Did he read my mind? Or was God sending me a message? To this day, I don't know why he chose that analogy to demonstrate his sermon, but it was just the nudge I needed. I hadn't worked out how we were going to get there, but I went home that day, grabbed a container out of the garage, and started packing. Sure enough, everything started to fall in line after that.

CHAPTER THIRTY-NINE

THE REMAINDER OF 2013 was filled with painful firsts that drained me emotionally. They were a constant reopening of an open wound. Every time I formed a scab, I would encounter another first and it would be ripped off again. The earlier ones had been hard, but none were as hard as my first holiday season without Garry. Of the two, Thanksgiving was his favorite. He could care less about the turkey and all the trimmings, but there were two things I dared not leave off the menu. As far as he was concerned, it wasn't Thanksgiving without my dressing and some cranberry sauce.

From the beginning of our marriage, I had strived to improve and perfect my recipe. It was a real source of pride for me that he loved my dressing, and his love for it made the holiday special for me. I looked forward to making it and seeing his appreciation every year. On the night before Thanksgiving, I would normally be preparing my turkey to go in the oven to slow-cook overnight, and making the cornbread for my dressing. It would have been a joy to prepare that meal in my new kitchen, but on November 27, 2013, I sat at my kitchen island staring at a cold oven. For the first time in thirty years, there would be no turkey, no ham, no greens or mac 'n cheese, and saddest of all, no dressing and cranberry sauce.

I had been invited to Staci's house for dinner, and while I appreciated the invitation and the fact that I wouldn't have to spend the holiday alone ... without Garry, the holiday just wasn't the same. Christmas hadn't been much better, but at least I'd had the joy of showering my grandbabies with presents to distract me from the sadness that engulfed me every time I acknowledged I would never share the holidays with him again. I was never so glad to see the year come to an end.

I'd spoken to the realtor just before Christmas and told her I wanted to put the house on the market around the first of the year. We finally got all the paperwork drawn up and signed by mid-January. I sat at my kitchen table staring at my copy of the contract after she left, thinking, *Well, there's no turning back now!* A couple of days later, I called Kenny.

"Hey, Mommy, how's it going?"

"Well, I did it. I put the house on the market. The sign went up yesterday. I want to come out there the first of March to look for a house. I've decided whether I have a buyer or not, I want to be out of here by the end of April. When I make my reservations, I'll let Anthony know I'm coming so he can be prepared to show me some houses. I have a list of some I definitely want to see."

"Okay, well just let me know. I'll be there to pick you up, and I'll go with you to look at the houses."

"Thanks, baby, I was hoping you'd say that."

I spent the rest of January packing and getting quotes from moving companies. Every day I got up and dedicated two or three hours to packing. I had a system: one pile to donate, one pile to throw away, and one pile to pack. I alternated between sobbing and laughing hysterically as I contemplated each item and realized my "to-pack" pile kept growing. *This is ridiculous, Arlita,* I admonished myself. *You know you can't keep all this stuff.* It took another week or so before I was finally able to sever the emotional attachment to the majority of my "to-pack" pile. I sat on the floor in the family room picking through my life, overcome by memories of each item and its special significance. The radio was blasting in the background. I was listening to the gospel station. "Let Go" by DeWayne Woods came on and I started to sing along. Somewhere in the middle of the song it hit me. *That's what you need to do, girlfriend,* I said to myself. *Let go and let God!*

Once that revelation washed over me and I embraced it, the packing got a little easier, and soon my other two piles increased. When I wasn't packing or talking to moving companies, I was making to-do lists. Finding a new bank, changing health insurance, and finding new doctors were at the top of the list. I had already sold most of my furniture that was outdated, and I planned to buy a few new pieces. I wouldn't know what or how much I could buy until I knew how much space I would have.

The house was listed on the realtor's website and available to view online. I checked the site every day. There were plenty of views, but so far no one had requested a showing. I tried not to be discouraged; it had only been two weeks. After the third week I met with the realtor, and she suggested we drop the price by five thousand dollars. Within a couple of days of dropping the price, the realtor called and said she had a couple who wanted to see the house.

They were a young couple in their midforties with a teenage son. They wanted to get him into a better neighborhood and school district. They really liked what they saw online and were interested in seeing the house in person. The wife really liked the kitchen, and she was in love with the floors. They went through every room of the house and on their way out had a question about the plants and the riding mower in the garage. I told them I would be leaving the larger plants if they wanted them, and we could talk about them purchasing the mower.

Garry had paid over a thousand dollars for that mower and had only used it one season. Technically I couldn't use it, but I wasn't going to just give it away. After they left, the realtor reminded me it was just our first walkthrough.

"They had a lot of positive feedback. I could tell the wife really liked the house and the neighborhood, but I want to caution you not to get your hopes up."

I'd already told myself the same thing as I sat in the family room and listened to the couple go through every room of my home. When she left, I went upstairs to my room and sat in my recliner. I sat there for a long time very quietly praying. "Lord, you know what I need. I'm not going to keep bugging you; I'm just putting this out here right now. It's in your hands!"

There were a couple more showings after the first one over the next couple of weeks, and each time I cautioned myself not to get stressed. I tried hard not to obsess, but I was seriously hoping we'd get an offer before we had to drop the price again. February roared in like a lion, and just when I started to get antsy, I got a call from the realtor.

"Mrs. Carter, I'm sorry to call you so late. I know I told you not to get your hopes up, but I just had to call and let you know—we got an offer on the house!"

I thought I was imagining things. I couldn't believe I'd heard her right. It had only been a week. "Did you say we got an offer?" I asked.

"Yes ma'am, we sure did."

"Which couple made the offer?" Even as I asked the question, I was sure I already knew the answer.

"It was the first couple who looked at the house. They have been preapproved. Their offer came in a little low, but we'll submit it to the bank anyway. If they don't accept it, then at least we'll have some idea what they will and will not accept. I told the couple this was a short sale, and they seem to be okay with that. They're motivated because they really want to be moved in before the new school year begins."

"Thank you so much for calling and letting me know. I'm planning to try and be out of the house by the end of April—the twenty-seventh of April, as a matter of fact. So I guess it's all up to the bank."

"I'll come by tomorrow with the offer if you're available, and we can get this show on the road."

"Oh, I'll be available. I know it might not happen, but I'd love to have this wrapped up before I leave."

I was so excited about getting the offer, I got up right away and sat down at the computer to look for airfare to Atlanta in March. I decided to go the second week of March and give myself five days to find a house. I prayed that would be enough time.

I called Kenny the next day to give him the news. "Hi, honey, I have some news. It may be too soon to celebrate yet, but we got an offer on the house."

"You did? Wow, that's great, Mommy!"

"The realtor is coming over later today with the paperwork. I'll hold my excitement until I see what the bank has to say about their offer. We're going to continue to show the house just in case, but it would be great if we could wrap it up with this offer. I'm thinking about coming down there March sixth through the tenth. How does that fit into your schedule?"

"That's fine. Just let me know what time your flight gets in."

"Okay. When I book it, I'll send you my itinerary. I'm going to look for an early arrival on the sixth so I can meet with Anthony and look at some houses right away. Hopefully, I can find something quickly. If I have to stay a little longer, I will. I really want to be out of here and moved in down there by April 28."

"Okay, Mommy. We'll help out any way we can."

After I hung up, I went to the computer and booked my flight, and then went to pack some more boxes. Later, after the contract had been signed, I went over to my mom's to see how she was coming with her packing. It only took a few minutes to see she was having a "letting go" issue as well. As gently as I could, I reminded her that we were going to be sharing a house.

"Unless you're planning to purchase a storage unit, Mom, I'm afraid you're going to have to do a little more purging. We're not going to need all of your dishes and all mine too."

I used the dishes as an example, but what really worried me were all her clothes. She had enough clothes to open a boutique, and she probably only wore less than a third of them. I had no idea how I was going to convince her to part with more of them.

I still had a lot do before my trip to Atlanta, the most pressing being finding a mover. When I returned home, I made a few more phone calls. I'd talked to four different moving companies, and they were all expensive. Whether I did my own packing or had them do it, the price would take a big chunk out of my budget. I was also disappointed to find they wouldn't move my plants, and it could be as much as a couple of days or over a week before our belongings arrived, because ours wouldn't be the only ones on the truck.

I had nightmares about our things getting mixed up with other customers'. Moving both me and Mom presented a logistical problem as well: it would cost more to have the truck pick up from more than one location. I decided I would have to move myself with the aid of my sons. I got both boys on the phone and presented my case.

"Getting a moving company to move us isn't going to work, guys. First of all, they are very expensive, they won't move my plants, and they can't guarantee when our things will arrive. If it were just me, I might consider it. I could stay with Kenny or in a hotel until they arrived, but that's not going to work for Mom, I already know that.

"If I rent a truck, the biggest one I can get, which one of you can drive it? I'll need one of you to help drive my car down too."

"I'll drive the truck," Kenny said. "I moved April's sister, so it's not a problem for me."

"I guess I'm driving the car, then," Kevin said, laughing.

"Okay, I'll pay for Kenny's airfare to come up here and for your airfare to return to Chicago. How does that sound?"

"Sounds good," they both agreed.

I started checking on the cost of renting a truck and found the price was a third of what the movers wanted. Even with the gas for the truck and my car, I would save a big chunk of money. Kevin and Kenny contacted some of their friends and asked for their help loading the truck when the time came. With a crew in place, the only thing left to do was decide on which rental place to use.

Over the next couple of weeks, I did more packing and decided to go with U-Haul. Before I knew it, it was time to leave for Atlanta. I prayed I'd find a house quickly and be able to wrap up all the paperwork in the time allotted. I didn't just want to be moved by the end of April, I needed to leave and leave on my own terms. I thought about my conversation with my attorney, and I agreed the key to finding some peace—to moving on with my life— was getting out of that house.

CHAPTER FORTY

AS THE PLANE RACED down the runway preparing to take off, I closed my eyes and tried to visualize all of the houses on my list, hoping they looked as good in person as they did in the pictures on the website. I tried not to think about what I would do if I didn't like any of them. In order to stick to my timeline, it was crucial that I find a new home on this trip.

Kenny and April picked me up from the airport. Anthony, the realtor they found for me, had another client to see and wouldn't be available to meet until later that afternoon. Just before I left home, I found another house that I hadn't had time to add to my list. I told Kenny where it was, and since it was close to his house and we had time to kill, we decided to go and take a look. I gave him the address, he put it in his GPS, and we set out to find it.

It was supposed to be in this little subdivision called Bridle Point, which was less than ten minutes from Kenny's house. We drove around and around in circles but couldn't seem to locate the house. I began to wonder if the website had published the wrong address. There were a lot of houses for rent in the subdivision, and April spotted one in particular that looked a lot like the house we were looking for.

We drove back to take a closer look and took down the information. We called Anthony and asked if we could add it to the list of houses I wanted to see. It wasn't in his inventory, but he knew the realtor handling the house and promised to call and see if we could get in to view it. It was a ranch, and from the pitch of the roof, it looked like it could possibly have the bonus room I was looking for. A little kernel of excitement rose up in me, and I wondered to myself, *God, could it really be that easy?*

While we were waiting for Anthony to finish with his other client, we took April home so she could wait for the kids to get out of school. Kenny took me to get some lunch, and all I could think about was the house we'd just seen.

"I really like that house, at least what I can see from the outside. I really hope we can get in to see the inside today and it's available to rent." Seeing the look on Kenny's face, I smiled. "I know what you're thinking. I still want to see all the other houses on the list, but I don't know, son . . . there's just something about *that* house. The fact that it's so close to you, I mean, that has to be an omen . . . right?"

"I know," he said, smiling. "I just don't want you to be too disappointed if it's not available."

After we finished our lunch, Anthony called and said he would meet us at a Starbucks close to the first house on my list. We met him, and I was instantly impressed by his easy professional manner.

"I'm still waiting to hear back from the other realtor about the house in Bridle Point. Hopefully you'll get a chance to see it today or tomorrow at the latest."

After telling him more about my situation and my desire to be moved in by the end of April, he assured me he would do everything in his power to help me find a new home as quickly as possible.

We looked at the first house, and while it looked good on the outside, the inside left a lot to be desired. While we were walking through the next house on my list, the other realtor called and said the house in Bridle Point was available for rent and unoccupied. She said she would text us the code to the lockbox and we could go in and take a look.

I could hardly contain my excitement, but I was determined to look at the rest of the houses. One house looked okay, but we were unable to get inside. The next house was too far away from Kenny. I should have been disappointed, but I was even more convinced that something or someone was pulling me toward the other house. I didn't want to waste any more time, I just wanted to go and see it right away.

Anthony gave us the code, and since he had another appointment, he said we could go and see it on our own. "Just make sure you turn off the lights when you're done and lock up. You can call me and let me know what you think. If you don't like it, I still have some other properties I can show you tomorrow."

On the way back to the subdivision, we stopped to pick up April and the kids so they could go with us to see the house. When we arrived, the girls had a fit as soon as they saw the house. They had already noticed how close it was to theirs and were very excited that Grandma would be so close. Kenny entered the code to the lockbox, retrieved the key, and opened the door. If I hadn't already believed in love at first sight, I would definitely have believed the minute we stepped inside. It was exactly what I was looking for.

The master suite was separated from the other bedrooms by the family room and the kitchen. It had a formal dining room, a small sitting room I could use as an office, and a bonus room. Including the master, there were three bedrooms and two bathrooms on the main floor, and the bonus room upstairs also had a full bath and walk-in closet. The kitchen was a decent size with an eat-in area. There was a nice little patio out back and a two-car garage.

I wasn't the only who fell in love with the house. While the grown-ups were looking at everything downstairs, the girls were checking out the bonus room upstairs. They came bounding down the stairs, excitedly claiming it as "their room." I knew from that moment that was the house I wanted. I could barely dial Anthony's number fast enough. He didn't answer, so I left a very simple message: "I WANT THIS HOUSE!"

It was an agonizing couple of hours before he returned my call. "I got your message, Mrs. Carter. So you liked the house?" he asked.

"Yes, I love it! So what do I have to do next?"

"Well, I'll give the realtor a call first thing in the morning and tell her you want to fill out an application. I'll give her your number, and she will take it from there. In cases like this, we will split the commission."

"Thank you so much, Anthony, for all your help. How much do I owe you for your time, and when do I need to pay you?"

"Let's get you in the house first, we'll worry about that later."

"Okay, thank you again. I'll definitely give you a call and keep you informed of my progress."

The leasing agent called the next day, and after answering a few questions over the phone, she gave me a link so that I could fill out an online application. She said it could take up to forty-eight hours to hear back from them. I prayed the whole time I was filling out the application: "Please Lord, let me get this house!" It was the longest weekend of my life waiting for a call back. I was like a teenager with a crush on the most popular boy in school. All weekend long, I wrote down my name with the Bridle Point address underneath it. I was trying to demonstrate to God that I believed in his power to answer my prayer by claiming the house was already mine.

Saturday and Sunday came and went with no word, and by Monday afternoon, I was climbing the walls.

"You need to calm down and stop worrying, Mom, I'm sure you're gonna get the house."

"I wish I was as sure as you are," I said. "I'm supposed to leave on Wednesday. What if they don't call me before then?"

"Well, then you'll just have to stay another day or two longer, but I'm sure you will hear from them before then."

Finally, around five that evening, just when I thought I was going to lose my mind, I got the call. "Mrs. Carter, I'm so sorry it took so long to get back to you. I have good news: your application was approved, and the house on Bridal Point Parkway is yours if you want it."

I was so excited I could barely breathe, let alone talk. It took me a moment, and I finally answered her. "Yes, I definitely want the house! So what do I do next?"

"Well, we will start working on drawing up a lease. I will call you tomorrow and let you know how much the rent will be. You will need to get a cashier's check for your security deposit and first month's rent. There is also a one-time nonrefundable pet deposit. You will also have to present proof of renter's insurance at the lease signing. I believe we can have everything ready by Wednesday morning. Will that be okay with you?"

"Yes, that will be fine," I said. "It will give me time to get everything together on my end."

When I hung up the phone, Kenny only had to look at the big grin on my face to know that I'd just received good news. He came over and hugged me. "I told you so," he said, laughing. "So what happens now?" he asked.

"Well, the first thing I need to do is call the airline and change my return flight to Thursday. I need to get some renter's insurance, and as soon as they give me the amount, I need to get a cashier's check for my security deposit, pet deposit, and first month's rent. They said they should have the lease ready for me to sign by Wednesday morning."

I changed my flight to Thursday afternoon, and then I called Kevin to let him know I'd be coming back a day later than I planned. "You found a house that fast, Ma? That's great!"

"Well, actually April found it. But I'm just glad, no matter who found it. I'll call Mom later and fill her in on all the details, but you can tell her if you want to." Since I had a long relationship with State Farm, I asked Kenny for a local office I could call to purchase the renter's insurance. He had the same insurance and gave me the name of his agent.

Wednesday morning I had everything I needed, and I was ready to sign the lease. We'd gone back to the house one more time so I could walk through and make absolutely sure it was what I wanted. I walked through the rooms more slowly, paying more attention to the size of the rooms, imagining our furniture there, imagining us there. I stood in the middle of the empty family room for a long time, thinking to myself, *This is where I'll start over. This is where I'll begin my new life.*

I told the property manager I wanted to move in on April 28 and arranged for Kenny to get the keys a couple of days earlier so he could get in and check out the house before we arrived. Kenny was also going to help by arranging to get the lights and water turned on before I arrived. With the lease signed and everything else in place, I slept like a log that night. When I boarded the plane the next day, I felt like I could fly all the way back without the plane. I was so excited I could hardly wait to get back and finish packing.

Besides packing, I had to find a new bank and secure a truck for the move. I also had to purchase plane tickets for Kenny and Kevin. There had been no word from the bank about our offer, but the realtor assured me that was not unusual, and if it came to that, they could overnight all the documents I would need to sign when the time came to close. Over the next several weeks, I checked off all the items on my to-do list and prepared myself mentally to move me and my mother over seven hundred miles away, to a new state, a new home, and a new life.

I thought I was ready, but the closer it got to the day, my excitement waned and was replaced by overwhelming sadness. I began to second-guess my decision. I sat in the family room surrounded by boxes and asked myself if I was really doing the right thing. Looking at Garry's urn, I talked to him. "We were supposed to do this together," I said. With tears running down my face, I asked him, "Why are you making me do this alone?" I sat there for hours until the tears on my face dried up and I began to feel cold through and through. I waited for an answer, and once again, there was none.

Finally, I dragged myself upstairs to my room and got into bed. *You're on your own, old girl*, I thought to myself, *and you've come too far now to turn around.* Three days later Kenny arrived, and he and Kevin staged all the boxes in the living room to make it easier to load the truck. Early on the morning of April 27, we drove to the U-Haul store to pick up the truck I had reserved the week before. The plan was to go to Mom's apartment and load all her belongings on the truck first. Kenny and his helpers would then bring the truck to my house and load up my things, and we would leave from there.

We wanted to arrive in Atlanta in the late afternoon, so we planned to leave at three in the morning. By six that evening, the truck was loaded and locked. Everything we couldn't take with us had been distributed between family, friends, and neighbors. There had been a steady stream of people coming by throughout the day to say goodbye and elicit a promise from us to stay in touch. We ate carryout because all the dishes and utensils were packed up. While I went from room to room making sure we hadn't forgotten anything, Kenny went to meet some friends. When he returned to the house with them, I realized I wasn't the only one having trouble leaving the house. Kenny walked through the rooms with his friends and recalled childhood memories. They took pictures coming in and leaving out of the house for the last time.

It brought tears to my eyes seeing how sad Kenny was leaving his childhood home. Once again I felt the pang of doubt, but like before I realized it was too late to turn around. There was no way I could keep the house even if I wanted to. I knew I should try and sleep, but I couldn't relax. I walked around the empty house, consumed with memories myself. I stood in the living room looking out at the street my children had played on. I could almost hear the sound of their laughter. It started to rain, and I worried about making the trip in the rain. I prayed for travel mercies and went to lie down again, hoping to get at least a couple of hours of sleep.

It seemed like as soon as my head hit the pillow, the alarm I set went off with a persistent buzz that would not be ignored. I woke my mom and folded up the blankets we'd slept on and put them in the car. It had continued to rain, and there was a definite chill in the air. After checking all the rooms one last time, I finally stepped out on the front porch and locked the door. I stood there for a while remembering all the times Garry and I had sat out there enjoying a summer evening. I could feel my eyes starting to water as I heard Kenny say gently, "Mommy, we need to get going." I walked to the car and got in, and as we pulled off the cul-de-sac following Kenny in the truck, I turned and looked at my house one last time, and whispered, "Goodbye."

Epilogue

I COULDN'T BELIEVE IT had been a whole year since I arrived here still grieving, still broken, and still plagued by doubt about my decision to uproot myself and my mother from the place I had lived my whole life. The rain never let up. In fact, it rained almost the entire trip, alternating between a pesky drizzle and a full-out windshield-wipers-on full-blast downpour.

I was bone tired from loading the truck the day before and lack of sleep, but I somehow managed to keep my eyes glued to the back of that U-Haul truck. The truck held almost all of my worldly possessions, the most precious among them my youngest son. Every time one of those eighteen-wheelers got too close, I held my breath. Every time Kenny changed lanes seemingly on two wheels, I bit my bottom lip so hard I was sure I would draw blood. It was a long, agonizing trip, and by the time we reached the Georgia state line, I had a full-blown migraine.

Mercifully the rain stopped just as we crossed over into Georgia. The rain clouds moved out of the way, revealing a beautiful, brilliant sunshine. The temperature had risen to a humid eighty-seven degrees. As planned, we arrived with plenty of daylight left. As we pulled into the driveway of our new home, I watched my mother's face, hoping to see a pleased expression. Instead I saw skepticism, and that pang of doubt reared its ugly head again.

I took the key from the lockbox and opened the door and let her in. Once inside, her expression changed to one of surprise. "It's a lot bigger on the inside than it looks from the outside," she said.

"Does that mean you like it?" I asked.

She didn't answer me right away, but as I walked her around giving her the tour, her smile got bigger and brighter. Finally, she turned to me and said, "Yes, I like it. It's a nice house, baby."

Relieved, I went back outside to help unloading the truck. We didn't have any bedroom furniture, so we slept on our mattresses on the floor. I was so tired I didn't notice if it was uncomfortable or not. I was out the minute my head hit the pillow.

The next several months were spent getting settled and dealing with the lingering grief that not even seven hundred miles could wipe away. I was grateful for the time I was able to spend with my son and my grandchildren. We comforted each other and helped each other get past the pain and sadness that was still very much at the forefront of our hearts and minds.

I changed my driver's license, bought Georgia plates for my car, finished transferring our funds to the new bank, switched health insurance, and found new doctors. I was slowly learning my way around town, and my GPS had become my new best friend. I found a new church, made some new friends, and reconnected with my Georgia relatives.

For forty years, my identity had been tied to the roles I assumed when I got married. I was Garry Carter's wife and Kevin and Kenny's mom. Over time, I got lost and forgot that before I became all that, I was simply me. I was a young woman with her whole life ahead of her and endless possibilities. I was a young woman who at the tender age of twenty had already been through a lot, a woman who would go on to survive and overcome so much more.

When my husband died, a part of me died with him. It had been a long and painful journey that was by no means over, but in the last twelve months, by the Grace of God, I had picked up the broken pieces of my life and put them back together. I'd lost my way, but I found it again. I rediscovered my strength and my power. I was no longer afraid, no longer plagued with doubt. I had proven to myself that I could put on my big-girl panties and get the job done, whatever was necessary.

Over the past year, I had learned there was no time limit on grief. Summer had been right—no one could tell me how long it would take to stop hurting, only that one day I would. Every day I woke up and realized although the pain was still there, it was no longer as sharp . . . as intense. It was no longer a heavy coat I wore each and every day, but instead a memory that snuck up on me from time to time. It was a reminder of the life I once lived, the love and joy I once experienced. As I let go of the pain and sorrow, those feelings were replaced with hope that one day God would see fit to bless me again. I clung to the belief that he would acknowledge the hole in my heart and fill it up with a new love and a new joy, just as he had blessed me with a new home.

Until then, I would wait patiently and nurture that seed of hope. The bank had taken so long responding to the offer, the young couple had to withdraw it. I was angry with the bank, but I understood that the buyers had to do what they had to do. They had to think about themselves and their son. We put the house back on the market and hoped we'd find another buyer soon. I refused to be discouraged. I remembered the words of my former pastor. He always told us, "Don't give up on God—'cause he won't give up on you!" I still believed in the power of prayer, and I knew if God made a way for me to make this move and secure this house, in time he'd take care of the rest as well.

I was comfortable in my own skin, comfortable in my new role. I was a single woman holding it down on my own. In addition to our new home, our new life, and our first year in Atlanta, I had much to be thankful for and much to celebrate on April 26, 2015. To mark the occasion, I invited friends and family over for a cookout. The house was full, and everyone was having a good time. I stood in my dining room looking out the window at my new yard, on my new street, with the sounds of my family and friends fellowshipping in the background.

I looked up at the sky and smiled, engulfed by a comforting warmth I knew did not come from the sun streaming through the window.

"Thank you, Lord," I said quietly. "Thank you for your divine peace and your protection. Thank you for keeping me and comforting me on this journey. Most of all, thank you for restoring my heart!"

The hole was still there . . . but it was getting smaller with each passing day!

About the Author

ARLITA CARTER IS RETIRED and currently resides in Snellville, Georgia, where she is enjoying the love and support of her family and the many new friends she has made there. She is living, loving, and thriving in her new life and adjusting well to her new reality.